THE NEW CROSS STITCHER'S BIBLE

THE NEW
CROSS _ _ _ _ _ _
STITCHER'S
Jane Greenoff # BIBLE

THE DEFINITIVE MANUAL OF ESSENTIAL CROSS STITCH AND COUNTED THREAD TECHNIQUES

D&C
David and Charles

CONTENTS

*To Bill, my husband
and best friend,
with love always.*

A DAVID & CHARLES BOOK
Copyright © David & Charles Limited 2007, 2010

David & Charles is an F+W Media
Inc. company, 4700 East Galbraith Road
Cincinnati, OH 45236

First published in the UK in 2007
This UK paperback edition first published in 2010

Text and designs copyright © Jane Greenoff
2007, 2010
Photography and layout copyright ©
David & Charles 2007, 2010

Stitch Library artworks © David & Charles 2007, 2010
adapted from originals supplied by the Cross Stitch Guild

Jane Greenoff has asserted her right to be identified as
author of this work in accordance with the Copyright,
Designs and Patents Act, 1988.

A catalogue record for this book is available from the
British Library.

ISBN-13: 978-0-7153-3771-4 paperback
ISBN-10: 0-7153-3771-8 paperback

Printed in China by RR Donnelley
for David & Charles
Brunel House   Newton Abbot   Devon

Executive Editor Cheryl Brown
Desk Editor Bethany Dymond
Project Editor Lin Clements
Senior Designer Charly Bailey
Chart Preparation Ethan Danielson
Production Controller Ros Napper

David & Charles publish high quality books on a wide
range of subjects. For more great book ideas visit:
www.rucraft.co.uk

INTRODUCTION

Since the extraordinary success of *The Cross Stitcher's Bible* published in 2000 (now in ten languages), I felt it was time to look at the book again, particularly in the light of my teaching experiences over the past few years. My classes are now almost without exception dedicated to cross stitch plus additional counted stitches. I still feel that pure cross stitch, worked perfectly, is beautiful to look at and simple to do but many stitchers are moving on and adding Hardanger, blackwork, hemstitch and other counted techniques to their projects, and these techniques require more detailed explanations. This unique book aims to provide you with useful, accessible information in an easy-to-use format.

Cross stitch is often our first love but I hope that by referring to *The New Cross Stitcher's Bible* you will be able to add to and enhance your cross stitch patterns and perhaps design for yourself. The book will add to your armoury of counted techniques whilst allowing you to pursue the pleasure of pure cross stitch.

I hope this book, with its clear instructions, computer-generated charts and extensive chart and stitch libraries, will become your essential manual, allowing you to perfect existing techniques and also explore other exciting companions to cross stitch, such as the use of beads, ribbons and embellishments and many other decorative stitches. The instructions and explanations in this book are the result of over 20 years of designing and stitching and I hope you enjoy sharing my experiences.

Jan Greenoff

HOW TO USE THIS BOOK

The book has been divided into sections with colour-coded pages to enable you to find the information you require easily and to provide a clear and comprehensive approach to all aspects of cross stitching.

❖ Getting Started is colour coded blue and gives advice on choosing and using equipment, fabric and threads, plus all the practical aspects of how to cross stitch on Aida and evenweave fabrics.

❖ Creative Options is colour coded yellow and describes cross stitching techniques using some of the many different fabrics and threads available.

❖ Exploring Choices is colour coded red and features exciting designs that show how easy it is to combine cross stitch with other counted embroidery techniques.

❖ In Getting Started, Creative Options and Exploring Choices, I have included boxes called Stitch Perfect, which focus on the important points in each section. There are also mini technique boxes to assist you.

❖ In Creative Options you will see illustrations of worked designs, many of which combine a number of techniques fully explained elsewhere. For example, the Anemone Floral Cushion (opposite) includes cross stitch with stranded cottons (floss) and linen threads on linen, crossed cushion stitch in space-dyed threads and French knots in pure silk and blending filament (full instructions on page 53).

❖ The extensive Stitch Library includes the stitches you need to work any of the designs in the book, with clear, coloured diagrams and explanatory text.

❖ In addition to the extensive Chart Library I have included some scrumptious samplers so you can create heirloom masterpieces, combining some of the techniques and stitches explained in the book.

❖ Most of the designs are charted in the Chart Library starting on page 166. Colour charts with black/white symbols have been used so you can photocopy and enlarge them. Most of the designs can be stitched on Aida or evenweave. Where evenweave is essential it is indicated in the picture caption. All the cross stitch designs have been stitched with DMC stranded cotton (floss) unless stated otherwise. When fabrics are specified, the thread counts are indicated as threads or blocks to 2.5cm (1in) i.e., 28-count or 14-count. All stitches are worked over two fabric threads or one fabric block unless stated otherwise.

❖ Measurements are given in metric with imperial conversions in brackets. Use either metric or imperial when working, do not combine them.

GETTING STARTED

You should find this section very useful as it contains a great deal of invaluable information on cross stitch basics, including how to choose equipment, use charts, manage threads and all the instruction you'll ever need on creating beautiful cross stitch on Aida and evenweave fabric.

Counted cross stitch is most commonly worked using stranded cottons (floss), often incorrectly referred to as 'silks'. This is probably the simplest way to start your stitching, adding different threads as you become more experienced. As you can see from the gorgeous pictures here, cross stitch is one of the most rewarding kinds of embroidery and the images that can be created are simply stunning. The kingfisher picture below is worked in stranded cottons and almost all full cross stitches. I have added some optional blending filament to the bird's plumage (see page 46) to make it glisten but the design could be worked even more simply on Aida with just stranded cottons. The two colourful kitchen tile pictures shown opposite use full cross stitch, with half cross stitch for the pale background.

KINGFISHER

Stitch count: 44h x 41w
Design size: 8 x 7.5cm
(3⅛ x 3in)
Fabric: Zweigart Cashel ivory linen 28-count or 14-count Aida
Needle: Tapestry size 24
Chart: Page 167

This lovely bird has been stitched using two strands of stranded cotton (floss) for cross stitch and one strand for backstitch. The water was stitched in half cross stitch using one strand of stranded cotton together with one strand of Kreinik Blending Filament 095. I used two strands of the blending filament with the stranded cotton to add a slightly frosted appearance to the bird's plumage.

GREEN CABBAGE AND RED PEPPER TILES

Stitch count: 56h x 56w (each design)
Design size: 11cm (4¼in) square
Fabric: Zweigart Dublin ivory 26-count linen
Needle: Tapestry size 24
Charts: Pages 166 and 169

These striking kitchen tiles are both worked in the same way. Use two strands of stranded cotton (floss) for cross stitch and one strand for backstitch. Stitch the light-coloured background in half cross stitch using one strand. The designs could be worked on 14-count Aida fabric but would be fractionally smaller.

FOLLOWING A CHART

I will never forget the day I discovered counted cross stitch, staring at the fabric expecting to find the design printed! Looking at blank fabric and not knowing what to do next was a bit scary – the secret is to take it in easy, bite-size pieces.

The designs in this book are counted designs and are worked from charts. A chart is really just a detailed map to be followed and if you follow these guidelines you will not get lost. The charts and keys for the majority of the projects are in the Chart Library (pages 166–209). The four celebration samplers have their charts included with the instructions. The charts are easy to follow as they are all in colour with a black and/or white symbol to aid colour identification (see Types of Charts, opposite).

CHART AND KEY BASICS

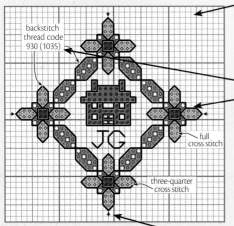

backstitch
thread code
930 (1035)

full
cross stitch

three-quarter
cross stitch

- ◆ Each square on a chart, both occupied and unoccupied, represents two threads of linen or one block of Aida unless otherwise stated. Each occupied square equals one stitch unless otherwise stated.
- ◆ Backstitch thread code – DMC (Anchor).
- ◆ Cross stitch charts generally consist of whole squares representing complete cross stitches, but you will see additional stitches added to some charts in the Chart Library indicating three-quarter cross stitches (sometimes called fractional stitches), French knots and so on. These stitches are labelled in the key or included on the chart. The Sampler Key Keeper chart (instructions on page 41) is shown here with the main parts identified.
- ◆ Traditionally cross stitchers begin to stitch from the middle of the chart and the middle of the fabric to ensure that the design is centred when it is mounted and framed. Find the middle by following the little arrows at the sides.

> ### JANE'S TIP
> *Check your position regularly to discover counting mistakes early and avoid lots of stitches to unpick – often referred to as reverse stitching!*

- ◆ Some counted thread stitches can be worked over any number of fabric threads although the stitch construction will stay the same e.g., Rhodes stitch may be formed over four, six or eight threads, so check the chart to clarify the number of fabric threads involved.
- ◆ The count of a fabric (the number of stitches to 2.5cm or 1in) affects the size of a finished piece even when worked from the same chart. This is useful when faced with a frame or card that is slightly too small for the chosen motif. You can increase the fabric count from, say, 14-count to 18-count, which reduces the design so it fits.
- ◆ To prevent serious counting errors, use a coloured pen to rule a line on the chart from arrow to arrow to find the centre and then add

a line of tacking (basting) to the fabric. If working a band sampler, work tacking lines down either side of the first band, to prevent your project wandering right or left.

- ◆ When looking at a chart, try to plan the direction in which you are going to stitch. If you count across the shortest distances of empty fabric each time you will avoid making counting mistakes. This sometimes means counting diagonally, vertically or horizontally across a pattern. Mistakes most often occur when counting across long sections of blank fabric. You can turn your work and the chart upside down if you prefer to work towards you, but never turn halfway – your stitches will end up facing the wrong way!

TYPES OF CHARTS

When stitching cross stitch designs from books, magazines and kits you may find different types of charts but don't panic – they all give the same information in a slightly different way. This Green Cabbage Tile could have been worked from a chart presented in various ways, as shown below. See also page 122, Computer-Aided Design.

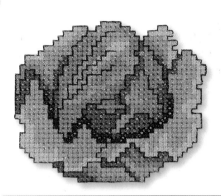

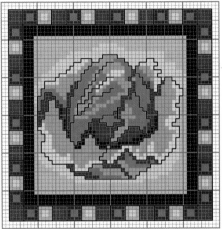

Coloured squares only

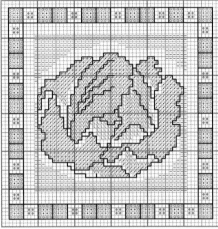

Black and/or white symbols

Coloured squares with
black and/or white symbols

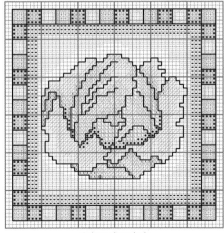

Coloured symbols

JANE'S TIP

I make a photocopy of a black and white chart so I can colour it in as I go to avoid looking at the wrong section. You may find a metal board with magnetic strips helpful. It keeps the chart in position and marks your place.

EQUIPMENT

The equipment needed for cross stitch couldn't be simpler – essentially just blunt tapestry needles and some sharp, pointed scissors. You will need other items for making up projects but these are given under the relevant finishing instructions at the back of the book. Remember that cross stitch need not be displayed as just cards and framed pictures: as you will see from the purse on the next page and from the photographs throughout, cross stitch can be transformed into all sorts of lovely decorative and useful items.

NEEDLES

◆ When working counted cross stitch you will need blunt tapestry needles of various sizes, depending on your fabric. A blunt needle is required because you should be parting the threads of the fabric rather than piercing the material. Aim to avoid splitting the fibres as you stitch.

◆ Occasionally I use a 'sharp' needle when adding backstitch outlining or when creating fractional stitches on Aida fabric. A 'sharp' size 10 is useful for this and will double as a small beading needle.

◆ The most commonly used tapestry needles for cross stitch are sizes 24 and 26, although needles are also available in sizes 20, 22 and 28. When using a size 28, use only the equivalent of one strand of stranded cotton (floss) because the eye is very delicate and will break. Adjust the needle size to match the project.

◆ Discard old needles with marks or rough areas as these can damage your threads and fabric.

◆ Avoid leaving your needle in the fabric when it is put away as it may leave a mark (unless you are working with gold-plated needles). The nickel plating on needles varies and some stitchers find they are allergic to the nickel and therefore prefer gold-plated needles.

◆ I only use gold-plated needles as I find they slip through the fabric perfectly and are essential if creating lots of French knots or bullion knots.

◆ If you are working on a floor-standing frame, you may find a double-ended needle helpful, where the eye of the needle is in the middle rather than the end. This means that the needle goes up and down rather like a shuttle in a loom.

◆ When the use of beads is suggested in a project they may be attached using a special beading needle or 'sharp' size 10. A blunt gold-plated beading needle size 26 has been specially developed for cross stitchers (see Suppliers).

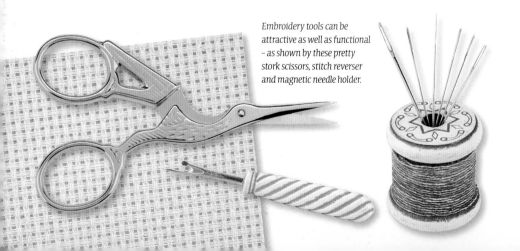

Embroidery tools can be attractive as well as functional – as shown by these pretty stork scissors, stitch reverser and magnetic needle holder.

THREADING A NEEDLE OR NEEDLING A THREAD?

Sometimes threading a needle can defeat you, usually when you are tired or distracted or when you have been stitching too long! So try needling the thread instead. Pass the thread across your index finger and hold it quite firmly. With your other hand holding the pointed end of the needle, rub the eye of the needle up and down the thread. The thread will pop up through the eye of the needle is if by magic.

SCISSORS

◆ Keep a small, sharp pair of pointed scissors exclusively for your embroidery. I wear mine around my neck on a ribbon so I know where they are at all times. There are magnets available to attach your scissors to the embroidery frame if you use one.

◆ Use dressmaker's shears for cutting fabric.

FRAMES AND HOOPS

◆ Frames or hoops are not essential for cross stitchers and I have worked without them for many years. I prefer to work my cross stitch in my hand as this allows a sewing action (see How to Hold Fabric page 22) but this is a matter of personal preference. I do use a frame when a project includes satin stitch.

◆ Generally, I avoid embroidery hoops as I find that they tend to mark the fabric but if you must use one, choose one large enough to hold the complete design – moving a hoop across your beautifully formed stitches is criminal!

◆ When I use a frame (such as when working the crossed cushion stitch and the spider's webs on the Anemone Floral Cushion on page 53), I use a padded, upholstered frame with a sandbag weight, shown below (see Sue Hawkins in Suppliers).

◆ Frames and hoops are useful when you are working in miniature and also when adding beads or combining cross stitch with silk ribbon.

An upholstered needlework frame with sand-bag weight is a useful accessory (see Suppiers).

13

PINK MALLOW PURSE

Stitch count: 33h x 32w
Design size: 6 x 5.8cm
(2⅜ x 2¼in)
Fabric: Zweigart Cashel
ivory 28-count linen
Needle: Tapestry size 24
Chart: Page 167

*This pretty purse makes a feature
of a simple design and could
be used for items of stitching
equipment. Work this floral motif
over two linen threads, using two
strands of stranded cotton (floss)
for cross stitch and French knots
and one strand for backstitch.
If working this project on Aida
fabric you may prefer to work the
three-quarter stitches using a sharp
needle. I made the embroidery into a folded
purse using Liberty lawn fabric but do feel free to
experiment. To make up as a purse see page 217.*

MAGNIFIERS

There are a number of different types of
magnifying contraptions on the market,
some of which will make you look like
something from the planet Zog but you will
be among friends! There are various factors
that will affect your choice.

◆ If you already wear glasses for close work
you may be able to find a cheap and simple
pair of magnifying spectacles that will be
just right for your stitching. There are also
small clip-on lenses that can be worn in
addition to your glasses. Lenses can be
worn around the neck and the position
adjusted with side cords. The success or
failure of these also depends on your bust
size as they do seem to need an adequate
'shelf' to be in the correct position!

◆ If you feel the need for something more
substantial you will be able to find many
excellent lenses with flexible arms which
clip to the table, chair or embroidery
frame. Some of these may be combined
with a lamp (see picture opposite).

◆ Do make sure you hold your work at the
correct distance from your eyes. To find
this distance, hold your work at arm's
length then gradually bring it towards
you until you can see it clearly. If you then
continue to bring it nearer, you will find
another point where it starts to become
indistinct again. Hold your work at a
distance between these two points where
you can naturally see it most clearly. When
they reach their forties, many people start
to find that this position gets further
and further away from their eyes. If this
is happening to you, you probably need
reading glasses, so consult an optician.

> ### JANE'S TIP
> When choosing magnifiers or
> magnifying spectacles, take some
> stitching with you as you may
> well hold your needlework in
> a different position to that
> of a book.

LAMPS AND DAYLIGHT BULBS

Your requirements here will vary depending on when you have the opportunity to stitch.

◆ An old-fashioned standard lamp is probably the most suitable as the soft light drops on your work from above and you are unlikely to burn yourself on the bulb!

◆ Some stitchers have great success with head torches (from camping shops). They vary but the most successful type seems to be those with an adjustable beam, which can be angled on your stitching.

◆ The list of lamps available grows daily but Daylight bulbs and Ott Lite are very helpful, particularly as domestic light bulbs distort colours, which can be very trying and lead to colour matching mistakes. I use Ott Lite, as the bulbs create a very clear light and do not get too hot.

You will find magnifiers and lamps very useful when working projects in miniature, such as this pansy key ring (instructions on page 58), where the finished design is less than 2.5cm (1in) square!

CHOOSING AND MANAGING THREADS

The most commonly used thread for counted embroidery is stranded cotton (floss) but you will see flower threads, linen threads, rayons, perlé cottons, assorted metallics and spaced-dyed specialist threads used throughout this book.

All the charts in the Chart Library were stitched using DMC stranded cotton (floss) unless stated otherwise. Anchor alternatives are given in brackets. If you do change to Anchor or another brand of thread, bear in mind that an exact colour match is not always possible. The following guidelines apply to stranded cotton (floss) as information about other yarns will be found in the relevant sections.

CHECKING FOR COLOURFASTNESS

Ensuring that threads are colourfast is important, particularly if you need to launder the piece or are planning to tea-dye it (see page 33). I have had experience of threads not just running but galloping! You should have no trouble with well-known reputable brands such as DMC, Anchor and Madeira but take extra care with Christmas reds.

To check for colourfastness, place the work face down on a clean surface and press the back of the stitches with a clean, damp white tissue. Any trace of colour on the tissue means the thread colours are not fast, so do not wash or tea-dye.

USING STRANDED COTTON

◆ When selecting threads, always have the fabric you are intending to use close at hand, because the colour of the background fabric will affect your choice of thread colours. When in a shop, check the colour of the thread in daylight as electric light can 'kill' some shades. Buy a daylight bulb to use in normal spotlights to help when working in the evening.

◆ Cross stitch is generally worked using two strands of stranded cotton when working on 14-count and 16-count Aida. It is perfectly acceptable to mix the number of threads used within the same project. You could alter the texture by working in one, two and even three strands.

◆ When using two strands or more for cross stitch, you will need to separate the strands and then realign them before threading your needle and beginning to stitch.

◆ If you're not sure how many strands to use on Aida, stitch a few complete cross stitches and look at the stitching in daylight. Some colours may need the number of strands adjusting to suit the project.

◆ If you are working on evenweave and do not know how many strands to use, carefully pull a thread from the edge of the fabric and compare the thread with the strands of cotton. Generally, the strands on the needle should be a similar weight, unless you want a more striking effect.

JANE'S TIP
In some cases there are no alternatives to the threads I've used but this should not hinder you in any way! Experiment with some of the many gorgeous threads available! See pages 38–50 for some mouth-watering examples.

TWEEDING

Where two shade numbers are quoted for one stitch this is known as tweeding. This straightforward practice is a simple way to increase the numbers of colours you have without buying more thread.

To tweed, simply combine more than one coloured thread in the needle at the same time and work as one – as I have for this little hedgehog (stitching instructions on page 66). You can also apply the tweeding technique to working French knots and bullion bars to great effect. Metallic threads and blending filaments can also be tweeded with stranded cotton.

ORGANIZING YOUR THREADS

It really does pay to start with good habits and have an organizer system for your threads. You will then be able to find a shade when you need it and you will be surprised by how many projects you will be able to stitch using left-over threads. There are many excellent organizer systems on the market but I make my own cards as shown here.

1 Take a piece of stiff card (I use the card from a packet of tights or panty-hose) and punch holes down each side of the card. Take a skein of stranded cotton (floss), cut the cotton into manageable lengths of about 80cm (30in), double them and thread them through the holes as shown. It is quite simple to remove one length of thread without disturbing the rest.

2 Label the card with the manufacturer's name and shade number. When the project is complete all the threads will be labelled ready for another project.

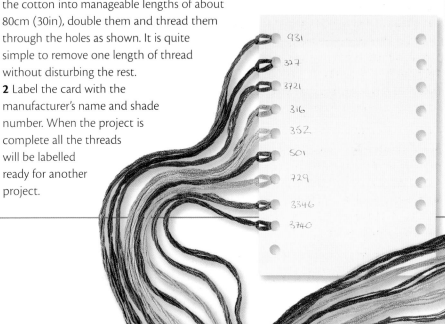

STARTING TO STITCH

This section of the book creates a background for the later sections, Creative Options and Exploring Choices. Whether you are an expert cross stitcher or just beginning, please read this section in case there are tips and hints you may not have heard before. You may be able to see the reasons for some of the things you do or perhaps the reasons why you should! Much of the advice here is from a personal perspective, so feel free to do your own thing. When stitching the designs, beginners might find Working Projects (page 30) useful as it provides a checklist to get your project started.

CROSS STITCH FABRICS

When I started to stitch back in the 1980s there was very little choice of fabric available for stitchers. In the UK, it was either fine linen or 14-count Aida fabric and that was about it! Now there is so much choice it can be quite confusing and leave the stitcher, particularly a newcomer, quite at a loss.

Counted cross stitch, and in fact any type of counted embroidery, can be worked on a variety of materials – not just popular fabrics like linen or Aida, but also Hardanger fabric (22-count), canvas, stitching paper, magic canvas and Afghan material. I describe fabric choices and uses in more detail in Creative Options (pages 32–36).

BUTTERFLIES AND BUDDLEIA

Stitch count:
71h x 60w
Design size:
12.7 x 11cm (5 x 4in)
Fabric: Aida ivory
14-count or Zweigart
Cashel ivory linen
28-count
Needle: Tapestry
size 24
Chart: Page 168

This picture is worked on Aida using cross stitch and backstitch only – see page 27 for a version on linen using massed French knots for the flower and the butterflies stitched over one thread. Use two strands of stranded cotton (floss) for cross stitch (and French knots if using) and one strand for backstitch.

STITCHING ON AIDA

All Aida fabrics are woven with threads grouped into bundles to form a square pattern, which creates obvious holes. The stitches are formed using these holes. Aida is available in many different colours and counts and is also available made of linen threads, which is lovely to handle.

Aida is wonderful for cross stitch as it creates very square stitches and projects seem to grow quickly. Beginners like it because it is so easy to see the holes and therefore where to put the needle. It is perfect for checks, tartan and gingham designs. It frays less than evenweaves, unless encouraged.

Aida has some disadvantages. You are limited to using the holes created by the fabric manufacturer, which can make fractional stitches more difficult to form. In addition, some counted stitches need more fabric threads for formation.

STITCHING ON EVENWEAVE

This range of fabrics, which includes linen, has threads woven singly rather than in blocks and are available in many colours and counts.

Many people like using evenweave for the aged-linen look and the way it handles. Working on evenweave is not difficult, just different. The blue posy design below illustrates this: the finished pieces are the same size on evenweave as on Aida because each stitch is formed over two threads instead of one block, therefore a 28-count evenweave has the same stitch count as a 14-count Aida – 28 threads to 2.5cm (1in) = 14 blocks to 2.5cm (1in). See overleaf for a more detailed explanation of fabric counts and working out design sizes.

Evenweave can be worked over one thread or for fine detail. See also Working with Linen on page 28.

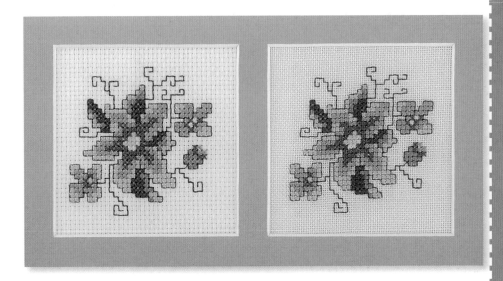

PRETTY BLUE POSY

Stitch count: 32h x 32w **Design size:** 5.8cm square (2¼in) **Fabric:** Zweigart cream 28-count Cashel linen and/or 14-count cream Aida **Needle:** Tapestry size 24
Chart: Page 169

The posy has been worked twice – on Aida over one block and on linen over two threads but the designs are the same size. Use two strands of stranded cotton (floss) for cross stitch and one for backstitch.

What is Thread Count?

All fabrics are sold by the yard or metre or part thereof and are described by the number of threads to 1in (2.5cm), i.e., their gauge or count. To check the count of a fabric, lay a ruler on the fabric and count the number of blocks or threads in 1in (2.5cm) – use a needle to help you follow the threads. If there are 14 blocks to 1in (2.5cm) then the fabric is 14-count. A 28-count linen will have 28 threads to 1in (2.5cm).

You can work counted cross stitch on anything that has a grid or is made up of squares. To translate a squared chart or pattern on to fabric accurately, you need material that is itself made up of squares. Therefore fabrics used for counted needlework are all woven in even squares. These fabrics are divided into two main groups: Aida, which is woven in blocks with obvious holes; and evenweave, which is woven in single threads. (See also Choosing and Using Fabrics page 32.) The butterflies and buddleia design on page 18 was worked on 14-count Aida.

How Many Strands?

The number of strands of stranded cotton (floss) used depends mainly on the stitch count of the fabric you are using. When in doubt, work a few cross stitches in the fabric margin and decide how many strands you prefer. If the chart does not indicate how many strands to use, check by pulling a thread from the edge of the fabric and compare it with the strands of cotton. They should be a similar weight to the threads in the fabric. As you experiment with your stitching you will be able to combine different threads in the same project with remarkable effects. (See also Mixing Thread Types page 52.)

How is Design Size Calculated?

If you are going to progress from purchased cross stitch kits to working from charts or better still, your own designs, you must know how to work out the finished size of the design. It is this calculation that decides how much fabric you will need to stitch your project or whether a particular motif will fit in a card aperture. There is nothing worse than working a project and realising belatedly that the whole design will not fit on the fabric!

All that determines the finished size of a cross stitch design is the number of stitches up and down and the thread count of the fabric. Calculate the size of a design as follows.

1 Look at your chart and count the number of stitches in each direction.

2 Divide this number by the number of stitches to 2.5cm (1in) on the fabric of your choice and this will determine the completed design size. For example, 140 stitches divided by 14-count Aida results in a design size of 10in (25.5cm).

3 Now add a margin for stretching, framing or finishing. I always add 13cm (5in) to both dimensions for a picture or sampler. This can be reduced to 7.5cm (3in) for smaller projects.

When calculating design sizes on linen or evenweave, remember that you will be working over two threads, so divide the count of the evenweave by two before you start calculating.

Jane's Tip

Remember when creating a card or trinket pot to allow the extra margin on the aperture size not the stitch count.

Stitch Perfect – PREPARING YOUR FABRIC

❖ Press the fabric before you start, to remove creases and check for marks and blemishes.

❖ Find the middle of the fabric by folding in four and pressing lightly. Open out and work a line of tacking (basting) stitches following the threads to mark the fold and the centre. Remove these stitches when work is completed. Now rule a line on the chart (if using a copy) to match the arrows and the tacking.

❖ Sew a narrow hem or oversew raw fabric edges to prevent fraying. This can be removed on completion. Avoid using adhesive tape or glue as they can 'creep' and attract grime.

❖ Work one large cross stitch at the top of your fabric some distance away from the stitching area – this will remind you which is the top of the work and which way the work is facing.

STITCHING FROM A KIT

Good quality cross stitch kits will supply you with enough fabric and thread to complete the whole design (see picture below). This will be based on you sorting the threads correctly and keeping them in a safe place away from cats and coffee! See also page 120.

◆ Always read all the instructions in the kit pack before starting to stitch.

◆ If the kit threads are supplied as a bundle or swatch, sort them before you start stitching and try to do this is daylight. I have mistaken blues, greys and greens many times when working under domestic electric light. Check that you have all the colours you need and mount all the threads on a thread organizer alongside its shade number (see page 17).

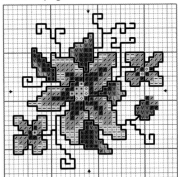

◆ Unless indicated otherwise by the kit designer, start stitching in the middle of a design to ensure an adequate margin for making up.

◆ Find the centre of the chart by following the little arrows at the sides to the centre stitch or the stitch nearest the centre point. You could circle this with a pencil.

JANE'S TIP

Be aware that the physical size of a chart doesn't bear any resemblance to the completed size of the project.

Cross stitch kits vary a little in their contents, depending on the manufacturer, but you should have a chart, embroidery threads, fabric and a needle, and perhaps also a thread organizer and a picture mount or card blank, if appropriate.

HOW TO START STITCHING

It is important to start and finish your stitching neatly, avoiding the use of knots which would create ugly lumps and bumps in your finished work.

KNOTLESS LOOP START

Starting this way (Fig 1) can be very useful with stranded cotton (floss), but only works if you are intending to stitch with an even number of strands, i.e. 2, 4, or 6.

1 Cut the stranded cotton to 80cm (31.5in) long and separate out one strand. Double this strand and then thread your needle with the two ends.

2 Pierce your fabric from the wrong side where you intend to place your first stitch, leaving the looped end at the back of the work. Return your needle to the wrong side after forming a half cross stitch and pass the needle through the waiting loop. The stitch is now anchored and you may begin to stitch.

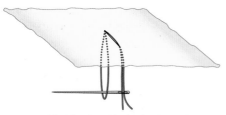

Fig 1 *Starting with a knotless loop.*

> ### JANE'S TIP
> *I don't think that the back has to be as perfect as the front but if you keep it neat you will not have to spend hours sorting out the spaghetti on the back.*

AWAY WASTE KNOT START

Start this way (Fig 2) if working with an odd number of strands or when tweeding threads (where you use one strand each of two or more colours to achieve a mottled, tweedy appearance – see page 17), or if you are a real perfectionist!

1 Thread your needle and make a knot at the end. Take the needle and thread through from the front of the fabric to the back and come up again about 2.5cm (1in) away from the knot.

2 Now either begin cross stitching and work towards the knot, cutting it off when the threads are anchored, or thread the end into your needle and finish off under some completed stitches. Avoid using this method with black thread as it may leave a shadow on the fabric.

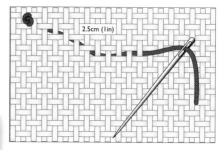

2.5cm (1in)

Fig 2 *Starting with an away waste knot.*

HOW TO HOLD FABRIC

If you are working on a frame or hoop this doesn't really apply but if you are using a sewing action it may be helpful. With a large piece of fabric, I roll the material towards the centre of the area where I am stitching so I'm holding the wrong side of the material.

WORKING A CROSS STITCH

A cross stitch has two parts and can be worked in one of two ways – a complete stitch can be worked, or a number of half stitches may be stitched in one line and then completed on the return journey. Your cross stitch may face either direction but the one essential rule is that all the top stitches should face the same direction to produce the neatest result.

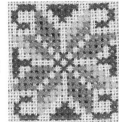

To create perfect cross stitches the strands of thread first need to be aligned. Take two strands of stranded cotton (floss), separate the strands completely and then realign them before threading your needle.

> ### JANE'S TIP
> When using some fibres it is helpful to pass the threads through a lightly dampened sponge to help remove unwanted static from the threads.

FORMING A SINGLE CROSS STITCH ON AIDA OR EVENWEAVE

Bring the needle up from the wrong side of the fabric at the bottom left of an Aida block or to the left of a vertical evenweave thread (see Fig 11 page 29). Cross one block of Aida or two threads of evenweave and insert the needle into the top right-hand corner (see Fig 3 and Fig 4 below). Push through and come up at the bottom right-hand corner. Complete the stitch in the top left-hand corner. To work an adjacent stitch, bring the needle up at the bottom right-hand corner of the first stitch.

Fig 3 Working a single, whole cross stitch on Aida fabric.

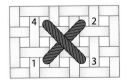

Fig 4 Working a single, whole cross stitch on evenweave fabric.

FORMING CROSS STITCH IN TWO JOURNEYS

Work the first leg of the cross stitch as usual but instead of completing the stitch, work the next half stitch and continue to the end of the row (Fig 5). Complete the cross stitches on the return journey. I recommend this method as it forms neater vertical lines on the back of the work. This method isn't suitable for cross stitching over one fabric thread (see Stitch Perfect – Evenweave in Miniature page 59).

Fig 5 Working cross stitches in two journeys (on evenweave).

> ### JANE'S TIP
> If you prick yourself whilst stitching (or should I say when) and mark your fabric, a dab of your own saliva will remove the stain.

FRACTIONAL CROSS STITCHES

Quarter and three-quarter cross stitches enable us to create curves and smoother lines. Three-quarter cross stitch creates a triangular shape allowing for more detail within small motifs (see examples in the picture below). These stitches are less easy to form on Aida because the needle passes down the central hole in the thread group. When forming these stitches on Aida, a 'sharp' needle is helpful.

Work the first half of the cross stitch as usual, sloping the stitch in the direction shown on the chart. Work the second, quarter stitch over the top and down into the central hole to anchor the first half of the stitch (Fig 6).

STITCH & PARK

When working with a number of different shades you can use several needles at a time to avoid stopping and starting over again. Work a few stitches in one shade, bring the needle out to the front of the work and 'park' it above where you are stitching. Introduce another colour, work a few stitches and then park that colour. Bring back the previous colour, working under the back of the stitches. Use a gold-plated needle to avoid any risk of the needle marking the fabric.

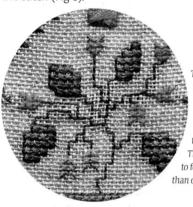

This motif from the *Beautiful Band Sampler* illustrates the use of three-quarter cross stitches very clearly on the little pink flowers. These are always easier to form on evenweave than on Aida.

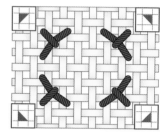

Fig 6 *Working three-quarter cross stitch on evenweave.*

Stitch Perfect – CROSS STITCH

❖ Use the correct size needle for the fabric and number of strands of thread required.

❖ When stitching on evenweave fabric, start to the left of a vertical thread (see Fig 11 page 29) to prevent counting mistakes.

❖ Start with a knotless loop start or away waste knot (see page 22), avoiding knots on the back of the work.

❖ Work the cross stitch in two journeys (see Fig 5 on previous page) forming neat vertical lines on the back of the work. Use a sewing movement – half cross stitch in one direction, covering these original stitches with the second row.

❖ To prevent thread twisting when working cross stitch in two journeys, either turn the work upside down and let the needle spin, or twist the needle as you stitch.

❖ Work cross stitch with all the top stitches facing the same direction.

❖ Come up through unoccupied holes to help keep stitches beautifully formed.

❖ Plan your route around a chart, counting over short distances to avoid mistakes.

❖ Do not travel across the back of the fabric for more than two stitches as trailing thread will show on the front of the work (see Stitch & Park above).

BACKSTITCH OUTLINING

Backstitching is a personal thing. Sometimes it is essential to the project because without it, you wouldn't be able to recognize the finished piece! It is used to add definition to a motif or for details like a cat's whiskers or a ship's rigging.

Stitch Perfect – BACKSTITCH

❖ Try using subtle shades for backstitch to avoid a hard edge to the cross stitches and avoid black unless needed for wrought iron or similar motifs.

❖ Generally, use one strand of stranded cotton and a slightly smaller needle size for backstitch outlining.

❖ Work backstitch after all cross stitching has been completed, to avoid breaking up the backstitch line.

❖ Work backstitch over individual blocks on Aida or pairs of threads on evenweave and avoid working long stitches, unless it is

appropriate or unless you are deliberately aiming for a 'sketchy' backstitch style which does not follow the cross stitch neatly.

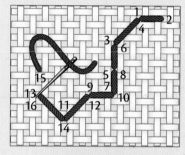

Fig 7 *Working backstitch.*

GOOSE AND PIG

Stitch count: 32h x 71w
Design size: 5.8 x 12.7cm (2¼ x 5in)
Fabric: Zweigart cream 14-count Aida
Needle: Tapestry size 24
Chart: Page 171

These two animals are from the Farmyard Fun Cushion on page 37, with the pig reversed to make a pleasing shape. The motif has been worked twice to show the use of backstitch. The lower version has backstitch added and you can see that the creatures have more character once outlined. Work the design using two strands of stranded cotton (floss) for cross stitch and the French knot, and then one strand for backstitch.

25

Working French Knots

French knots are small but important little stitches often used for eyes and other details. In this book they are shown as coloured circles or knots, with colour and code given in the chart key or on the chart. The design opposite uses massed French knots to great effect.

French knots can cause some distress as they can disappear to the back of the work or end up as a row of knots on the thread in the needle! To work perfect French knots, follow Fig 8. Bring the needle through to the front of the fabric and wind the thread around the needle twice. Begin to 'post' the needle partly through to the back, one thread or part of a block away from the entry point (to stop the stitch being pulled to the wrong side). Now gently pull the thread you've wound, so it sits snugly at the point where the needle enters the fabric. Pull the needle through to the back to have a perfect knot in position.

For bigger French knots, add more thread to the needle as this gives better results than winding more times around the needle.

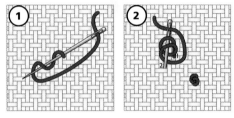

Fig 8 *Creating a French knot.*

Changing Threads and Finishing Off

Changing threads and finishing your work off correctly will pay dividends, creating a neat appearance and a safe, lasting piece of stitching.

At the back of the work, pass the needle under several stitches of the same or similar colour and snip off the loose end close to the stitching (see Fig 9). Small loose ends have a nasty habit of pulling through to the right side! If you are a perfectionist, try finishing the stitches in the direction that you are working – this is particularly relevant when working band samplers, where you don't want to distort the fabric or create a gap in the centre of a band.

When the thread needs replacing, stop stitching and 'park' the needle above the design. Thread a new needle with the replacement thread and form a few stitches. Now un-park the needle and finish the old thread under the new stitches. This will prevent any stitch distortion on the front of the work.

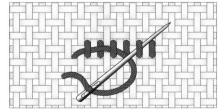

Fig 9 *Finishing off a thread neatly.*

This buddleia and butterfly design is the same as the one on page 18 but has been worked over two threads of a 28-count linen, with the buddleia flower stitched in massed French knots instead of cross stitch, effectively imitating the many small flowers of the plant. The butterflies have been worked over just one linen thread and so are half the size of those in the previous design. To ensure the butterflies are worked in the correct position, stitch them from the flower outwards.

WORKING WITH LINEN

Linen is made from the fibres of the flax plant *Linium usitatissimum*. Unlike other fabrics, linen increases in strength when wet and it is the perfect choice for cross stitch on table or bed linen and for pulled and drawn thread work. Today, linen fabric is used extensively by the fashion industry as pure linen clothing is in great demand. I wear linen clothing and as a result spend plenty of time clutching a steam iron!

Linen manufactured for embroidery is generally an evenweave fabric, which means there are the same number of vertical and horizontal threads to 2.5cm (1in); it does not mean that the threads are all the same thickness or that there are no slubs or wobbly threads! These naturally occurring irregularities can dissuade some stitchers from using it but stitching on linen is not difficult, just different. It is also the fabric of choice when working pulled thread embroidery (see page 106) because you *want* the threads to stay pulled or creased. It is also possible to stitch poems or other text within a small sampler if the border is worked over two threads and the text over one thread.

ROSY APPLES

Stitch count: 45h x 51w   **Design size:** 8.8 x 10cm (3½ x 4in)   **Fabric:** Zweigart Dublin ivory 26-count linen   **Needle:** Tapestry size 24   **Chart:** Page 185

This charming little picture is worked over two threads of linen, using two strands of stranded cotton (floss) for cross stitch and then one for backstitch.

RAILROADING

This technique is used to force two strands of stranded cotton (floss) to lie flat and parallel to each other (Fig 10). When pushing the needle through the fabric, pass it in between the two strands of stranded cotton. You can railroad both parts of the cross stitch or only the top stitch.

Fig 10 *Using the railroading technique.*

STITCH PERFECT – EVENWEAVE/LINEN

The general instructions for working on evenweave fabrics also apply to linen.

❖ Use the correct size needle for the fabric (see page 12).
❖ Separate each strand of stranded cotton (floss) and then re-combine them, ensuring the twist is running in the same direction on each strand.
❖ To avoid reversing the twist, start stitching with an away waste knot (page 22) rather than the loop start method.
❖ On linen and evenweave start stitching to the left of the vertical thread (Fig 11) as this will help prevent counting mistakes.

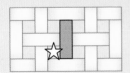

Fig 11 *Starting to the left of a vertical thread on linen/evenweave.*

❖ Work cross stitches over two threads in each direction to even out any discrepancies. If more detail is required, stitches can be formed over one thread.
❖ When stitching over one thread, work the stitches singly rather than in two journeys, to prevent the stitches sliding under the fabric threads.
❖ Learn to railroad (see above): although time-consuming, it produces effective results. Even simpler, as you take the needle out of the fabric, give it a half turn: this will keep the thread from twisting and the stitches will lie flat.
❖ When working across the fabric, for example, on a band sampler, it is good practice to finish the stitches in the direction that you are working.

WORKING PROJECTS

This book is full of projects you can stitch, some of which are shown opposite. This page gives stitching information in a nutshell, which will be particularly helpful for less experienced stitchers. The idea of stitching a project from scratch is sometimes daunting but these basic instructions will get you on track. See also Getting Started pages 10–29.

WHAT THREADS DO I NEED?

The majority of the project designs in this book are charted in the Chart Library (with a few in the main chapters), with the colour keys listing the colours and threads needed. You can use different colours to the ones listed but remember to check that all the colours work well together.

WHICH FABRIC AND HOW MUCH?

The fabric used, the stitch count and the finished design size are given in the caption under the colour pictures of the projects. If you are working the design as photographed just add a margin of 12.5cm (5in) to the design size and you can move on to 'Where Do I Start' (below).

If using alternative fabrics, check the stitch count of the material and if this is different to that of the stitched sample you must work out the finished design size – refer to page 20. A higher thread count will produce a smaller stitched design.

WHERE DO I START?

Start stitching in the middle of the design to ensure an adequate margin for stretching and framing. To find the middle of the fabric, fold it in four and press lightly. Open out the fabric and work a narrow line of tacking (basting) stitches following the threads to mark the fold and the centre. These tacking stitches should be removed on completion of the work.

HOW MANY STRANDS?

If the design you wish to stitch does not indicate in the chart or stitching instructions how many strands of stranded cotton to use, check by carefully pulling a thread from the edge of the fabric and comparing it with the strands of cotton – they should be a similar weight. If using alternative threads to the ones used in the stitched sample, work a few stitches in the fabric margin to check the effect.

BEFORE YOU START

◆ Prepare your fabric for work – see also page 21. Sew a narrow hem or oversew the raw edges to prevent fraying. This can be removed on completion of the project.

◆ Rule a line on the chart (if using a copy) to match the tacking (basting) stitches on your piece of fabric.

◆ Check you have all the thread colours you need and mount all the threads on a piece of card or a thread organizer, adding the shade numbers beside the threads.

◆ Work one large cross stitch at the top of your work away from the stitching to remind you which is the top and which way the work is facing.

This selection of projects gives you some idea of the exciting designs you can create using the comprehensive advice in this book. From the top, clockwise: Hardanger and Honesty Picture (stitching instructions on page 51); Zigzags and Ladders Sampler (page 110); Hellebore Card (page 132); Assisi Dragonfly Sachet (page 93); Blue Ribbon Flower Card (page 86) and Rainbow Alphabet Sampler (page 49).

CREATIVE OPTIONS

This section takes a closer look at some of the fabric and thread options open to the cross stitcher. You will see how easy and rewarding it is to cross stitch on a variety of materials, including perforated paper, silk, waste canvas, non-evenweave fabric and double canvas. Some of the many threads available are explored, showing how effective cross stitching is with yarns other than stranded cotton (floss), such as flower threads, space-dyed threads, rayons, metallics and blending filaments.

CHOOSING AND USING FABRICS

Today there is so much choice, both in fabric thread count and colour, and the next few pages show you a variety of fabrics to whet your appetite and encourage you to look further – the only limit is your imagination and perhaps your eyesight!

The important message is to remind you to choose the appropriate fabric for the job in hand i.e., soft washable cotton Afghan fabric for a baby rather than crisp, crunchy linen and so on. Another example of this would be using pure linen for pulled thread embroidery, as you are creating the holes and therefore the decorative effect by creasing the fabric threads. This would not be as satisfactory if worked on an easy-care material that does not crease!

Bear in mind whether the fabric is for decoration or a more functional use, and select a thread count you can manage without the frustration of working on material that strains your eyes. Most charted designs will adapt to suit different fabrics, for example, you can transfer cross stitch patterns on to canvas and vice versa.

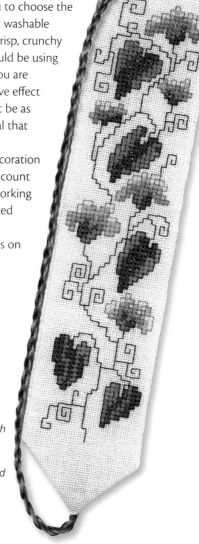

CLIMBING CREEPER BOOKMARK

Stitch count: 98h x 23w
Design size: 18 x 4cm (7 x 1½in)
Fabric: 4.5cm wide (1¾in) ivory 28-count linen band
Needle: Tapestry size 26
Chart: Page 173

This pretty bookmark has been worked on a length of linen band. Work the design over two linen threads, using two strands of stranded cotton (floss) for cross stitch and one for backstitch. I used a simple hemstitch across the top edge (see page 119) and folded the lower edge to a point and stitched it in place invisibly, adding a twisted cord (see page 41).

I would add a note of warning: if you are going to spend hours stitching personal masterpieces – do resist the temptation to economize on fabric quality. I prefer Zweigart and use all the fabrics across their range. I have visited their factory in Germany and have seen how the fabric is woven, dyed and the quality controls that are in place.

LINEN AND AIDA BANDS

Fabric is woven in a variety of widths, but one specialist area is that of bands. Linen band is widely used in Europe for home decorations, door bow embellishments, shelf edging and so on. Linen and Aida bands are also ideal for creating small projects, such as the bookmark opposite, as only two raw edges need to be finished.

You will see in this section that fabrics for counted thread embroidery are excitingly varied. Evenweave linens are available in some lovely colours, from soft and subtle to deep and vibrant, as you can see by the picture here. The range of linen and Aida bands also continues to improve. See page 60 for examples of canvas fabrics.

AGEING LINEN

It is easy to add the appearance of age to linen by dipping it in black tea. The fabric must be a pure, natural fabric such as 100% cotton or linen. Tea-dyeing can be done on the fabric before you start stitching or to the completed embroidery, although you need to make sure that threads used are colourfast (see page 16). After dipping the fabric or needlework in the tea, dry naturally and then press.

JANE'S TIP
To avoid waste and keep fabric costs down, try to buy a 'fat quarter', which is generally 50 x 70cm (20 x 27½in).

COLOURED AND PATTERNED FABRICS

The range of fabrics available to the stitcher is quite overwhelming and I can't illustrate them all here, but hopefully will set you thinking about some of the options available to you. There are fabrics that combine damask fabric with Aida patches forming stitchable areas; others are hemmed as tablecloths and in a myriad of colours, textures and fibre content.

COLOURED FABRICS

Some of the fabric colours just make your fingers itch to stitch, but there are factors to consider. When selecting threads you do need daylight and the fabric of choice at hand as the background fabric colour will have a profound effect on the finished piece. Some of the new, bright colours are simply wonderful to look at, as these bold pincushions show. Take care though with some unusual colours to select threads carefully.

CROSS STITCH HEART PINCUSHIONS

Stitch count: 46h x 45w each   **Design size:** 8.5cm (3¼in) square
Fabric: Zweigart Annabelle 28-count shade 487 (peach) or Zweigart
Cashel linen 28-count shade 227 (lemon)   **Needle:** Tapestry size 24   **Charts:** Page 175

These two bright pincushions are worked on different fabrics but both have the same thread count so the projects are the same size. Use two strands of stranded cotton (floss) for cross stitch. See page 216 for making up a pincushion.

PATTERNED FABRICS

These fabrics have been woven using different coloured threads rather than weaving in white and then dyeing to suit and this offers us all sorts of options. You could use the pattern as part of your project, incorporating it into your design as I have done in this Baby Photograph Keepsake. Alternatively, ignore the pattern and use it as a background, as in the Bouquet and Buttons picture below.

BABY PHOTOGRAPH KEEPSAKE

Stitch count: 15h x 15w
(maximum for each patterned square)
Design size: 2.5cm (1in) square (for each square)
Overall size of case 9 x 11.5cm (3½ x 4½in)
Fabric: Zweigart blue check 14-count Aida, 30 x 18cm (12 x 7in) approx
Needle: Tapestry size 24
Chart: Page 183

This little case is perfect for photos. Change the blue shades to pinks if you prefer. If using the fabric as part of your design, centre the motif within each square. If working on plain fabric, fold the fabric into three to gauge where to place the motifs – see diagram on page 217. Use two strands of stranded cotton (floss) for cross stitch and one for backstitch. To make up the case see page 217.

BOUQUET AND BUTTONS

Stitch count: 41h x 44w
Design size: 7.5 x 8cm
(3 x 3⅛in)
Fabric: Zweigart pink check 14-count Aida
Needle: Tapestry size 24
Chart: Page 171

This charming design uses two strands of stranded cotton (floss) for cross stitch and French knots and one strand for backstitch. Add four mother-of-pearl buttons with contrasting thread.

AFGHAN FABRICS

Afghan fabrics are generally used for making decorative throws or cot blankets although the fabrics do lend themselves to lovely cushions, as shown opposite. I use pure cotton fabrics when making throws as I like the way they handle and wash.

When working an Afghan intended as a throw, remember that the back of the project will be in view so try to be tidy as you work. I work all the design over two fabric threads so that I can work the crosses in two journeys (see page 23) thus forming nice straight lines on the back of the work. It will also grow satisfyingly quickly.

Afghan fabrics do vary – some restrict the areas that can be stitched while others allow you to extend your stitching over the squares. On the two folk-art cushions, I have worked the central parts of the design over two threads within the Afghan squares and the smaller border motifs over one thread.

Cross stitching over one fabric thread (unless on interlocked fabric) is not satisfactory when worked in two journeys; so form each cross stitch individually or perhaps work the border motifs in tent stitch. (See also Stitching in Miniature on page 59.)

I have included a corner of an Afghan throw (the Black-Eyed Susan design, below) to illustrate the frayed edge possible with this fabric. You would need to either hand stitch or use a sewing machine to work a line of stitches invisibly to avoid fraying too far. The frayed edge may then be knotted to create a more decorative effect.

JANE'S TIP

If working on an Afghan fabric with a high acrylic content (which many of the 'easy care' ones have), you may need to use hand cream prior to stitching to smooth your skin and help avoid snagging the fabric.

FARMYARD FUN AND HEARTS AND HOUSES CUSHIONS

Stitch count: 38h x 42w maximum motif size **Design size:** 10.7 x 11.8cm (4¼ x 4½in) maximum motif size   **Fabric:** Zweigart pure cotton Anne 18-count **Needle:** Tapestry size 22
Charts: Pages 170–173

These cushions are both made in the same way. Work the larger motifs over two fabric threads, centring each design within an Afghan square (although this Afghan fabric allows you to extend your stitching further than 44 x 44 stitches if desired). Use three strands of stranded cotton (floss) for cross stitch and two for backstitch. Work the smaller border motifs repeatedly over one fabric thread, using two strands of stranded cotton and completing each cross stitch individually. Work a heart in each corner. Add a grid around the large motifs in cross stitch or double cross stitch over four threads using two strands of Appletons crewel wool.

BLACK-EYED SUSAN

Stitch count: 43h x 48w
Design size: 12cm (4¾in) square
Fabric: Zweigart pure cotton Anne 18-count
Needle: Tapestry size 22
Chart: Page 183

Work the design over two fabric threads, using three strands of stranded cotton (floss) for cross stitch and two for backstitch. Before fraying, work a row of backstitch in thread matching the fabric to define the frayed edge.

EMBROIDERY THREADS

There is now a vast range of thread types available for cross stitch embroidery and some of the most common are shown here. Threads may be supplied in hanks, skeins or wound on to cards or spools and this can be a bit confusing for the less experienced if you do not know what the thread is going to look like.

There are no rules about what you can and cannot do with which threads: the trick is to try the thread on the fabric you intend to use, experiment with the number of strands if appropriate and then see what happens.

It is worth keeping left-over threads clearly marked with the manufacturer and shade number (see page 17) but all is not lost if you have not done this. You can create a sampler using odds and ends (although you won't be able to repeat the project when it is much admired by friends and family!).

A mouth-watering selection of embroidery threads from various manufacturers to tempt you – and there are lots more to choose from!

STRANDED COTTON – Mercerized, divisible, six-ply cotton thread with a soft sheen. Available as solid colours, variegated and multicolour.
STRANDED RAYON – Very shiny, non-metallic, divisible four-ply thread.
PERLÉ COTON OR PEARL COTTON – Glossy single-ply pure cotton thread often used in Hardanger embroidery. They have different names depending on manufacturer. Available as solid colours, space-dyed and in hanks or balls.
SPACE-DYED THREADS – Generally made from cotton or silk and may be stranded or supplied as single threads. They have different colours (or shades of one colour) along their length and are sometimes referred to as hand painted.
FLOWER THREADS – Pure cotton with a matt appearance, available in solid or space-dyed colours.

SPACE-DYED
SILKS

STRANDED RAYONS

SPACE-DYED
FLOWER
THREAD

STRANDED
PERLE RAYON

HAND-PAINTED
SYNTHETIC
THREAD

VARIEGATED
RAYONS

SPACE-DYED
THREADS

SOLID COLOUR
STRANDED
COTTONS

LINEN
THREADS

MULTICOLOURED
STRANDED COTTONS

MULTICOLOURED
PERLE COTTONS

STRANDED COTTONS

Choosing and Managing Threads (page 16) gave detailed information on the use of stranded cotton (floss) in cross stitch embroidery. The pictures on the previous page and the bright needlecase below show you some of the colour range available. Stranded cottons are also perfect for making twisted cords, as shown by the little key keeper opposite. The major thread manufacturers produce solid and variegated stranded cottons. Some Variations threads are shown here.

Stitch Perfect – STRANDED COTTON

✤ Before starting to stitch, separate the strands and realign them before threading your needle.

✤ Work with a length of stranded cotton about 80cm (30in).

✤ If you are not sure how many strands to use, stitch a few complete cross stitches and look at the stitching in daylight – see also page 20.

✤ Cross stitch is generally worked using two strands of stranded cotton on 14-count and 16-count Aida but you can, of course, mix the number of threads used within the same project. For example, you could alter the texture of a piece by working in one, two and even three strands. Try working French knots with different strands..

✤ Before laundering a piece of work, ensure that the threads are colourfast by following the advice on page 16.

BRIGHT NEEDLECASE

Stitch count: 32h x 37w
(front flap, cross stitch only)
Design size: 6.3 x 6.7cm (2½ x 2¾in)
Fabric: Zweigart 14-count cream Aida
Needle: Tapestry size 24
Chart: Page 174

Remember to allow extra fabric for the back flap of the needlecase. Work the design using two strands of stranded cotton (floss) for cross stitch. Use two strands to work the hemstitch (page 119) around three sides of the design and then use two strands to work the two rows of four-sided stitches (page 154) down the 'spine' of the case. My version was completed by stitching two flannel 'pages' to the inside of the four-sided stitches, with a twisted cord (see opposite) added to finish.

SAMPLER KEY KEEPER

Stitch count: 34h x 34w   **Design size:** 6.2cm (2½in) square   **Fabric:** Zweigart Cashel 28-count tea-dyed linen   **Needle:** Tapestry size 24   **Chart:** Page 174

This little project illustrates how a twisted cord made from stranded cottons can add a perfect finishing touch. The ends of the cord can be teased out to make a little tassel. Work the design using two strands of stranded cotton for full and three-quarter cross stitches and one strand for the backstitch outline and initials. Change the initials using the backstitch alphabet on page 198.

MAKING A TWISTED CORD

A twisted cord is perfect for embellishing projects as you can see by the key keeper above, and they are very easy to make.

1 Choose a colour or group of colours in stranded cottons (floss) (or other threads) to match your embroidery.

2 Cut a minimum of four lengths at least four times the finished length required and fold in half. Ask a friend to hold the two ends while you slip a pencil through the loop at the other end.

3 Twist the pencil and continue twisting until kinks appear. Walk slowly towards your partner and the cord will twist.

4 Smooth out kinks from the looped end and secure with a knot at the other end.

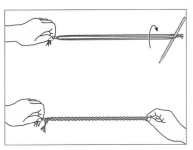

Making a length of twisted cord from embroidery threads.

Metallic Threads and Blending Filaments

There are now dozens of wonderfully vibrant metallic, sparkly and glow-in-the-dark threads available to the cross stitcher. The Christmas Bell Pull (overleaf) has been stitched combining metallics and stranded cottons (floss). In the past, metallic threads have been regarded as rather difficult threads to use but there are now metallics that are much more user friendly. I have included tips from Kreinik, who produce the largest range of metallic and blending filaments – so they should know!

This eyecatching selection of dazzling and colourful metallic threads, braids and blending filaments is sure to make your fingers itch to stitch!

FINE METALLIC THREADS

STRANDED
LIGHT EFFECTS
THREADS

STITCH PERFECT – METALLIC THREADS

❖ When using metallic threads stitch more slowly and more attentively, and use a needle large enough to 'open' the hole in the fabric sufficiently to allow the thread to go through easily.

❖ Use short lengths of thread 46cm (18in) or less to avoid excessive abrasion when pulling the thread through the fabric.

❖ Let your needle hang frequently (after one or two stitches) so the thread can untwist.

❖ Stitch using the 'stab' method rather than the 'hand sewing' method, working your stitches in two movements – up vertically, and down vertically through the fabric.

❖ To vary the amount of shine, change the number of strands of metallic thread – more strands give a greater sheen.

❖ If using DMC Light Effects threads, treat these as space-dyed threads (see page 48) to avoid disrupting the colour pattern.

❖ When using blending filaments, instead of combining the thread with stranded cotton you could overstitch existing cross stitched areas with the filament.

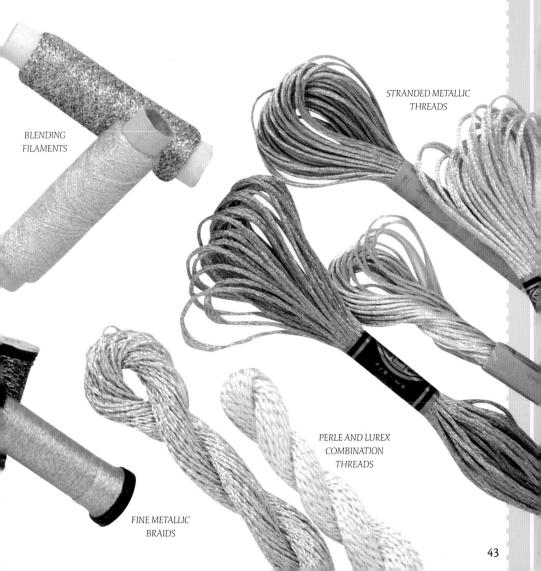

BLENDING FILAMENTS

STRANDED METALLIC THREADS

PERLE AND LUREX COMBINATION THREADS

FINE METALLIC BRAIDS

USING METALLIC THREADS

The projects on these two pages will allow you to explore metallic threads and their effects on different fabrics, and also create some attractive gifts and keepsakes.

I think the secret of using metallic threads is to find the style and thickness needed for the project by looking at the threads when you make your selection. Some fine yarns are referred to as 'braids' but look like normal thread, so it is much easier to select by eye, unless you have a specific list of requirements from the designer.

Some yarns are stitched using a needle and some are thicker, so are added to the surface of the design and then stitched or couched in place, so be prepared to experiment. (Silk ribbon and fine lace may also be treated in this way.)

When using very glossy metallic gold or silver threads, it is vital that you work with short lengths, about 46cm (18in), and a needle large enough help the threads through the fabric. If you work with long lengths you will find that the gold or silver flakes away from the core thread as you work and you lose the metallic effect.

JANE'S TIP

Metallic braids, such as Kreinik #4 braid, can be moistened with a damp sponge to help relax the thread and reduce twisting and knotting.

CHRISTMAS BELL PULL

Stitch count: 62h x 30w
Design size: 11.3 x 5.5cm (4½ x 2⅛in)
Fabric: Zweigart Cashel linen 28-count shade 513
Needle: Tapestry size 24
Chart: Page 180

This pretty little project could be stitched on sparkly Aida fabric if preferred. Work using two strands of stranded cotton (floss) for cross stitch, double cross stitch and French knots. Where the Anchor Lamé metallic thread is used, divide and use as described on the chart. Work the backstitch using one strand. See page 214 for making up the bell pull. Make a hanging cord using the left-over threads (see page 41), teasing out the ends into little tassels.

CHRISTMAS PARCEL NAPKIN RING

Stitch count: 27h x 20w
Design size: 5 x 3.6cm (2 x 1½in)
Fabric: Zweigart 14-count Star Aida
Needle: Tapestry size 24
Chart: Page 179

Work the cross stitch using three strands of DMC Light Effects. Work the darker area of the bow with three strands of Anchor Lamé. Work the lighter part with one strand of stranded cotton and three strands of the lamé together. Add backstitch with one strand of navy blue stranded cotton. To make up as a napkin ring, fold in the raw edges, hem them invisibly and join them at the back to make a continuous ring.

BLUE BOW AND BERRIES

Stitch count: 40h x 40w
Design size: 7.5cm square (3 x 3in)
Fabric: Zweigart 14-count linen Aida
Needle: Tapestry size 24
Chart: Page 179

Work the design using two strands of stranded cotton (floss) and six strands of Anchor Lamé for cross stitch and one strand of stranded cotton for backstitch. The card was made using handmade blue paper, red card and a decorative ribbon. See page 215 for making cards.

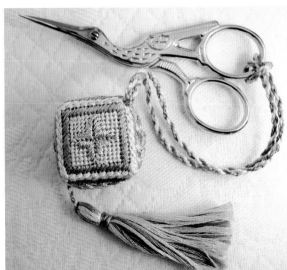

A sparkly cube like this makes an interesting scissor or key keeper or a decoration for a Christmas tree and is a great way to experiment with metallic threads. It is worked as a flat embroidery on single canvas and is shown on page 61 in a red/green/gold colourway, where you will also find the stitching instructions.

Using Blending Filaments

Blending filaments are light, delicate threads intended to be combined with other fibres, usually with stranded cotton (floss) to add a glisten or sparkle. For example, pearl blending filament is ideal combined with white stranded cotton to create snow effects, as you can see in the exquisite little Snowy Bird House Card opposite. You can see blending filament used alone to create delicate spider's webs on the Anemone Floral Cushion on page 53. Refer to the Stitch Perfect box on page 43 for advice on working with metallic threads.

Jane's Tip

Blending filament is perfect for adding reflective highlights to areas of sunlight, moonlight, dew and water. It was used in this way for the water in the kingfisher design on page 9.

Threading Blending Filament

When combining blending filament with stranded cotton (floss) in one needle, follow the four-part diagram here, as this method anchors the thread firmly in the needle.

1 Loop the thread and pass the loop through the eye of the needle, leaving a short tail.

2 Now pull the loop of thread over the point of the needle.

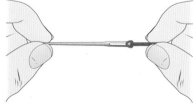

3 Tighten the loop at the end of the eye of the needle by pulling the two ends of the thread.

4 Gently stroke the knotted thread to 'lock' it in place. Add the stranded cotton by threading it on to the needle in the usual way.

SNOWY BIRD HOUSE

Stitch count: 39h x 38w
Design size: 7cm (2¾in) square
Fabric: Zweigart 14-count ivory
linen Aida
Needle: Tapestry size 24
Chart: Page 174

*Work this charming motif using two
strands of stranded cotton (floss)
for cross stitch, adding three strands
of Balger Blending Filament to the
stranded cotton when working the
snow on the roof. Use two strands of
DMC Light Effects E321 for the holly
berries and robin's breast. Add the
backstitch in one strand of stranded
cotton. Make up into a card by framing
the embroidery with strips of gold card
secured with double-sided adhesive
tape and add a festive bow to finish.*

SPACE-DYED THREADS

One of the joys of working cross stitch is that the stitch stays the same throughout the project but the effect can be changed by clever use of different fibres. Space-dyed threads, sometimes called variegated threads, have different colours (or shades of one colour) along their length. They change colour at regular, spaced intervals so you can decide where you want a particular shade to appear in your stitching. It is a very relaxing way to stitch as a whole project is worked from just the one skein of thread. Follow the basic guidelines below for using space-dyed threads and the effects will be stunning – and sometimes surprising! Your work will definitely not be the same as any other stitcher.

In a way, working with space-dyed threads is a type of designing without the angst! There are dozens of manufacturers of these specialist fibres so feel free to experiment and some are shown here and overleaf to give you some idea of the yummy colours available. If you can't find the exact version used in my projects do try something else – there will be dozens of alternatives.

The Rainbow Band Sampler opposite has been stitched using space-dyed threads throughout, with the addition of a little gold metallic. In this instance I have used De Haviland Flower Thread and the sampler was very relaxing to stitch as the whole project was worked from the same skein. I have used space-dyed threads in other parts of this book and love to combine them with other fibres, for example, the Hardanger and Honesty design shown on page 51 uses Anchor Multicolour Pearl thread, and you will see space-dyed thread used in the blackwork section later in the book.

> ### JANE'S TIP
> Not all space-dyed threads are colourfast so you need to consider the end use when selecting them. After spending dozens of hours on a Hardanger tablecloth, it would be heartbreaking to ruin it in the first wash (see Checking for Colourfastness on page 16).

Stitch Perfect – SPACE-DYED THREADS

✤ When combining stranded cottons (floss) with space-dyed threads, compare the colours along the length of the thread to check that the shades tone successfully.

✤ Look at the skein and cut the thread to see where colours start and finish.

✤ Irrespective of the number of strands used for the project, always start with an away waste knot and not the loop start, as the colour order will be disrupted.

✤ When threading the needle, check the colour you intend to use is near the away waste knot.

✤ When working cross stitches always complete each cross as you go and do not form cross stitches in two journeys.

✤ Use a length of thread only whilst the colours suit the project. Do not attempt to use the whole length of thread if the colour of that section is not appropriate.

RAINBOW ALPHABET SAMPLER

Stitch count: 69h x 28w
Design size: 12.5 x 5cm
(5 x 2in)
Fabric: Zweigart 14-count
linen Aida
Needle: Tapestry size 24
Chart: Page 181

Work the cross stitches using one strand of De Haviland English Flower Thread in rainbow shades, adding twirls in backstitch. Work Rhodes stitches with one strand. Use one strand of Madeira gold metallic for the adapted double cross stitch. Frame as desired.

Stitch Perfect
– FLOWER THREADS

❖ Experiment with the thread thickness of Flower Thread as it varies slightly.

❖ Use the correct number of strands for the fabric in question (see page 20).

❖ You may need to use stranded cotton (floss) rather than the Flower Thread for backstitch as it may be too heavy for the project.

❖ Use shorter lengths when working with Flower Thread as it becomes rather fluffy if pulled through the fabric too many times.

UNUSUAL THREADS

Space-dyed or variegated threads vary enormously, not only in price but also in fibre content and colour variation. Some have quite simple colour patterns, while others have more complex or subtle arrangements of colour. The Hardanger and Honesty picture opposite uses a pretty Anchor variegated thread for the Kloster blocks. Your local needlecraft shop will probably have examples of interesting and unusual threads from many different manufacturers, perhaps including Caron, Stef Francis, Thread Gatherers and Oliver

Twists. A word of warning though: some manufacturers do not always give their colour ranges different code numbers, which makes it rather difficult to find more of a thread you have been working with – so make sure you buy enough for your project!

Using variegated threads to introduce a different look to your work is great fun. Some are completely randomly dyed, so choosing different sections of colour and predicting how they will change as the thread is used is not always possible but they can be useful for working mixed greenery, brick walls etc.

HARDANGER AND HONESTY PICTURE

Stitch count: 54h x 50w   **Design size:** 9.8 x 9cm (3¾ x 3½in)   **Fabric:** Zweigart cream 28-count linen (not suitable for Aida)   **Needle:** Tapestry size 22 and 24   **Chart:** Page 182

Work the design using two strands of stranded cotton (floss) for cross stitch and one for backstitch. Use one strand of Anchor Multicolour Pearl No.5 for the Kloster blocks and one strand of cream Pearl No.12 for the filling stitches (see pages 96–105 for Hardanger instructions). Mount and frame as preferred.

These two details show the Kloster blocks formed in a pretty variegated thread, with various filling stitches added in a similar colour to the fabric, including dove's eyes, corner dove's eyes, spider's webs and corner needleweaving.

51

MIXING THREAD TYPES

There are no rules about which threads go with which and there's no limit to what you can achieved by mixing fibres. This has been common practice in the machine embroidery and free embroidery worlds but perhaps has been slower coming to those who count!

A chart is the map we use to transfer the design from the paper to the fabric and the key may be simply a list of shades or in the case of the Anemone Floral Cushion shown opposite, the key also refers to types of thread and thread thicknesses. The idea of this design is to tempt you to look at charts in a different way and try new threads with at least a little gay abandon. Stitchers who enjoy counted thread embroidery are by their nature used to following patterns, or in our case charts, and hopefully this pretty cushion will tempt you to push the boundaries, just a little.

ANEMONE FLORAL CUSHION

Stitch count: 69h x 69w   **Design size:** 12.5cm (5in) square   **Fabric:** Zweigart ivory 28-count linen
Needle: Tapestry size 24 and 26   **Chart:** Page 178

The central panel on this cushion has been stitched using stranded cotton (floss), linen thread, Pearsall silk, Kreinik blending filament and De Haviland Tudor Twist. Refer to the Stitch Library for working the stitches. Work the cross stitch first using two strands of stranded cotton, Pearsall silk and linen thread. Work the outer border of crossed cushion stitch in one strand of Tudor Twist, adding the spider's web in Kreinik blending filament 034. It might help to use a frame when adding the web. Add a dragonfly charm (see Suppliers) using one strand of matching thread and make up as a cushion (see page 219).

The central panel of the Anemone Floral Cushion uses an attractive combination of mixed threads, including a variegated blending filament for the delicate cobwebs. The crossed cushion stitch border is very colourful.

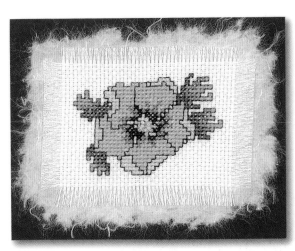

ANEMONE CARD

Stitch count: 26h x 39w
Design size: 4.6 x 7cm
(1¾ x 2¾in)
Fabric: Zweigart Star
14-count Aida
Needle: Tapestry size 24
Chart: Page 178

This card uses the flower from the chart on page 178 (with a few ad libs!). Use two strands of stranded cotton (floss) for cross stitch and one for backstitch. The card is made by layering a fluffy, handmade paper on green card using double-sided tape.

Stitching on Non-Evenweave

So far we have seen how cross stitching looks on evenweave fabrics but non-evenweave or un-evenweave linen was used to create samplers and counted masterpieces long before the concept of evenweave had been invented, and it is exciting to attempt to recreate a design on non-evenweave material. The little violet card below has been stitched on linen scrim, a non-evenweave but pure linen fabric, which usually ends up as tea-towels or dish-cloths and isn't normally intended for embroidery.

The term 'evenweave' refers to the method used to manufacture the fabrics we use for cross stitch and does not mean that the material will have no lumps and bumps! This misunderstood term means that when the fabric is woven, the number of warp and weft threads (along the length and across the width) are the same. This is why when you work a cross stitch on evenweave fabric, the stitch appears square rather than squashed, shortened or elongated. However, cross stitches worked on non-evenweave fabric *will* be affected by the uneven weave, becoming slightly shortened or elongated; therefore you will need to experiment with the characteristics of the fabric to achieve the best results. And the results can be wonderful, especially if you are aiming to replicate the authentic look of antique samplers. If you love that aged look, as I do, refer to *Cross Stitch Antique Style Samplers* (D&C, 2005) for a wealth of designs.

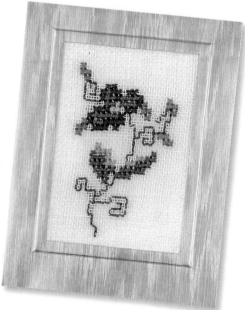

VIOLET CARD

Stitch count: 29h x 19w
Design size: 7.5 x 4.5cm (3 x 1¾in)
Fabric: linen scrim 22/24-count
Needle: Tapestry size 24
Charted motif: Page 177

This card uses the left-hand violet from the Willow Tree Sampler chart. Use three strands of stranded cotton (floss) for cross stitch and two for backstitch. Mount into a double-fold card.

BUMBLEBEE FLY SWAT

Stitch count: 18h x 34w
Design size: Depends on your swat or item being used!
Fabric: Use your imagination
Needle: Tapestry size 24
Chart: Page 173

I have added this amusing little project just to make the point that you can add stitching to anything with a grid! Use four strands of stranded cotton (floss) for cross stitch and two strands for backstitch.

WILLOW TREE SAMPLER

Stitch count: 67h x 66w   **Design size:** 11.5 x 9.5cm (4½ x 3¾in) approx
(will vary depending on the non-evenweave)   **Fabric:** Cross Stitch Guild non-evenweave 28/32 linen
Needle: Tapestry size 28   **Chart:** Page 177

*If you look at the stitch count of this project it would be square on an evenweave fabric but you can
see that it is portrait shaped. Work the design on Cross Stitch Guild non-evenweave fabric, using two
strands of stranded cotton (floss) for cross stitch and one for backstitch. Use two shades of green and
two strands for the random French knots added to the willow. Frame as desired.*

Stitch Perfect – Non-Evenweave

❖ To know non-evenweave fabric and its
foibles, work a square of 20 tacking stitches
counting over two threads, to see whether
a landscape (long) or portrait (tall) shape
is created.

❖ Work a small test piece on the fabric and
check you have the effect you require.

❖ If you are planning a traditional sampler,
it is important to select motifs that are
of the right style and weight and which
will benefit from the effect produced by

non-evenweave fabric e.g., a rabbit when
stitched may look more like a hare!

❖ Don't be afraid to experiment with different
motifs that will alter depending on the
fabric direction. Trial and error is the way
you will achieve the most successful results.

❖ If you want the design to fit a certain frame,
be aware that design size may vary as the
thread count may not be constant.

❖ Non-evenweaves can be given a lovely aged
look by tea-dyeing (see page 33).

Using Stitching Paper

Fabric isn't the only material you can cross stitch on. Stitching paper (perforated paper) can be stitched, folded, glued and cut to make pretty cross stitch projects and used to fill scrapbooks and treasure albums. I have collected items stitched on early perforated paper for many years, including samplers, bookmarks and needle cases.

Stitching paper is based on early Victorian punched paper, also called Bristol Board, made in England as early as 1840. The Victorians used it to work bookmarks, needle cases, pincushions, glove and handkerchief boxes, notebook covers and greetings cards.

Stitching paper is generally the equivalent of a 14-count fabric, so you can transfer cross stitch charts on to this medium as long as the design does not include three-quarter cross stitches. I have used stitching paper here to create a gift card and a hollyhock design.

I have also included an example of Stitching Cards produced by Tokens & Trifles (see Suppliers), which are the closest examples of the ready-formed bookmarks and paper scraps available during Victorian times (see opposite). These stitching cards are available in different stitch counts.

HELLEBORE GIFT CARD

Stitch count: Not appropriate here
Design size: 8 x 12cm (3¼ x 4¾in)
Fabric: Stitching paper gold 14-count
Needle: Tapestry size 24
Chart: Page 183 (elements charted separately)

Work the motifs using three strands of stranded cotton (floss) for cross stitch, one strand of gold metallic for the centre detail and two strands of stranded cotton for the backstitch outline. To make up, cut out the motifs leaving a small margin around the edge as shown in the hollyhock detail photograph below and then arranged on a double-fold card with a green insert, fixing the various parts in place with double-sided adhesive tape.

HOLLYHOCK

Stitch count: 29h x 34w
Design size: 5 x 6.2cm (2 x 2½in)
Fabric: Stitching paper black 14-count
Needle: Tapestry size 24
Chart: Page 180

Work an individual flower using three strands of stranded cotton (floss) for cross stitch. I have started to cut out the flower leaving one row of paper at the edge. You could create a remarkable effect by working individual flowers on paper, cutting them out and applying them to a cross-stitched stem.

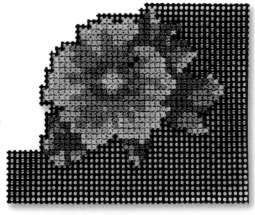

Stitch Perfect – STITCHING PAPER

- Stitching paper is quite strong but it does need to be handled with care.
- There is a right and a wrong side to the paper: the smoother side is the right side.
- Avoid folding the paper unless this is part of the design.
- Find the centre of the paper with a ruler and mark with a pencil. Pencil lines can be removed with a soft rubber.
- On stitching paper, use three strands of stranded cotton (floss) for the cross stitch and two strands for backstitch outlining and lettering.
- Complete all stitching before any cutting.
- Draw the cutting lines on the back of the completed stitching using a soft pencil.
- Use small, sharp-pointed scissors or a good craft knife to cut out the design and any decorative elements of the pattern.
- Where appropriate, stick completed sections together using double-sided adhesive tape, unless stitching is required.

TUDOR ROSE HEART

Stitch count: 40h x 49w
Design size: 5.6 x 7cm (2½ x 2¾in)
Fabric: Heart-shaped stitching card 18-count (see Suppliers)
Needle: Tapestry size 28
Chart: Page 184

Work the motif using one strand of stranded cotton (floss) for cross stitch, half cross stitch and backstitch. Join the two cards together using a running stitch around the existing perforations using one strand of DMC 3685 (Anchor 1028).

Stitch Perfect – STITCHING CARDS

- Stitching Cards are often much finer than stitching paper.
- Check your stitch count before you start – you do not want to run over the edge!
- When using Stitching Cards you can use the ivory side or the antique finish on the reverse.
- Use a size 28 needle to avoid distorting the ready-made holes in the cards.
- Use one strand of stranded cotton (floss) for cross stitch and backstitch.
- The cards are supplied with an un-perforated blank which may be used to cover the wrong side of the stitching.
- If you are tempted to add beads you will need to select Petite Glass beads because of the finer stitch count.

Stitching in Miniature

I mentioned on page 20, the connection between stitch counts and design size and you can see by the photographs below and opposite the scale change achieved by working a charted design on very fine fabric. I have used silk gauze and evenweave linen to create some tiny counted projects. Indeed, in the dolls' house world stitching in miniature is the norm. Little samplers, pictures, pole screens, cushions and so on can be created from using counted charts and fine-count fabrics. Look in dolls' house embroidery books and you'll see what I mean.

Silk gauze is very expensive but you only need small amounts and it can be purchased in small squares ready mounted. Cross stitchers generally think stitching on silk gauze 40 stitches to 2.5cm (1in) is out of the question because it sounds so fine but it is much less taxing than first imagined. Silk gauze is constructed in such a way that although the stitch count is high, the holes in the fabric are large and easier to see than you think! The secret is to prepare the fabric as described right and work in a good light with the correct size gold-plated needle. I use a size 28 needle and work under a standard lamp which gives a wonderful light but doesn't get too hot.

I have included two flower motifs that have been stitched in miniature using two different stitches to suit the specific fabric – the pansy has been cross stitched on silk gauze and mounted into a key ring, while the rose card is worked on linen in tent stitch.

Mounting Silk Gauze

When working on silk gauze you will need to use a simple mount-board frame.
1 Cut two pieces of stiff mount board to the size of your fabric.
2 Cut two sections or windows out of the centre of each piece of board – these sections need to be just big enough to work the embroidery.
3 Using double-sided adhesive tape, sandwich the silk gauze piece between the two boards. The frame can easily be removed once stitching is completed.

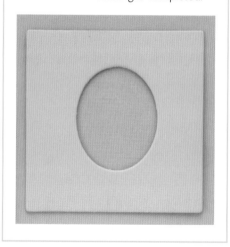

PANSY KEY RING

Stitch count: 25h x 25w
Design size: 1.6cm (⅝in) square
Fabric: 40-count silk gauze
Needle: Tapestry size 28
Chart: Page 179

Work the design using one strand of stranded cotton (floss) for cross stitch and mount into a purchased key ring (see Suppliers).

Stitch Perfect – SILK GAUZE IN MINIATURE

❖ Silk gauze is constructed in a similar way to interlock canvas, to ensure that the threads will not slide.

❖ Silk gauze should be worked in a small mount-board frame to prevent the fabric distorting (see opposite).

❖ Half cross stitch or full cross stitch may be used successfully.

❖ Try stitching a small section to check your tension because you may find that half cross stitch is adequate.

❖ Avoid carrying threads across the back of work because it will show from the front.

❖ You can work long stitches and half cross stitches on silk gauze without distortion because it is interlocked.

ROSE CARD

Stitch count: 32h x 23w
Design size: 3 x 2cm (1⅛ x ¾in)
Fabric: Zweigart Cashel antique white 28-count linen
Needle: Tapestry size 28
Chart: Page 179

Work the rose over one thread using one strand of stranded cotton (floss) for the tent stitch (rather than half cross stitch) and then add the backstitch in one strand. Mount the design into a double-fold card with a circular aperture to fit the embroidery. The partly worked rose is cross stitched over two fabric threads, showing the change in design size by working over two threads not one.

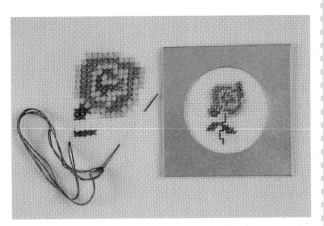

Stitch Perfect – EVENWEAVE IN MINIATURE

❖ If working cross stitch over one thread on evenweave, work each cross stitch individually rather than in two journeys to stop the stitches sliding under neighbouring fabric threads.

❖ If working over one thread on linen (or any evenweave) use tent stitch rather than half cross stitch, as tent stitch will give

better coverage of the fabric and keep the stitches in position. If half cross stitch is used the threads will slide under neighbouring fabric threads.

❖ Select your evenweave fabric with care, with the minimum of slubs and imperfections, which are less easily disguised when working over one thread.

WORKING ON CANVAS

I enjoy the contrast of working cross stitch designs on canvas for a change of effect and have designed projects commercially using canvas as an alternative to Aida or evenweave. Stitchers are sometimes nervous of transferring designs on to canvas when they were designed for fabric but the principles are the same. Early French samplers were generally stitched on canvas with the background left unstitched, to great effect – so have a go! Just remember to count the thread of the canvas and not the holes. Canvas can be made from cotton, linen and plastic and is available in four mesh sizes – 10-, 12-, 14- and 18-count (threads to 2.5cm/1in). Any gauge of canvas can be used with any chart. Canvas is available in two main types: double-thread (duo) canvas and single-thread (mono) canvas. See page 63 for working on single canvas. The material with blue lines shown below is waste canvas, a removable background fabric – see page 66.

See page 63 for working on single canvas. ... see page 66.

> ### JANE'S TIP
> Your choice of fabric to stitch on will depend on the stitches you plan to use, your eyesight and whether the project is decorative or functional. For example, canvas is perfect for cushions, chair seats and so on, which need to be harder wearing.

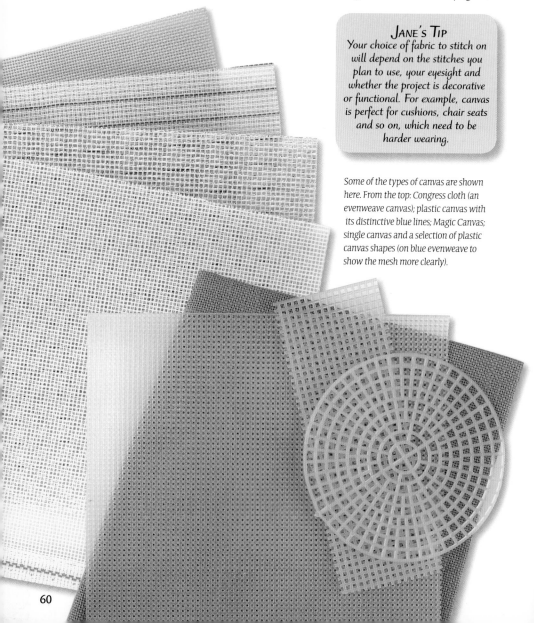

Some of the types of canvas are shown here. From the top: Congress cloth (an evenweave canvas); plastic canvas with its distinctive blue lines; Magic Canvas; single canvas and a selection of plastic canvas shapes (on blue evenweave to show the mesh more clearly).

SPARKLY CHRISTMAS CUBE

Stitch count: 16h x16w each face   **Design size:** 2.5cm (1in) cube   **Fabric:** 18-count single canvas
Needle: Tapestry size 22   **Chart:** Page 176

A sparkly cube (made by Sue Hawkins as a Christmas tree decoration) would make an interesting scissor or key keeper. It is shown on page 45 in a blue/silver colourway. Work the design as a flat embroidery over different numbers of canvas threads as shown on the chart. Use six strands when working with stranded cotton (floss) and six strands of Anchor Lamé for all the counted stitches, referring to the Stitch Library for working the rice stitch, tent stitch, satin stitch and Rhodes stitch. Make up into a cube as described on page 213. See page 41 for making a twisted cord and page 218 for making a tassel.

*The Sparkly Christmas Cube features three designs, each stitched twice:
these three pictures show the different faces of the cube.*

WORKING ON DOUBLE CANVAS

This type of canvas, also called Duo or Penelope is the same as mono canvas except that the threads are grouped in pairs in each direction and are usually finer. As with an evenweave fabric, stitches are worked over the double threads but if you want to put more detail into part of a design, you can make four times as many stitches by using every canvas thread. Half cross stitch, full cross stitch and tent stitch can be worked on double canvas.

Cross stitch charts may be used to work designs on canvas and vice versa as I have done with this pretty bluebell motif, worked once on Aida and mounted as a book patch and once on double canvas.

 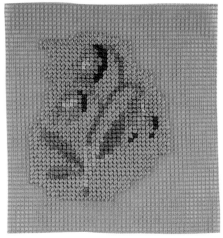

BLUEBELL ON AIDA AND DOUBLE CANVAS

Stitch count: 36h x 28w   **Design size:** 5.7 x 4.5cm (2¼ x 1¾in) on 16-count Aida
Fabric: Cream 16-count Aida or double canvas 10-count   **Needle:** Tapestry size 22   **Chart:** Page 185

This motif has been worked on Aida and also on double canvas to show that charts may be transferred on to canvas if preferred. The cross stitch version uses two strands of stranded cotton (floss) for cross stitch. The canvas version uses six strands for cross stitch and DMC 352 (Anchor 9) for the tent stitch background colour.

Stitch Perfect – CANVAS

❖ Before stitching on double canvas, use a thick tapestry needle to push apart the double threads. This is known as pricking out the canvas and will make stitching easier if you intend to combine working one and two threads.

❖ Using double canvas when adding beads to a design creates the most satisfactory results as the beads stay nicely in position, not wobbling as they tend to do on single canvas.

❖ When counting canvas, always count the *threads* and not the holes, because your stitches are made over threads and not in holes. This is a common stumbling block but you will always get it right if you remember it this way – holes in canvas cannot be counted because they are empty and therefore do not exist!

❖ When working on single canvas it is best to use continental or diagonal tent stitch because if you use half cross stitch some of them may slip under the weave of the canvas and will be very uneven.

WORKING ON SINGLE/MONO CANVAS

Single-thread or mono canvas is constructed of simple, even weaves and is also available in a deluxe quality, where the threads are polished before the canvas is woven and so the yarn passes smoothly through the canvas as you stitch. Single-thread canvas is suitable for any piece of work but especially upholstery, such as seat covers where the embroidery will be stretched unevenly when the seat is in use. The canvas threads are free to move a little on each other and so adjust to the stress rather than tearing. You will find both ordinary and deluxe canvas in white or brown (the latter is known as antique) and you should choose according to the colours of yarn that you will be using.

A word of warning: some commercial kits tell you to work half cross stitch on single canvas. A much better result is obtained by using tent stitch, but you will probably run out of wool as tent stitch uses about half as much yarn again as half cross stitch. You have to decide whether to buy more wool or settle for a rather thin-looking finished piece with inferior wearing qualities.

JANE'S TIP
Deluxe canvas is always worth the extra expense as the polished threads help to prevent the yarn snarling up.

WORKING ON INTERLOCK CANVAS

Single/mono canvas is also available as interlock canvas, with the threads along the length doubled and twisted together to hold the cross threads firmly in place. This produces a more stable canvas, ideal for designs that include long stitches, which might otherwise pull loose canvas threads together and make holes in your work. The Topiary Trees Needlecase, with its satin stitch,

benefitted from being stitched on interlock canvas. The disadvantage of interlock canvas is that it is only available in white so you must take care not to stitch too tightly or the white will show through. Interlock is easy to make up once the embroidery is finished because it does not fray, unlike mono deluxe canvas which will very quickly fray right to the edge of the stitching unless great care is taken.

TOPIARY TREES NEEDLECASE AND PENDANT

Stitch count: 53h x 46w for case;
21h x 21w for pendant
Design size: 7.5 x 6.5cm (3 x 2½in) for case;
3cm (1⅛in) square for pendant
Fabric: 18-count single canvas
Needle: Tapestry size 22
Chart: Page 184

Work the satin stitch borders with one strand of Anchor Multicolour Pearl No.5 and the rest of the pattern with two strands in tent stitch, with a cream tent stitch background. (You could omit the background and work the design as cross stitch on evenweave or Aida.) Work the spine and outside edge of the case in long-legged cross stitch and attach the pendant with a twisted cord (see page 41). Line the case and pendant with dark green felt invisibly hemmed with matching thread.

USING MAGIC CANVAS

This specialized product is a treated interlock single canvas that does not fray. It can be folded and so is excellent for three-dimensional projects. It has an attractive appearance, so it isn't necessary to cover the background with stitching. I have used a sparkly version for some window light catchers but Magic Canvas is also available in a variety of colours, including white, red, yellow, green, blue, black, gold and silver.

LIGHT CATCHERS

Stitch count: 28h x 28w
(each project including eyelets)
Design size: 4cm (1½in) square
Fabric: Zweigart Magic Canvas 18-count
in white and silver
Needle: Tapestry size 22   **Chart:** Page 185

Work the motif on one half of the canvas then fold the other half to cover the back of the stitching. Cross stitch the darker blue and brown in two strands of stranded cotton (floss) and work the lighter blue in half cross stitch in two strands. Add the eyelets in two strands and the backstitch in one.

BEADED PICTURE FRAME

This fun project takes no time at all and you can use the frame for a little photo or a tiny piece of stitching. I keep a jar of assorted glass beads in a glorious array of colours for just such a project. No chart is needed – just do your own thing. Fold a 10cm square (4in) of Magic Canvas into four and then fold in all four corners and press firmly. Now fold out the points to meet the outside edge. I joined the seams at the sides with matching threads and assorted Mill Hill seed beads, adding a few to the folded points. You could use Nymo thread to attach the beads, a specialized beading thread.

USING PLASTIC CANVAS AND PERFORATED CANVAS

These materials are very popular and are used in great quantities and in many ways, particularly in the United States of America. Plastic canvas is made from sheets of plastic punched with a mesh of holes and you use these holes to stitch a design just as you would on Aida. Perforated plastic canvas is very similar to stitching paper (see page 56).

Because these materials are stiffer than Aida they are often used for three-dimensional projects, such as festive decorations, napkin rings, picture frames, boxes and trinket pots. The plastic pieces can be trimmed to a shape with sharp scissors, joined together by stitching and can also be used to support a design already stitched on Aida or evenweave. Plastic canvas is available in 7-, 10- and 14-count and as pre-cut shapes. I have used a ready-made plastic canvas heart for the project shown below, concealing the edge of the canvas with blanket stitch.

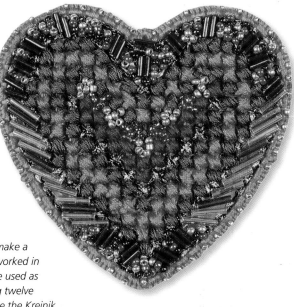

> ### JANE's TIP
> If you accidentally cut a bar on your plastic canvas, it can be repaired with superglue or a hot glue gun.

BEADED CHRISTMAS HEART

Stitch count: 18h x 19w
Design size: 7.6 x 7.6cm (3 x 3in)
Fabric: Plastic canvas heart 7-count
Needle: Tapestry size 22
Chart: Page 181

This project is fun to do and would make a pretty Christmas tree decoration. If worked in cross stitch without beads it could be used as a coaster. Work the cross stitch using twelve strands of stranded cotton (floss). Use the Kreinik 1/8in Ribbon to add the backstitch and the cross stitch as shown on the chart. Work blanket stitch around the edge of the heart, adding the Mill Hill Petite beads (using one strand of stranded cotton) to cover any gaps. Add the seed and bugle beads at random in the remaining spaces on the canvas (see picture for guidance).

> ### JANE's TIP
> If you want the edge of the plastic canvas to be well covered, use more strands of thread when working the blanket stitch edging.

Using Waste Canvas

Waste canvas is a really useful material that enables the cross stitcher to transfer charted designs on to fabrics that were not intended for that purpose and therefore do not have an even, countable weave. Today, the most commonly used application for this technique is to add designs to sweatshirts, T-shirts and baby clothes. Before waste canvas was produced commercially this technique was worked using linen as the waste fabric and if a very fine stitch count is needed this would still be the fabric of choice.

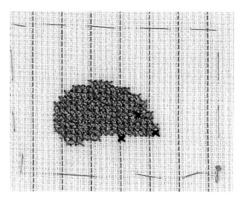

Waste canvas is a double canvas treated with a water-soluble starch product, which makes it simple to remove the threads after stitching but is therefore unsuitable for any other type of use. It is easily distinguished by the blue line running through the fabric. The waste material is applied to the garment or fabric and the grid is used to count whilst the design is stitched and then the threads of the canvas are removed.

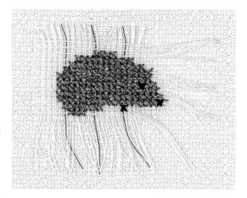

As you can see by the photographs here, the technique is worked in three stages and is described fully in Stitch Perfect opposite.

1 Tack the waste fabric in position.
2 Stitch the design from the chart.
3 Remove the waste threads.

Once all the waste threads have been removed, check for any missed stitches and add any additional backstitch outlining that might be needed to complete the design. Press the finished piece of stitching from the wrong side on soft towels (see page 210).

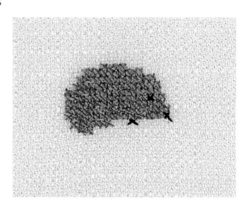

LITTLE HEDGEHOG

Stitch count: 11h x 18w   **Design size:** 2 x 3.3cm (¾ x 1¼in)
Fabric: 14-count waste canvas and viscose dress fabric in cream (or your garment)
Needle: Tapestry size 26 and crewel size 5   **Chart:** Page 167

This little creature has been stitched to illustrate the process of working with waste canvas. He is also a good example of tweeding threads – combining more than one shade in the needle to add texture and shading (see page 17). His prickles are worked at random using two thread combinations. Use one strand each of two shades of stranded cotton (floss) in the needle at any one time, with the exception of the eye, nose and foot.

Stitch Perfect – WASTE CANVAS

❖ Select the correct stitch count waste fabric for the design and if unsure, work a small test piece confirming the number of strands of stranded cotton (floss) required.

❖ Use the best quality thread (e.g., DMC, Anchor or Madeira) to avoid colour runs.

❖ Cut waste canvas at least 5cm (2in) larger than the completed design size.

❖ Tack (baste) the waste fabric in position carefully using horizontal and vertical tacking lines – it must stay put whilst you work.

❖ Work the cross stitch design from a chart, working each stitch individually though the grid of the canvas and the ground fabric.

❖ When working on a large count waste material, work through the small holes on the canvas to keep the stitches firmly in position and prevent variable tension.

❖ When the stitching is complete, trim away any excess waste canvas and lightly spray with cold water. This releases the starch and makes removing the threads easier.

❖ The starch released can be very sticky so use tweezers to remove the fabric threads and wash your hands regularly.

❖ Pull out the threads one at a time, varying the direction from which you are working to avoid any distortion.

❖ When all the waste canvas has been removed check for missed stitches, which may be added carefully with a sharp needle.

❖ If using this technique on clothing, wash on the normal wash cycle for the garment but press the stitched section on the wrong side where possible.

BLUE BUTTERFLY ON SILK

Stitch count: 29h x 24w
Design size: 5 x 4.5cm (2 x 1¾in)
Fabric: 14-count waste canvas and raw silk background fabric
Needle: Tapestry size 26 and crewel size 5
Chart: Page 168

I have added this decorative butterfly to a piece of hand-dyed raw silk. The silk has been washed to remove excess dye and to give an antique appearance. The motif has been worked in two distinct sections. The body has been worked through the small holes in the waste canvas using three strands of stranded cotton (floss). The wings are then worked through the large holes on the canvas thus forming a slight gap between the wings and body. The legs and antennae were added in backstitch in one strand of Kreinik Fine #8 Braid 393 and the backstitch added in two strands of stranded cotton (floss).

Exploring Choices

This section features a range of exciting designs showing how easy it is to combine cross stitch with other counted embroidery techniques. You will discover how much fun it is to bring a whole new dimension to your embroidery with the addition of buttons, charms, beads and ribbon, and how simple it is to enhance your cross stitch with other techniques such as blackwork, pulled work, drawn thread work, Hardanger embroidery and hemstitching.

I love adding different stitches to my cross stitch projects and using unusual threads, lace, ribbon, buttons and charms. The limit to choosing embellishments is really only your imagination, and successful treasure hunting. I trawl through bric-a-brac stalls, antique markets and junk shops and have used French paste jewellery, hand-painted Venetian glass and even the odd real pearl! Do experiment with embellishments and search for alternatives if you can't source the charm or button that I've used.

This section also includes advice on adapting cross stitch kits and designing projects, either on the computer or using paper and coloured pencils.

Using Embellishments

Charms, buttons and other embellishments may be added to a completed piece of stitching to great effect, although there are pitfalls to avoid. The scale of a charm or button needs to be correct for the project, and look good together if combined on the same piece of stitching (see the tiny bee charm on the card below). I have included a charm on my Anemone Floral Cushion (page 53) in addition to some of the projects in this section. In some cases I've used buttons alone or combined with charms and silk ribbon embroidery.

Charms

When selecting metal charms, avoid cheap, stamped versions as your work deserves the best. Brass charms are manufactured using strong processes and there will be chemical residues left on a charm if it has not been 'finished'. A process of 'dip, tub and roll' is the scouring method used to clean charms for use on embroidery, which prevents potential damage. If a completed piece of stitching is exposed to a damp atmosphere, a chemical reaction may cause the fabric to discolour. It is possible for blue fabric to have an orange patch where the charm touches the fabric. Where I have used antique embellishments to my own pieces, I have cleaned them very thoroughly, as virdigris marks may be impossible to remove.

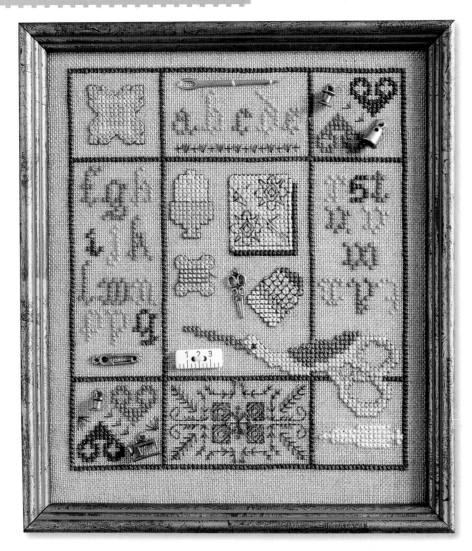

SUMMER FLOWER CARD (left)

Stitch count: 25h x 21w including button
Design size: 4 x 3.5cm (1½ x 1⅜in)
Fabric: 14-count white Aida
Needle: Gold-plated tapestry size 24
Chart: Page 202
Embellishments: Flowerpot button and gold-plated charm

Work cross stitch, bullion knots, French knots and lazy daisy stitches with two strands of stranded cotton (floss) and a gold-plated needle. Refer to the chart for the length of the bullion knots and lazy daisies. Sew on the button and charm with cream sewing cotton and complete the card with a gold card frame and coloured card. See page 215 for making up a card.

STORK SCISSOR SAMPLER

Stitch count: 90h x 80w
Design size: 16.5 x 14.5cm (6½ x 5¾in)
Fabric: Zweigart Cashel 28-count
Needle: Tapestry size 24
Chart: Page 195
Embellishments: Five pewter charms, two brass charms, a novelty button and gold-plated needle

This charming design has a real antique look. It is worked over two threads of linen (or one block of a 14-count Aida), using two strands of stranded cotton (floss) for cross stitch and French knots and the backstitch in one strand. Sew on the assorted charms, button and needle with matching thread. Mount and frame as preferred.

BUTTONS

There is an increasing array of buttons available, in the craft shops and through mail order, and some decorative buttons were used on the Summer Flower Card (page 68) and the Tea for Two Picture (overleaf). Mother-of-pearl or shell buttons create a lovely effect added to cross stitch and may also be combined with charms and beads. A charming result is created in the Stitcher's Treasure Picture (page 73) by using a combination of ribbon, lace, buttons and charms, which transform the small cross stitch motif into a much more complex project.

> ### JANE'S TIP
> Even if you do not have a computer at home, they are available in local libraries, allowing you to search for decorative items on the Internet.

> ### JANE'S TIP
> To tear handmade paper, place a ruler against the edge and tear. Dampening the paper before you tear will create a nice fluffy edge.

LILAC BOOT CARD

Stitch count: 31h x 31w
Design size: 5.6cm (2¼in) square
Fabric: Zweigart Dublin 25-count ivory linen
Needle: Tapestry size 24
Motif charted: Page 193
Embellishments: six mother-of-pearl buttons

The motif for this card is from the Little Shoe Sampler opposite (see chart key on page 193 for the changed colours). You could make an exquisite card for a bride by altering the colours to suit the bridal flowers. Work over two threads of linen, using two strands of stranded cotton (floss) for cross stitch and one for backstitch. Sew on the buttons using strong sewing thread. I completed the card with a tattered patch, some handmade paper and a ribbon trim. See page 215 for making up a card.

LITTLE SHOE SAMPLER

Stitch count: 53h x 74w
Design size: 9.5 x 13cm (3¾ x 5¼in)
Fabric: Zweigart 14-count pale grey Aida
Needle: Tapestry size 24
Chart: Page 193
Embellishments: Heart button, six mother-of-pearl buttons and a gold-plated charm

Work over one block of Aida, using two strands of stranded cotton (floss) for cross stitch and backstitch in one. Sew on the buttons and charm with strong sewing thread and mount and frame.

> ### JANE'S TIP
> When adding buttons use a strong thread that matches the button rather than the ground fabric, so the decorative effect is not spoiled.

OTHER EMBELLISHMENTS

Other embellishments, such as lace and ribbon, are fun to use with cross stitch. You could also use ribbon roses, tiny artificial flowers and even doll's house miniatures. Why not try adding cutlery charms to a kitchen sampler, with buttons for plates on a dresser and flowerpot charms on the fireplace? The Tea for Two Picture below could have the addition of coloured lace or broderie anglaise above and below the design if desired. Unless the lace or other embellishment is added with decorative stitches as part of the design, it should be attached invisibly with tiny stitches and matching thread, using a sharp needle if necessary.

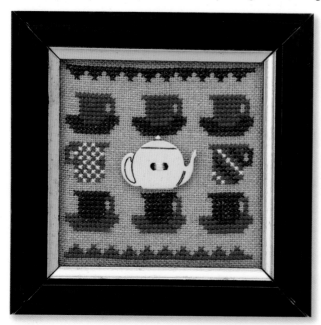

TEA FOR TWO PICTURE

Stitch count: 43h x 42w
Design size: 8cm (3¼in) square
Fabric: Zweigart Dublin 25-count unbleached linen
Needle: Tapestry size 24
Chart: Page 194
Embellishments: Teapot button

This little kitchen project is worked in pure cross stitch over two fabric threads (or one block of 14-count Aida). Use two strands of stranded cotton (floss) for cross stitch. Sew on the button with strong sewing thread. Mount and frame the design as preferred.

Stitch Perfect – EMBELLISHMENTS

❖ The size and scale of charms and buttons should match or balance with the scale of the cross stitch design.

❖ Clean a metal charm thoroughly with a paper towel before applying it to your stitching and if concerned, coat the back of the charm with clear nail varnish.

❖ Attach charms and buttons using a thread colour that matches the fabric.

❖ To attach a button or charm, starting with a loop start (see page 22), position the charm or button and pass the needle through the hole in the charm from the right side, thus marking the position. Slip the charm off the eye of the needle and pass the needle in

and out of the fabric and then through the loop on the right side.

❖ When stitching a charm into position, ensure that the threads on the needle stay taut and do not form an unsightly loop in the hole of the charm.

❖ If additional stitches are to be added in direct relationship to the charm or button, stitch the button in position first and then carefully add the additional stitches (see the flowers on the Summer Flower Card).

❖ When adding lace and ribbons to a cross stitch design, use invisible thread or a colour that matches the ribbon or lace, and use tiny stitches.

STITCHER'S TREASURE PICTURE

Stitch count: 31h x 32w (cross stitch only)
Design size: 5.8cm (2¼in) square (12cm / 4¾in finished frame size)
Fabric: Zweigart 28-count Cashel unbleached linen
Needle: Tapestry size 24   **Chart:** Page 194
Embellishments: Assorted mother-of-pearl buttons and
ivory lace and a gold-plated bow charm

*Work the cross stitch over two threads of linen (or one block of 14-count Aida) with two strands of
stranded cotton (floss). Add the backstitch outline in one strand. Arrange the lace and ribbon in a
pleasing way and stitch in position using tiny running stitches and matching or invisible thread.
Add the buttons and charm with strong sewing thread. Frame as preferred.*

JANE'S TIP

*I try to use ivory or antique white cotton
lace rather than manmade fabrics, as
nylon and polyester tend to be a bright
white with an unattractive sheen.*

Counting with Beads

Using beads is one of the most satisfying embellishment techniques when you are straying away from pure cross stitch. Their use is highly effective, whether you intend to combine the beads with your cross stitches or completely replace the stitches with beads, like the gorgeous Beaded Iris Chatelaine opposite. You will find designs using beads instead of stitches or beads complementing stitched areas elsewhere in this book, but the basic guidelines are included in this section.

The best bit about counted embroidery is that you have so many choices and are free to express your artistic tendencies, and nowhere is this more evident than when stitching with beads. In many cases you will simply be exchanging beads for stitches, because you can adapt any cross stitch chart to allow the use of beads, as long as the chart does not contain fractional cross stitches – it's not possible to attach half a bead!

Substituting beads for stranded cottons on parts of a charted design as in the Sunflower Card overleaf is a wonderful way to explore your creative powers. Working with beads in this way is easier than you can imagine: as all the beads are stitched on using only one colour thread you can work across the pattern row by row instead of working blocks of colour as you would for cross stitch.

Basic Bead Types

There is a huge range of beads available today and obtaining catalogues from some suppliers will reveal an irresistible array. For the cross stitch designs in this book I have used the smaller types of beads and some of the basic ones are described here. Beads are measured at the widest point and they do vary slightly.

Seed beads – these are small beads, between 1.8–2.5mm. The Mill Hill range includes petite glass beads, glass seed beads and seed beads with special finishes, such as antique and frosted.

Magnifica beads – these are very uniform, cylindrical beads, about 2.25mm in diameter, with larger holes than seed beads and thin walls. They are commonly used for bead weaving but also look good with cross stitch.

Bugle beads – these are rods of cut glass in a variety of lengths, colours and finishes. The sizes vary between 2–30mm long and they are usually 2.5mm wide.

Pebble beads – these are larger than seed beads and almost round in shape, about 5.5mm in diameter. Being a little heavier than seed beads, they can be attractive added to tassels and fringes.

Jane's Tip
Select the correct size bead for the fabric of your choice. If the beads are too large, they will crowd on top of each other and the design will distort. Most seed beads are perfect for 14-count Aida and 28-count evenweave. If unsure, work a small square in beads to see if the beads fit the space.

BEADED IRIS CHATELAINE

Stitch count: 46h x 79w
Design size: 14.3 x 8.3cm (5½ x 3¼in)
Fabric: Zweigart Cashel linen 28-count shade 224
Needle: Tapestry size 24 and beading needle or size 10 sharp
Chart: Page 186

This iris chatelaine was designed by Sue Hawkins (see Suppliers) using a combination of beads to create an exquisite effect. Sue stitched this motif by working the flower and decorative top border in Mill Hill glass seed beads using one strand of matching thread. A simple twisted cord (see page 41) and beaded tassel completes the project (see page 218 for making up).

> ### JANE'S TIP
> You could attach beads using Nymo thread, a strong, waxed thread created especially for beadwork. It is available in various colours.

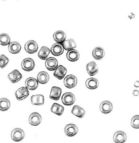

Different Effects

You can see two very different effects created by beads in this section. The Sunflower Card below is worked with all the beads attached in rows, all facing the same direction and creating a very formal effect, whereas the Lily of the Valley opposite is a copy of an early Victorian piece (taken from a hand-painted Berlin pattern) and here the beads were added in a less formal fashion. This gives a rather attractive aged appearance.

Jane's Tip

Beads are lively things and will end up all over the floor if you are not careful. There are excellent bead holders on the market but putting the beads on a square of cotton velvet on the table is the ideal solution, making them easy to pick up with your needle.

Attaching Beads

Attach seed beads and bugle beads with a fine 'sharp' needle or a beading needle using half cross stitch and thread that matches the fabric background. Bugle beads make excellent flower stamens and, because they are longer, are best attached after the cross stitch has been completed.

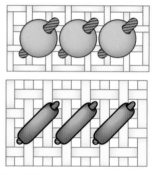

SUNFLOWER CARD

Stitch count: 31h x 23w
Design size: 5.6 x 4.1cm
(2¼ x 1¾in)
Fabric: Zweigart Cashel antique white linen 28-count
Needle: Tapestry size 24 and beading needle or size 10 sharp
Chart: Page 187

This sunflower motif has been embellished by working the flower head in Mill Hill glass seed beads, leaving the leaf and stem in pure cross stitch. Work the cross stitch over two threads of linen with two strands of stranded cotton (floss). Attach beads with matching thread and a beading needle.

BEADED LILY OF THE VALLEY

Stitch count: 58h x 54w   Design size: 9.8 x 10.5cm (3¾ x 4⅛in)
Fabric: Zweigart Cashel cream linen 28-count   Needle: Tapestry size 24 and beading
needle or size 10 sharp   Chart: Page 186

Work the leaves and stems in cross stitch over two linen threads using two strands of stranded cotton (floss). Add the beads using one strand of matching thread. I used a combination of shiny (silver-lined) and opaque beads to create an antique effect.

Stitch Perfect – BEADS

❖ To substitute beads for stranded cottons (floss) on a chart design, gather together the stranded cottons and match the beads to the threads. Choosing beads in isolation can be difficult.

❖ Treat bright yellow and orange beads with a little caution as they can outshine more subtle colours.

❖ Use a size 10 'sharp' needle instead of a blunt tapestry needle to attach beads. Specialist beading needles are available, which are longer and thinner.

❖ Apply beads using ordinary sewing thread matched to the fabric colour. To make sure you cannot see the thread through the beads, experiment by stitching a few on the corner of the fabric.

❖ Polyester mixture threads are stronger than pure cotton and thus are useful for attaching beads securely.

❖ Choose your fabric carefully. Beads will sit better on evenweave fabric than Aida, and on double canvas than on a single weave canvas.

❖ Consider using a frame or a hoop when working with beads. This will keep the fabric taut and you can pull the thread firmly as you work to keep the beads in position.

Introducing Blackwork

I have called this section an introduction to blackwork because it would take a much larger book than this one to cover the subject properly. I hope this will give you a real taste for this fascinating technique.

The name blackwork is very misleading as the technique may be worked in any colour or combination of colours. Blackwork is often used to depict flowers or stylized historical patterns but, as you can see by the elephant on page 81, the technique is very versatile. Blackwork consists of geometric patterns built up using Holbein stitch (double running stitch) and was traditionally worked in black thread against a contrasting (usually white) background with gold metallic highlights added for extra impact. During Tudor Elizabethan times blackwork was used to decorate clothing to imitate the appearance of lace. Many different effects can be achieved by varying the thickness of the thread, and careful selection of patterns with dark, medium and light tones. You will see from the blackwork designs on page 83 that you can select different patterns to create the dark and light effects.

Modern blackwork can make good use of different colours and even space-dyed threads can be used with great effect – see the Blackwork Poppy on page 82.

JANE'S TIP

When designing band samplers, I sometimes include a section of holbein stitch as this creates a striking contrast to the areas of cross stitch.

BLACKWORK TULIP

Stitch count: 82h x 31w
Design size: 14.9 x 5.6cm (5¾ x 2¼in)
Fabric: Zweigart Cashel ivory linen 28-count
Needle: Tapestry size 26
Chart: Opposite

The charts show an outline and then a version complete with blackwork patterns. You could use any of the patterns on page 83 to make your own version. The motif was stitched in a combination of cross stitch and blackwork over two threads of linen. Work the cross stitch with two strands of stranded cotton (floss) and the black backstitch outline with one strand. Outline the tulip head in two strands of black and then use a selection of green and gold filling stitches in one strand to complete the design. Make up as desired.

Blackwork Tulip

DMC (Anchor)

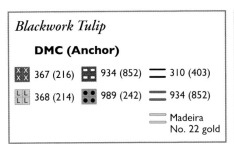

367 (216) 934 (852) 310 (403)

368 (214) 989 (242) 934 (852)

Madeira
No. 22 gold

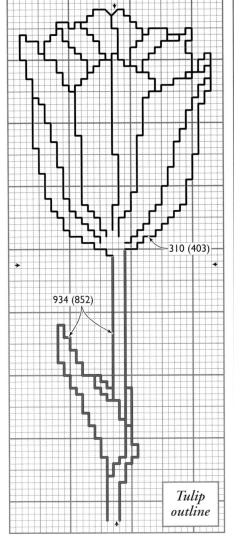

310 (403)

934 (852)

Tulip outline

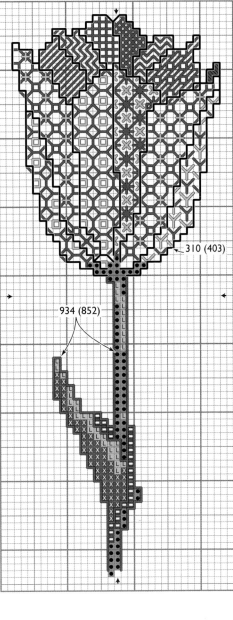

310 (403)

934 (852)

I'm often asked to explain the difference between blackwork and backstitch and the answer is to look at the back of the stitching. As I have said before, I'm not of the strict school that suggests that the back of your work should look like the front, but in the case of blackwork I do make the exception. If you work the stitches correctly, you will not know the back from the front. In truth, you may find it necessary to combine backstitch and Holbein as you can end up at the end of a row with nowhere to go!

Traditionally the outline of the pattern is worked first, often in a heavier thread weight (i.e., two strands) and then the filling patterns are worked from the middle of any section using Holbein stitch (double running) – see diagram below. The blackwork tulip design charted on the previous page, shows the outline separately, and then with the blackwork filling patterns.

The clever thing about blackwork is that you can use cross stitch patterns and adapt them to blackwork very simply. All you need is a clear outline. The tulip design occurs later in the book as a darning pattern (see page 84), where I have used the same outline and altered the filling technique. The Blackwork Elephant opposite has a very distinctive outline, with easy filling stitches.

Working Holbein Stitch

To work this stitch, also called double running stitch, begin by working a running stitch under and over two fabric threads if working on evenweave or one block if working on Aida (a). Now stitch the return journey, filling in the gaps (b).

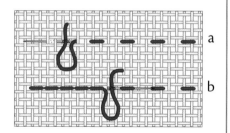

a

b

Stitch Perfect – BLACKWORK

❖ Blackwork is traditionally worked using double running stitch or Holbein stitch, rather than backstitch.

❖ Holbein stitch will give a smoother effect and the back of your work will look almost as good as the front, so it is particularly useful for table linen.

❖ Before starting to stitch you will need to plan the direction you are working so that you can return to fill the gaps without ending up a blind alley!

❖ You may find it useful to use a finer needle than usual – I use a size 28 gold-plated tapestry needle for the filling stitches.

❖ Use slightly shorter threads, particularly when using one strand of black. The thread tends to fluff up as it is used and this can spoil your lacy effect.

❖ When stitching blackwork, aim to create a stitched line like a thin, pen-drawn line; split the thread if necessary and work with a small, sharp needle.

BLACKWORK ELEPHANT

Stitch count: 36h x 41w
Design size: 6.5 x 7.5cm (2½ x 3in)
Fabric: Zweigart Cashel ivory linen 28-count
Needle: Tapestry size 26
Chart: Page 193

This fun design would be an easy project to begin to explore the joys of blackwork. Work over two linen threads, stitching the outline first in two strands of stranded cotton (floss) and then adding the filling stitches in black and gold in one strand.

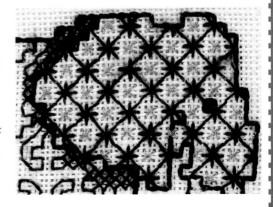

MULTICOLOURED BLACKWORK POPPY

Stitch count: 117h x 100w   **Design size:** 21.5 x 18cm (8½ x 7⅛in)
Fabric: Zweigart Dublin 26-count ivory linen   **Needle:** Tapestry size 26
Chart: Pages 190–191

*Stitch the poppy outline over two strands of linen using two strands of black stranded cotton
(floss). Work the areas of multicoloured cross stitch with one strand. Add the blackwork
filling stitches in the multicoloured stranded cotton and gold thread in one strand. Work the
cross stitched stems in two strands of black. Work the blackwork border of leaves in two
strands of multicoloured stranded cotton.*

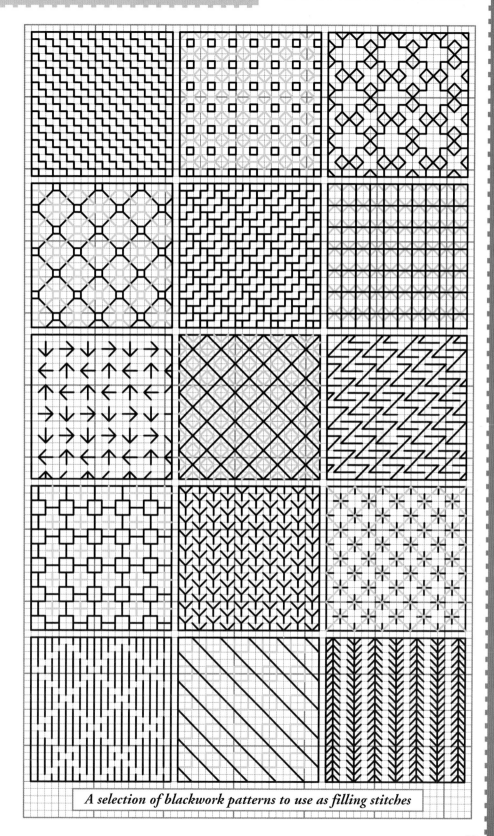

A selection of blackwork patterns to use as filling stitches

Pattern Darning

This decorative counted technique isn't new and was, in fact, taught to girls in schools in England in the mid 19th century. With modern textiles, much of our clothing is more durable than in earlier times so darning isn't considered a necessary skill, but in the past it was highly valued. The idea of darning, particularly socks, leaves me cold but pattern darning for fun is so satisfying. The trick is to follow the pattern very carefully to begin with and then, as you see the pattern begin to take shape and how the repeats occur, you will need the chart less. In a similar style to blackwork, the outline of the motif is created first and then the darning patterns are worked from the centre of each section.

The projects in this section are very pretty: you could start with the Flowerpot Button darn design opposite and then move on to the elegant tulip and stylized flower.

Stitch Perfect – Pattern Darning

❖ This is a difficult technique to work on Aida, so use evenweave.
❖ You will find it helpful to use a frame to hold the fabric taut.
❖ Work all darning patterns in running stitch, working in one direction only.
❖ Avoid the temptation to use satin stitch as it will spoil the effect.
❖ Count the fabric threads carefully as some patterns will use a variety of stitch lengths.
❖ Use shorter lengths of thread to avoid the thread fluffing, which will spoil the look of the patterns.
❖ If you make a mistake, it is easier to cut out the offending thread than attempt to unpick the error.

PATTERN DARN TULIP

Stitch count: 83h x 31w
Design size: 15 x 5.6cm (6 x 2¼in)
Fabric: Zweigart Cashel 28-count ivory linen
Needle: Tapestry size 26–28
Chart: Page 204

Work over a variety of fabric threads, as indicated on the chart, stitching the stem and leaves with two strands of stranded cotton (floss) for the cross stitch and one strand for the backstitch outline. Outline the flower head in two strands of stranded cotton and then add the filling stitches with one strand.

FLOWERPOT BUTTON DARN

Stitch count: 58h x 58w **Design size:** 10.5cm square (4⅛in)
Fabric: Zweigart Dublin 26-count ivory linen **Needle:** Tapestry size 26–28 **Chart:** Page 187

Work over a variety of fabric threads, as indicated on the chart, stitching cross stitch with two strands of stranded cotton (floss) and backstitch outlining with one strand. Work all the darning patterns with one strand. Add the lattice flowerpot button with matching thread when the stitching is complete.

PATTERN DARN FLOWER

Stitch count: 43h x 41w
Design size: 7.8 x 7.5cm
(3 x 2⅞in)
Fabric: Zweigart Cashel
28-count cream linen
Needle: Tapestry size 26–28
Chart: Page 202

Work over a variety of fabric threads, as indicated on the chart, stitching the stem with two strands of stranded cotton (floss) for the cross stitch and one strand for the backstitch outline. Outline the flower head with two strands of stranded cotton and then add the filling stitches with one strand.

SILK RIBBON AND CROSS STITCH

Adding silk ribbon embroidery to cross stitch can introduce a wonderful new dimension and variety to a piece of stitching, creating a fresh, three-dimensional look. Silk ribbon embroidery grows quickly, so it is also a very speedy way to produce the emergency card needed for a special friend. I use YLI silk ribbons (see Suppliers).

Silk ribbon is used as it comes, as it is fine enough to pass through the fabric in the same way as thread does. Other ribbons made from rayon and viscose can be used for surface stitches, like gathered ribbon stitch in this Peach Blossom Card, but are not suitable for some stitches.

If you wish to develop the use of silk ribbon embroidery in your work make the Blue Ribbon Flower Card and the Wedding Shower Card shown here. Try other stitches using silk ribbon, such as tent stitch, satin stitch or bullion stitches, and invest in a good ribbon embroidery book.

PEACH BLOSSOM CARD

Stitch count: 21h x 11w
Design size: 5 x 3cm (2 x 1¼in) including flowers
Fabric: Zweigart Cashel 28-count cream linen
Needle: Tapestry size 24 and gold-plated chenille size 7   **Chart**: Page 176
Embellishments: Heart button, 2mm and 7mm YLI silk ribbon and Madeira No.8 colour 8011

This pretty card was stitched over two fabric threads, using two strands of stranded cotton (floss) for cross stitch. Add the silk ribbon embroidery using 2mm ribbon in pale peach and dark rose for French knots and 7mm ribbon in pale peach for the gathered ribbon stitch (see overleaf). Mount the design in a silver card, then into a gold card and trim with gold thread.

BLUE RIBBON FLOWER CARD

Stitch count: 32h x 29w including button and flowers
Design size: 5.7 x 5cm (2¼ x 2in)
Fabric: Zweigart Cashel 28-count cream linen
Needle: Tapestry size 24 and gold-plated chenille size 7
Chart: Page 197
Embellishments: Lattice flowerpot button and silk ribbon

This ribbon-trimmed card was fun to make. Create the blue flower first in silk ribbon lazy daisy stitches (see page 89). Add random French knots to the flower centre and stem stitch stalks with two strands of stranded cotton (floss). Work the leaves in ribbon stitch (page 89), sew on the button and add ribbon French knots. Fray the edges of the linen and mount on blue card, adding a silk ribbon running stitch around half of the blue card and then mount on a single-fold card. See page 215 for making cards.

WEDDING SHOWER CARD

Stitch count: 31h x 16w including silk ribbon flowers

Design size: 5.7 x 3cm (2¼ x 1⅛in)

Fabric: Zweigart Cashel 28-count cream linen

Needle: Tapestry size 24, gold-plated chenille size 7 and size 10 sharp

Chart: Page 195

Embellishments: Seed pearls and 7mm YLI silk ribbon

Work over two linen threads (or one block of 14-count Aida), using two strands of stranded cotton (floss) for cross stitch and one for backstitch. Using the pink and peach ribbon add the ribbon flowers in gathered ribbon stitch (diagrams overleaf). Add the seed pearls at random using a 'sharp' needle and cream thread. Mount the finished design in a silver card frame, trim diagonally and then mount on a pink card, cutting off two corners for a decorative effect.

Stitch Perfect – SILK RIBBON EMBROIDERY

❖ The use of an embroidery hoop is recommended for silk ribbon embroidery.

❖ Use a large chenille needle (size 20) for ribbon embroidery, and size 24 tapestry needle when using stranded cotton (floss).

❖ If working silk ribbon French knots you will find a gold-plated needle helpful.

❖ Work over two threads of the fabric or as stated on the chart.

❖ Use pure silk ribbon, readily available in 2mm, 3mm, 4mm and 7mm widths.

❖ Work with 30cm (12in) lengths of ribbon, cutting the ends at an angle to prevent fraying and make needle threading easier.

❖ To begin, make a knot at one end of the ribbon and come up through the fabric from the back. Remove any twists in the ribbon before stitching.

❖ Work with a loose tension to give the required effect – as a guide, the eye of the size 20 needle should pass under the ribbon with ease.

❖ When finishing off silk ribbon embroidery, take the ribbon through to the back of the fabric and using sewing thread, backstitch the end of the ribbon to the nearest stitch of ribbon to secure it and then cut off close to the fabric.

❖ When framing ribbon embroidery, you must ensure that it does not get squashed by the underside of the glass, which would spoil the effect. Insert very narrow strips of board (spacers) into the edges of the frame, between the glass and the mounted embroidery to hold them apart, before you assemble the frame.

GATHERED RIBBON ROSE

I have used this stitch in the Wedding Shower Card and it creates a beautiful effect. You can also create a two-tone rose by placing two ribbons, in different colours and widths, one on top of the other and then working a running stitch through them both, before creating the rose by following the steps below.

1 Cut a piece of ribbon long enough to complete the whole rose. Using a sewing thread with a knotted end, work small running stitches along one edge, leaving the thread end long.

2 Thread one end of the ribbon on to a chenille needle and take the ribbon through to the back of the fabric.

3 Now use a new length of sewing thread to secure the ribbon to the back of the fabric, bringing the thread out to the front.

4 Start to pull up the gathers and begin to couch the ribbon in place.

5 Carry on gathering, forming a spiral and continuing to couch the ribbon as you go.

6 When the end of the ribbon is reached, tuck the end under the rose, couch in place and then take the thread through to the back of the work and secure.

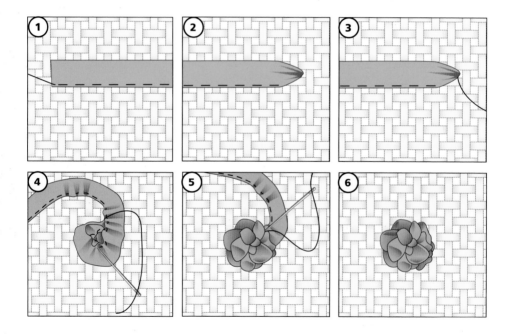

Gathered ribbon roses create a lovely effect on the Wedding Shower Card and are very easy to create. Try using multicoloured or variegated ribbons for a different effect. The picture also shows French knots worked with silk ribbon.

LAZY DAISY STITCH

This stitch worked in silk ribbon is very effective when combined with cross stitch in the Blue Ribbon Flower Card. The stitch can also be worked in stranded cotton or other threads.

1 Bring the ribbon to the front of the fabric (at point 1 on the first diagram), and then take it to the back of the fabric, close to where it first emerged, and re-emerge some distance away (at point 2). Leave the ribbon as a slack loop.

2 Now loop the ribbon behind the tip of the needle and begin to pull the needle and ribbon through the fabric.

3 Carry on pulling until the loop is the shape you want.

4 Take the needle to the back of the fabric, just beyond the loop, making a little anchoring stitch.

5 Pull the needle through to the back of the fabric to complete the stitch.

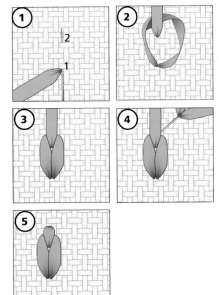

RIBBON STITCH

This stitch is very simple to do and is ideal for creating leaves, as you can see on the Blue Ribbon Flower Card shown on page 86.

1 Bring the ribbon to the front of the fabric, where you want the base of the stitch to be (at point 1).

2 Hold the ribbon flat against the fabric.

3 Put the needle under the ribbon and ease it upwards, smoothing and spreading the ribbon.

4 Put the tip of the needle in the centre of the ribbon, in the place where you want the tip of the stitch to be (at point 2).

5 Take the needle through to the back of the fabric, using your thumb to keep the stitch untwisted. Now slowly and gently pull the ribbon through.

6 The ribbon will fold back on itself, curling at the edges. Secure the stitch at the back of the work.

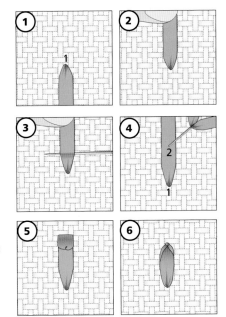

COUNT ANYTHING BUT CROSS STITCH

This is an unusual section to find in a cross stitch book but it demonstrates that counted embroidery is not just cross stitch but lots, lots more. The three projects here illustrate some of the variety of stitches included in the counted repertoire. Some of these stitches can be worked on Aida fabric, as you can see from the Tiny Band Sampler opposite, while others need the additional fabric threads available on evenweave fabric. Working the Little Floral Garden or the Queen Stitch Sampler will be the perfect opportunity to try evenweave.

The trick when working rows of these counted stitches is to be consistent and to construct the stitches in the same way each time. When you refer to the Stitch Library you will see that some stitches may be worked over different numbers of fabric threads even though the construction stays the same; for example, Algerian eye may be worked over two, four or more threads. Refer to the chart you are working from each time to confirm the number of fabric threads involved.

LITTLE FLORAL GARDEN

Stitch count: 32h x 24w   **Design size**: 6.2 x 5cm (2½ x 2in)
Fabric: Zweigart Dublin 25-count cream linen   **Needle**: Tapestry size 24   **Chart**: Page 197

This design is worked with two strands of stranded cotton (floss) for all the stitches except the Madeira No.22 gold, which is used as supplied. Work the Algerian eye, adapted double cross stitch, rice stitch and four-sided stitch (worked last) over four fabric threads. Work the long-legged cross stitch over two threads. Work the three satin stitch flowers following the chart for stitch length.

QUEEN STITCH SAMPLER

Stitch count: 34h x 38w, including four-sided stitch border   **Design size**: 6.2 x 7cm (2½ x 2¾in)
Fabric: Zweigart Cashel 28-count cream linen   **Needle**: Tapestry size 24   **Chart**: Page 196

*Work this pretty sampler using two strands of stranded cotton (floss) over four fabric threads for Queen
stitch, double cross stitch, Rhodes stitch, Algerian eyes, rice stitch and four-sided stitch (worked last).
Work the half Rhodes stitches over six threads and backstitch in one strand over two threads. The
Queen stitch, Algerian eyes and four-sided stitch are pulled stitches and should form holes if pulled
firmly – see page 106 for more advice.*

TINY BAND SAMPLER

Stitch count: 36h x 12w
Design size: 6.5 x 2.2cm (2½ x ⅞in)
Fabric: Zweigart 14-count cream Aida
Needle: Tapestry size 24
Chart: Page 196

*This is about the smallest band I have ever stitched and was great fun to
do – perfect for practising some new stitches, and only a few of each to
make! I used eyelets, half Rhodes stitch, rice stitch, long-legged cross stitch,
double cross stitch, satin stitch and Algerian eyes. Work all the stitches with
two strands of stranded cotton (floss) and the backstitch with one strand. I
bordered the design with some simple hemstitch (see page 119) and then
trimmed away the excess fabric to the edge of the stitching.*

ASSISI EMBROIDERY

This style of cross stitch takes its name from embroideries made in Assisi, Italy during the 13th and 14th centuries. Early examples can still be seen in Italian churches and museums and were worked by nuns and monks. The altar cloths they made were worked on white linen with a single colour silk thread, usually red, blue, yellow, green or brown. Designs included stylized birds, animals, flowers, foliage and also classical and biblical scenes.

In the last 20 years, a modern version of Assisi embroidery has evolved. Many different colours and patterns are used for the background, and the motifs are extremely varied. However, the traditional version is still practised in the town of Assisi, where the local women can be seen sitting in front of their houses and embroidering items for the local co-operative embroidery shop, which was established in 1902 to give employment to poor women to supplement their income.

Assisi work can be described as pure cross stitch although in reverse. The design is transferred to the fabric by working a backstitch outline first, and then the background of the design is stitched, leaving the motif void, remaining as blank fabric. In the past, stitches other than pure cross stitch were used, for example long-legged cross stitch and even four-sided stitch.

The Assisi Dragonfly Sachet shown opposite illustrates the versatility of a cross stitch chart, showing how the outline used for the motif can be used as the framework for the Assisi embroidery. I have worked the original design in cross stitch for the little pill box below and then taken the dragonfly motif and completed that as Assisi embroidery. You can see that I have used a slightly darker outline colour for the Assisi version as I wanted to be able to see the dragonfly's legs clearly. You could choose almost any design from the Chart Library and work it in the same way.

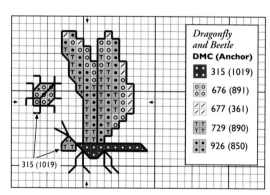

Dragonfly and Beetle DMC (Anchor)	
■	315 (1019)
○	676 (891)
╱	677 (361)
T	729 (890)
∷	926 (850)

315 (1019)

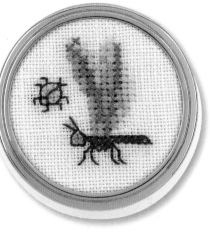

DRAGONFLY AND BEETLE PILL BOX

Stitch count: 19h x 17w **Design size:** 2.5cm (1in) square **Fabric:** Zweigart Newcastle 40-count ivory linen **Needle:** Tapestry size 28 **Chart:** above

Work this design over two fabric threads, using one strand of stranded cotton (floss) for the cross stitch and the backstitch. The insect's wings are not outlined. This tiny project was finished by mounting it into a tiny enamel pill box following the manufacturer's instructions.

Stitch Perfect – ASSISI EMBROIDERY

❖ Work the outline in backstitch or Holbein stitch (see page 80), carefully counting from the chart.

❖ Experiment with the number of strands needed to create the effect required.

❖ Work the cross stitch in two journeys to keep a neat tension throughout and perfect vertical lines on the reverse. If using a brighter coloured variegated thread with more distinctive colour changes, it would be best to work the cross stitches individually to maintain the colour sequence.

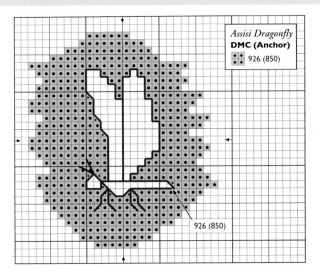

Assisi Dragonfly
DMC (Anchor)
∷∷ 926 (850)

926 (850)

ASSISI DRAGONFLY SCENTED SACHET

Stitch count: 29h x 26w
Design size: 5 x 4.5cm (2 x 1¾in)
Fabric: Zweigart Cashel 28-count in ivory
Needle: Tapestry size 24
Chart: Above

Work this design over two fabric threads, beginning with the outline of the dragonfly's body in Holbein stitch using one strand of stranded cotton (floss) only. Work the cross stitch around the edge of the outline as shown on the chart using one strand of stranded cotton, adding the legs and antennae in the darker colour as shown on the chart. Fray the edges of the finished stitching and sew it on to a sachet (see page 213 for making a bag). The sachet was made from patterned linen and finished with a simple hemstitch across the raw top edge (see page 119). Make a twisted cord made for a tie (see page 41) and fill the bag with scented pot-pourri to finish.

DECORATED INITIALS

Decorated initials are an ideal way of giving an emergency gift or card to a special friend. One of these initials could be stitched in an evening and made in to a simple patch to attach to a card or you could create a very different look if you work the initial on fine silk gauze and mount it in a pretty pot or pendant. I have designed a traditional alphabet and embellished it with a daisy head and poppy face but you could add your preferred flower to a favourite alphabet.

Decorative initials have a myriad of uses, as either single motifs or grouped together as a word, name or phrase. Try some of the following project ideas.

◆ Plan the letters of your name on graph paper and then stitch and make up as a door plate or book cover.

◆ Stitch a child's initial and mount it into a pretty frame for their bedroom.

◆ Stitch a friend's initial and mount it into a coaster for when they call round for a cup of tea.

◆ Work the whole alphabet as a sampler and frame it or make up as a cushion.

◆ See the illustrated suggestions below for changing the fabric or design colours.

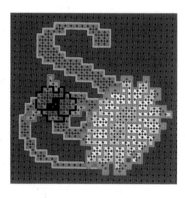

The charted letters from the Daisy Alphabet could be worked on different, perhaps bolder-coloured fabrics to change the look, as shown above. You could also experiment with changing the thread colours completely to others of your choice, as the picture below shows.

CRYSTAL POT

Stitch count: 33h x 25w
Design size: 4.5 x 6.5cm (1¾ x 2½in)
Fabric: Zweigart cream 28-count Cashel linen
Needle: Tapestry size 24
Chart: Pages 206–209

Work this design using two strands of stranded cotton (floss) for cross stitch and one for the backstitch. Mount into the pot following the manufacturer's instructions.

WOODEN POT

Stitch count: 27h x 34w
Design size: 5 x 6.5cm (2 x 2½in)
Fabric: Zweigart cream 14-count Aida
Needle: Tapestry size 24
Chart: Pages 206–209

Work the design using two strands of stranded cotton (floss) for cross stitch and one for the backstitch. Mount into your pot to finish.

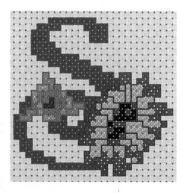

JANE'S TIP

Remember that alphabet letters vary in physical size so check the letter of choice fits the pot or card in question. The W is much wider than the letter B in my stitched examples. See page 20 for calculating design size.

HARDANGER EMBROIDERY

Hardanger, a town in Norway, gave its name to this type of counted embroidery, where cut work was a feature of the local dress. Hardanger embroidery or cut work is easy to do and is extremely effective when combined with cross stitch but it seems to strike terror in the hearts of cross stitchers, possibly because they have snipped a fabric thread in error whilst unpicking!

As with many of the techniques covered in this book I can only give you taste of Hardanger, sure in the knowledge that once you have had a go at this deceptively easy range of stitches you will, like me, become hooked! The Multicolour Hardanger Bookmark shown below would be a perfect starter project. To experiment further, go on to create the three other stunning projects in this section, and see page 51 for another Hardanger project.

When you work the basic stitches that make up Hardanger embroidery your stitching will not disintegrate and fall apart! When done correctly this type of embroidery can be machine washed if need be. Hardanger embroidery can be worked on evenweave fabric of any thread count or on Hardanger fabric which is supplied with 22 blocks to 2.5cm (1in). If working on Hardanger fabric, treat each block as one thread. At its simplest, Hardanger work

consists of three stages which are described over the next few pages:

1 Stitching Kloster blocks.

2 Cutting threads.

3 Decorating the remaining threads and spaces.

The secret of successful cut work embroidery is working Kloster blocks (the framework needed for the decorative filling stitches) and to count these blocks correctly. If they are in the right place the threads may be cut out and the stitching will not fall to pieces!

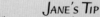

JANE'S TIP

When you are working up the second side of the Kloster block pattern, run your needle across the fabric to check that your stitches are still in line.

MULTICOLOUR HARDANGER BOOKMARK

Stitch count: 87h x 18w
Design size: 15.8 x 3.3cm (6¼ x 1¼in)
Fabric: Unbleached 28-count linen band
Needle: Tapestry size 24 and 22
Chart: Page 204

Stitch the Kloster blocks with one strand of Anchor Multicolour Pearl No.8. Check the Kloster blocks are in the correct positions and then cut the threads as shown on page 98. Withdraw the loose threads and then stitch the needleweaving and dove's eyes with one strand of Pearl No.12 in ecru. Work the backstitch in one strand of stranded cotton (floss). Neaten the top of the bookmark with one row of hemstitch in cream Pearl No.12 and trim to the stitching (see page 119). Make a simple tassel (see page 218) with the remaining multicolour threads and see page 214 for making up.

STITCHING KLOSTER BLOCKS

Kloster blocks form the framework for the cut areas in Hardanger embroidery. You will be, in fact, binding the fabric edges prior to cutting. Start with an away waste knot, far enough away so as not to interfere with your progress. When you need a fresh thread finish off under a number of blocks and then cut very close to the stitching. If you make a small counting error on a cross stitch project it's often possible to hide the fact but this is **not** the case when working the Kloster blocks. If you make an error you will need to find the problem and put it right. I will give some tips as you work through this section.

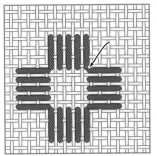

Working Kloster blocks

These are worked in patterns, formed with 5 vertical or 5 horizontal straight stitches, each of them over 4 threads on evenweave or 4 blocks on Hardanger fabric. The stitches are worked side by side, following the grain of the fabric. When counting Hardanger, count the threads never the holes. To see why, hold up four fingers – if you count the gaps between fingers you could count five or three depending on where you started counting!

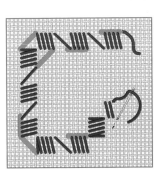

Kloster blocks from the back

When travelling to the next block (if it is not immediately next door to your last stitch) do not travel across the surface of the material, as this trailing thread on the back may be cut in error and you'll have to waste time on repair work! To move between the blocks, pass your needle under the back of the Kloster block (through the tunnel) and not only will the whole thing look neat and tidy but you will also avoid potential panic! In this diagram, the blue route is to be avoided.

> ### JANE'S TIP
>
> When forming Kloster blocks, take the time to snip off the knot and weave in the remaining trailing threads as you go. This is much better than having dozens to sort out before you can cut the fabric threads.

Stitch Perfect – KLOSTER BLOCKS

❖ Count the threads **not** the holes.

❖ To form Kloster blocks, work the stitches side by side so that they look the same on the wrong side of the fabric. The back stitches will have a very slight slant.

❖ The vertical and horizontal blocks must meet at the corners, sharing the corner hole. Check as you work to avoid unpicking.

❖ Check that you have counted correctly as you stitch and check that each block is in the correct position.

❖ Check that vertical Kloster blocks are opposite one another and horizontal blocks are opposite horizontal ones.

❖ Work all Kloster blocks in a pattern, checking the blocks meet where they should.

❖ Never start cutting until all Kloster blocks are completed and match everywhere.

❖ Do not travel between blocks at the back unless under existing Kloster blocks.

CUTTING THREADS

When the Kloster blocks have been stitched, the threads between them are cut and pulled out. The secret to successful cutting is to work all the Kloster blocks, checking that you have counted correctly and that all the blocks are exactly opposite each other. Looking at the photographs of the Hardanger projects in this section you can see that the Kloster blocks are formed in vertical and horizontal lines.

Cutting threads Once you have completed the first set of Kloster blocks, study this diagram to see where to cut the fabric threads. The threads should be cut in pairs, with very sharp, pointed scissors at the end of the Kloster blocks, not at the side. Remember to cut where the needle has pierced the fabric. You will see the reason the horizontal lines are opposite each other and why the Kloster block stitches have to be in the correct place. You will be cutting two ends of the same thread.

JANE'S TIP

Before cutting a pair of threads, check that you can see both points of the scissors and then count the threads on the blade – this way you cannot make a cutting mistake.

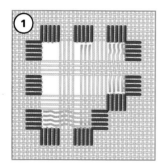

Removing threads Pull out the cut threads carefully. This diagram shows Kloster blocks stitched with some threads cut and some awaiting removal.

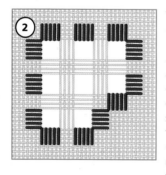

Threads removed This diagram shows the Kloster blocks stitched and with all the correct threads cut and pulled out, ready for decorating. After cutting, don't worry if you can see some small whiskers at the cut sides. Leave these until the piece is finished: many will disappear as the work is handled, but if necessary they can be carefully trimmed when all the stitching is complete.

This detail shows part of the Christmas Hardanger Heart (shown in full opposite), with the Kloster blocks completed, the needleweaving worked and the filling stitches completed. You can also see the silver calligraphy paper I used as a background beneath the embroidery to complement the Hardanger.

CHRISTMAS HARDANGER HEART

Stitch count: 48h x 54w
Design size: 8.7 x 9.8cm (3½ x 3¾in)
Fabric: Zweigart Cashel antique white
28-count linen
Needle: Tapestry size 24 and 22
Chart: Page 203

*Stitch the Kloster blocks with one strand of
Anchor Pearl No.5 (with metallic silver). Work the
filling stitches with one strand of Pearl No.12 in
ecru. Work the cross stitch with two strands of
stranded cotton (floss) over two fabric threads,
with the backstitch candle wick in one strand.
Mount and frame as desired.*

JANE'S TIP

*Be disciplined at the cutting stage
and avoid distraction. Start at a
shared corner hole and cut two
threads away from you. Cut the
second two threads and then
turn your work so you continue to
cut in the same direction – two
threads at a time because then
you cannot cut three!*

REPAIR WORK

If you do make a mistake and
cut a thread unintentionally it is easy
to correct this.

1 Remove the fabric thread you've cut
by mistake.

2 Take a strand of stranded cotton
(floss) the same colour as your fabric or
a fabric thread if working on linen, and
darn it in and out so that it replaces the
accidentally cut thread, leaving a long
thread hanging on the wrong side.

3 Needleweave or wrap this section
next to anchor the threads, then the
loose thread can be trimmed.

MINI HARDANGER SAMPLER

Stitch count: 26h x 26w   **Design size:** 5cm (2in) square
Fabric: Zweigart Dublin 26-count antique white linen
Needle: Tapestry size 24 and 22   **Chart:** Page 205

Stitch the Kloster blocks with one strand of DMC Perlé No.5 in cream and the filling stitches in one strand of Perlé No.8 in cream. Work the double cross stitch with one strand of Perlé No.5 in cream and the four-sided stitch in one strand of Perlé No.8 in cream. Hemstitch around the edge using one strand of Perlé No.8 in cream. Fray the raw edge, trim to shape and frame.

Stitch Perfect – CUTTING THREADS

❖ Work slowly, in a good light and with small, sharp, pointed scissors.

❖ The cutting side is where the long straight stitches enter the fabric. Never cut alongside the long edges of the stitches.

❖ Cut the threads at the end of each Kloster block, working from a corner out. You need to cut four threads, but cut them in pairs.

❖ Pass the point of the scissors into the corner-shared hole and lift the threads. Check that you can see both points of

the scissors and that you are only cutting two threads, then lean slightly towards the Kloster block and cut.

❖ It is easier to cut all the relevant threads in one direction first then turn the fabric to cut in another direction.

❖ Pull out the loose threads using tweezers if necessary. The stitching should look like the final diagram on page 98, with groups of four threads vertically and horizontally left to decorate.

DECORATING THREADS AND VOIDS

When Kloster blocks are completed and the threads are cut and removed, you are left with groups of threads and spaces or void areas to decorate. It is also an important function of this decorative element that the remaining fabric threads are reinforced and strengthened after cutting. There are dozens of ways to do this but I have worked a few examples for you to see the finished effect. Traditionally, all these decorative filling stitches are worked in a finer thread than the Kloster blocks. To work any of these filling stitches, follow the sequence in the diagrams provided over the next few pages, ensuring that you work each section in the same manner, counting the wraps or weaves.

NEEDLEWEAVING

This is one of the most commonly used methods of embellishing threads left after cutting, especially over larger areas, and creates covered bars, which can be worked alone or be combined with filling stitches such as dove's eye and picots. The stitch is formed by starting from a void area and weaving in and out of two pairs of fabric threads – see the stages below. The aim is not to distort the bar but to form a neatly woven or plaited appearance. If adding dove's eye or picots these are traditionally worked during the needleweaving process rather than afterwards.

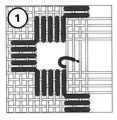 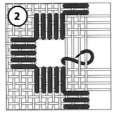 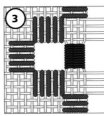 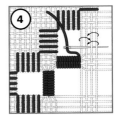

1 Start by anchoring the thread under adjacent cross stitch or hemstitch on the back of the work.

2 Beginning from a cut area, bring the needle up through a void area.

3 Weave the needle under and over pairs of threads to form a plaited effect. The stitches should not distort or bend the threads.

4 When one set of threads has been woven, move on to the next set.

CORNER NEEDLEWEAVING

As the name implies, corner needleweaving is the same stitch as needleweaving but instead of working across a bar (a set of four threads), the stitch is formed across a corner and depending on where you choose to do this the effects can be stunning.

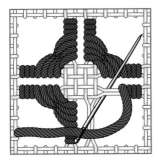

Use an away waste knot and start by wrapping a pair of threads until you are a few stitches away from an intersection. Needleweave the wrapped bar and the bar running at right angles for a few stitches, then continue with the wrapping. Keep a record of how many weaves you work so that they all look the same.

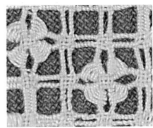

WRAPPED BARS

Wrapping bars simply means that the thread is wound round and round two or four threads after cutting. After Kloster blocks have been formed and the threads have been cut and removed, the four remaining threads may be wrapped in pairs and possibly embellished with spider's webs or corner dove's eyes. As you wrap each bar you will need to hold the threads you are wrapping quite firmly to prevent them from unravelling as you work. It does take a little practise – follow the stages below.

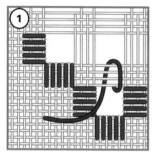

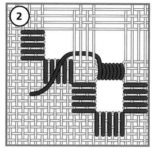

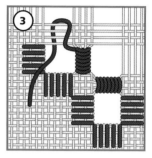

1 Start by anchoring your thread under adjacent stitches and then begin wrapping, working horizontally across the fabric.

2 Wind the thread around and around the remaining fabric threads, then travel to the next group of threads and repeat. As you wrap each bar, hold the threads you are wrapping quite firmly, to prevent them unravelling as you work.

3 Continue wrapping the bars, noting how many times each set is wrapped and keeping the stitches consistent.

DOVE'S EYE STITCH

Dove's eye stitch is a traditional Hardanger stitch that is usually constructed whilst needleweaving or wrapping bars. It is possible to add it afterwards but this is not recommended. The stitch creates a diamond-shaped hole in the centre of the void left by cutting. When forming the stitch, watch for the last twist as without this the diamond will look rather strange. Forming a dove's eye takes a little practise and a little 'pinching and pulling' will be needed to achieve perfect results – follow the stages below.

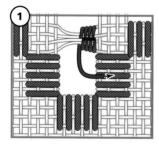

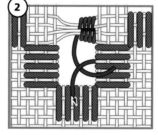

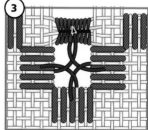

1 Whilst working the last side of a square, needleweave to the centre of the bar, bringing the needle out through a void area.

2 Pierce the neighbouring needlewoven bar (or wrapped bar) halfway along its length, bringing the needle up through the void and through the loop formed by the thread.

3 Continue around the square, but before resuming needleweaving or wrapping, loop the needle under the first stitch to form the final twist in the dove's eye.

CORNER DOVE'S EYE

An adaptation of the dove's eye previously described, this stitch is formed across the corners of the square rather than through the side bars.

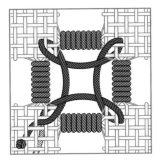

To create a corner dove's eye, follow the route taken by the needle in the diagram and remember to make the last twist to complete the square.

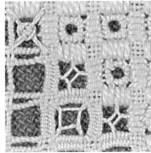

This detail shows a corner dove's eye (centre bottom), with dove's eyes and eyelets.

SPIDER'S WEB STITCH

Spider's web is a traditional filling stitch used to decorate the voids left by cutting threads and it is often used with wrapped bars – follow the stages below. As with all these stitches, although they are not counted it is a good idea to keep notes of the numbers of winds and weaves to ensure that the stitches are uniform.

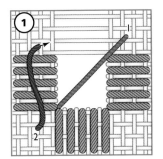

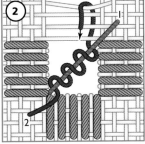

1 Work three sides in Kloster blocks, wrapped bars or a combination of both, bringing the needle out at the position marked 1 on the diagram. Cross the square, bringing the needle out at 2.

2 Return to position 1, winding the thread around the diagonal just formed, ready to complete the final side (shown as a wrapped bar in next diagram).

3 Bring the needle up at 3 and pass diagonally to 4, then wind the thread around the diagonal to the centre (as shown in the previous diagram).

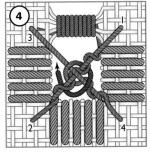

5 After three winds you may need to tighten and adjust the position of the winds to ensure that they are even and in the centre of the square. When the web is complete, leave the stitch by winding around the diagonal, as before.

4 Start weaving the web around the diagonals.

Picots

These pretty, decorative elements (rather like a sideways French knot) are worked as you wrap or needleweave the remaining threads after cutting. Take care to work each section in a uniform style. It will take a little practise to perfect these stitches but when worked they are very effective.

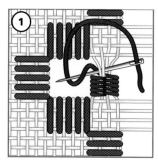
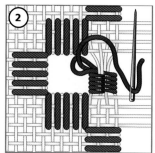
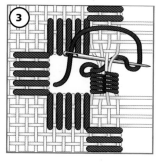

1 Needleweave halfway along a set of four threads and bring the needle out at the side to form the picot. Pass the needle under two threads on the same side and wrap the thread around the needle as shown.

2 Pull the needle through carefully, holding the wrapped thread in position – don't pull too tightly. Pass the needle through the centre of the four fabric threads, ready to make another picot along the other edge in the same way.

3 Once both picots have been formed, complete the needleweaving. To keep all the stitches consistent, make a record of how many weaves you make either side of the picots.

Buttonhole Edging

Buttonhole stitch is a very useful and versatile stitch and has been used to edge the Hardanger Diamond project (opposite). Once all the Hardanger embroidery and any cross stitch has been completed, the buttonhole stitches are worked around the perimeter, so the shape can be cut out without fear of the design falling to pieces!

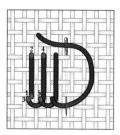
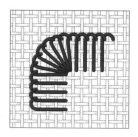
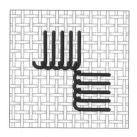

To work buttonhole stitch, start with an away waste knot (see page 22) and work long stitches over four threads (similar to Kloster blocks). Keep the stitches flat against the fabric and as consistent as possible. From the back, the stitches will look like a series of straight lines.

When you turn outer corners in buttonhole stitch, note that the corner hole holds seven threads.

When turning internal corners, note the way that the corner stitches are connected.

COMPLETING HARDANGER PROJECTS

The very nature of Hardanger embroidery means that you can see through it and so the final challenge is to use a complementary background to the piece. You may be surprised by what does and doesn't look good when you come to mount and frame. I have tried all sorts of background fabrics and was amazed at how effective Hardanger looked on tartan! In the projects in this chapter I have used some plum-coloured linen, stone-coloured card and some decorative parchment covered in Latin script written in silver pen.

HARDANGER DIAMOND

Stitch count: 58h x 62w (excluding buttonhole edge)
Design size: 10.5 x 11.3cm (4⅛ x 4¼in)
Fabric: Zweigart Cashel 28-count linen shade 224
Needle: Tapestry size 24 and 22
Chart: Page 192

Stitch Kloster blocks with one strand of ecru DMC Perlé No.8 and the filling stitches and eyelets in one strand of ecru Perlé No.12. Work the buttonhole edge in one strand of ecru DMC Perlé No.8 and then trim to the edge of the stitching. Mount and frame as desired.

Stitch Perfect – HARDANGER FILLING STITCHES

❖ For all filling stitches, use a slightly finer thread than for stitching the Kloster blocks.

❖ To weave a bar, bring the needle up in a void area and work over and under pairs of threads. After completing one bar, weave the next one at right angles to it, working around the design, taking care not to run threads across the back of the cut areas.

❖ Needleweaving shouldn't alter the shape of the bar, which should stay flat and straight.

❖ When wrapping a pair of threads, hold the wrapped thread firmly so it doesn't unravel.

❖ When working filling stitches, plan your route around the project and if necessary pass the needle under Kloster blocks but never across voided areas.

❖ When working dove's eyes, work in the same direction every time and remember to make the last twist.

❖ Count the number of winds of the spider's webs to keep them consistent.

❖ Finish off waste ends as you progress.

PULLED AND DRAWN THREAD EMBROIDERY

These are techniques that can cause a little confusion so I am going to look at them in detail in this section of the book. The two techniques can create such wonderful effects that they are well worth exploring. Both drawn and pulled thread embroidery are counted thread techniques and so they combine very well with traditional cross stitch. If you look at early antique band samplers you will find a myriad of counted stitches as well surface embroidery stitches combined, with stunning effects.

PULLED THREAD EMBROIDERY

In this technique the decorative effect on the fabric is created by forming stitches that are pulled to form holes in the fabric.

DRAWN THREAD EMBROIDERY

In this technique fabric threads are withdrawn from the fabric prior to decorating remaining threads with counted stitches.

PULLED THREAD EMBROIDERY

This is a type of embroidery where the pattern is created by pulling the fabric threads together using the construction of the stitch to create the effect. No fabric threads are removed to create the holes – it is all done by the tension in the embroidery. The holes produced by the pulled work stitches form patterns that are, perhaps confusingly, referred to as fillings! For this reason, some cross stitchers can find this technique a little difficult to master simply because they do not pull the stitches tightly enough. This habit comes from working pure cross stitch beautifully and not allowing the stitches to create holes!

Another secret to producing lovely pulled thread embroidery is to work on pure linen. Linen creases: if you wear linen clothes, you will know that it is not easy-care and creases very easily. When working pulled thread embroidery, you *want* the fabric to crease where the stitches are pulled and you want them to *stay* creased!

Traditionally, pulled thread embroidery is worked in the same colour as the fabric, as it is the holes that you create which are of interest, rather than the stitch itself. Pulled stitches, such as four-sided stitch, Algerian eye and Queen stitch can be worked alone or combined with cross stitch to create very pretty decorated motifs, as in the Strawberries and Cream Sampler opposite. They can also be used as filling stitches, as shown in the Lacy Flower Face on page 109. Using satin stitch in different formations can create very decorative pulled effects as long as the stitch is pulled firmly.

JANE'S TIP

If you work on an evenweave with a lot of synthetic content, the tendency is for the fabric to spring back to its original position. These easy-care materials are ideal for baby clothes or bibs that need constant washing and ironing but are less successful when working pulled stitches.

STRAWBERRIES AND CREAM SAMPLER

Stitch count: 54h x 54w   **Design size**: 10.5cm (4¼in) square
Fabric: Zweigart Dublin 26-count ivory linen   **Needle**: Tapestry size 24
Chart: Page 198

To work this delicate-looking sampler, work the cross stitch and queen stitch centre panel first using two strands of stranded cotton (floss). Now work the framework in four-sided stitch and cross stitch. Use filling stitches to complete each section: I used pulled satin stitch, Greek cross stitch, honeycomb stitch, double faggot stitch and coil stitch over four threads (refer to the Stitch Library). Work the eyelets over eight fabric threads using two strands of pink. All the pulled stitches are worked in two strands of stranded cotton (floss), with the backstitch added in one strand only.

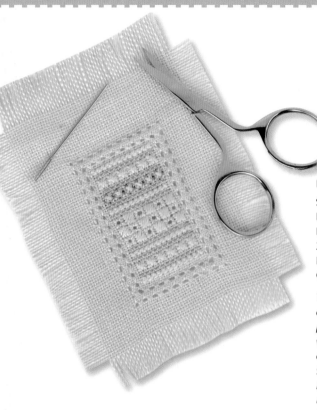

MINI CREAM SAMPLER

Stitch count: 30h x 18w
Design size: 5.5 x 3.3cm (2⅛ x 1¼in)
Fabric: Zweigart Cashel ivory
28-count linen
Needle: Tapestry size 24
Chart: Page 199

This tiny band sampler is worked in a combination of counted stitches and pulled threads. All stitches have been worked in two strands of stranded cotton (floss) (DMC 712 or Anchor 926), with the exception of the Madeira No.22 gold thread, which is used as supplied. Stitches used include long-legged cross stitch, double cross stitch, rice stitch and satin stitch (refer to the Stitch Library). The Algerian eyes and the four-sided stitch border are the pulled elements in this project (shown in the detail below).

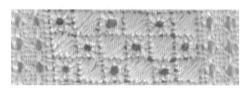

JANE'S TIP

Pulled thread embroidery is generally worked in thread the same colour as the fabric, but you could try using the stitches as decorative elements, as I did for the hemstitch edge in the needlecase on page 40. I also enjoy using linen thread for pulled thread embroidery.

Stitch Perfect – PULLED THREAD EMBROIDERY

❖ Use linen for pulled thread work, particularly for table linen, samplers and pillow covers.

❖ Pull the stitches so that the threads of the fabric are drawn together to form holes.

❖ With some stitches in pulled work, e.g., Algerian eye, the central hole is formed by pulling the thread firmly and always passing down the central hole in the stitch.

❖ Examples of special pulled stitches are described in the Stitch Library but you can produce very effective pulled thread embroidery by using the same stitch repeated in different formations. Satin stitch is a versatile stitch to try this with.

❖ Hemstitch is another pulled stitch (covered on page 111) and is used in conjunction with thread removal.

LACY FLOWER FACE

Stitch count: 38h x 38w **Design size**: 7.5cm (3in) square
Fabric: Zweigart Dublin 26-count ivory linen
Needle: Gold-plated tapestry size 24
Chart: Page 199

To work this simple flower face, backstitch the outline of the flower first in two strands of stranded cotton (floss). Now, using a variety of pulled stitches, fill each petal with a different stitch: I used pulled satin stitch, coil stitch over two threads, double faggot stitch, Greek cross stitch and honeycomb stitch (refer to the Stitch Library). Using two strands of thread, add random bullion and French knots to the flower centre. Border the flower with four-sided stitches worked over four fabric threads. Frame as desired.

DRAWN THREAD EMBROIDERY

Drawn thread embroidery is one of my personal favourites – it looks so clever but is in fact very simple to do. The trick is to take it in small stages, use a fabric you can see clearly and work in a good light. Drawn threads may be worked in bands, as shown in the samplers below and overleaf; in squares, as in the Corner Flowers and Hemstitch Square on page 115; or as part of a decorative hem around a project. The lovely Rose and Violet Sampler on page 116 uses all of these techniques, as well as some pulled stitches.

Essentially, a number of fabric threads are removed and/or re-woven and the remaining threads are then decorated. Withdrawing fabric threads is often combined with hemstitching of one sort or another. You will see examples of decorative hemstitch bands on the sampler on page 136 as well as some small examples in this section of the book.

Drawn thread work may superficially look like pulled work but their methods are quite different because in drawn thread work, fabric threads are cut and drawn out from the ground fabric.

ZIGZAGS AND LADDERS SAMPLER

Stitch count: 46h x 23w   **Design size**: 9 x 4.5cm (3½ x 1¾in)
Fabric: Zweigart Dublin 26-count ivory linen   **Needle**: Tapestry size 24 and 22   **Chart**: Page 200

Work cross stitch with two strands of stranded cotton (floss) and backstitch with one. Referring to the chart, withdraw the fabric threads using Method 2 described opposite. Work ladder hemstitch, simple hemstitch and zigzag hemstitch using two strands of stranded cotton DMC 712 (Anchor 926). Mount with a contrasting background fabric to display the drawn thread work and then frame as preferred.

PREPARING TO HEMSTITCH

I describe two ways here of removing fabric threads, prior to stitching hemstitch bands: Method 1 is suitable for wider bands, while Method 2 is better for narrower bands.

Method 1

1 On a wide band you can work roughly from the centre of the band because the cut threads will be long enough to work with. Carefully snip two horizontal fabric threads and gently unravel these threads to the edge of the band sampler.

2 Working in pairs, re-weave these threads as follows. Remove one fabric thread entirely, creating a ladder in the fabric. Using a size 22 needle, weave the needle in and out of the fabric threads as if to replace the missing thread.

3 Slip the loose fabric thread into the eye of the needle and pull gently.

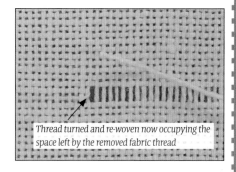

Thread turned and re-woven now occupying the space left by the removed fabric thread

Method 2

If you are working on a narrow band, it is easier to remove the fabric threads from the edge of the band because this leaves longer fabric ends to work with and re-weave.

1 Carefully snip *one* horizontal fabric thread at the margin of the band. Unravel it across the band to the other side, where you cut another adjacent fabric thread and unravel in the opposite direction. You will now have a ladder in the fabric and two fabric whiskers, one at either edge.

2 Working in pairs, re-weave these threads as follows: lift the fabric thread carefully and you will see the cut end of the other whisker. Remove this completely. Using a needle, weave the point in and out of the fabric threads and slip the loose fabric thread into the eye of the needle and pull gently. When done satisfactorily, you cannot tell where the linen threads have gone.

3 Repeat this process until all fabric threads are gone. Refer to the chart for the number of threads to remove. When the threads are re-woven, you will have created a new selvedge. The final picture would look the same on a wide band.

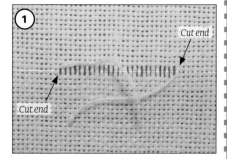

Cut end

Cut end

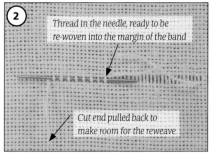

Thread in the needle, ready to be re-woven into the margin of the band

Cut end pulled back to make room for the reweave

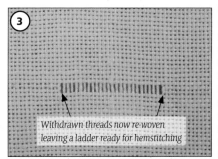

Withdrawn threads now re-woven leaving a ladder ready for hemstitching

SIMPLE HEMSTITCH

Once you have prepared the fabric by removing and re-weaving threads, as previously described in Method 1 or Method 2, you can begin to work a simple hemstitch band. Follow the steps and diagrams below, using two strands of stranded cotton (floss).

1 This hemstitching is over two threads in each direction. Work a straight stitch across two threads, turning the needle to face horizontally.

2 Make another straight stitch across two

threads, at right angles to the first, then pass the needle down diagonally under two threads.

3 Repeat the straight stitches along the row, counting carefully.

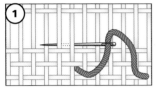  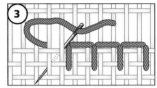

LADDER HEMSTITCH

This is the simplest decorative hemstitch. Cut the horizontal threads, as described in Method 1 or Method 2 and re-weave the threads. Now work two rows of hemstitch, as described above and shown in this diagram: the vertical threads that remain form a ladder pattern.

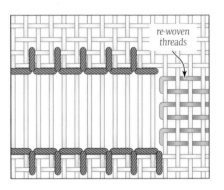

re-woven threads

WHITE HEMSTITCH SAMPLER

Stitch count: 42h x 24w
Design size: 8.5 x 4.5cm (3¼ x 1⅞in)
Fabric: Zweigart Dublin 26-count ivory linen 26-count
Needle: Tapestry size 24 and 22
Chart: Page 201

This project features some straightforward hemstitch bands, as well as pulled stitches in the four-sided stitch border. Using stranded cotton (floss) DMC 712 (Anchor 926), work all the counted stitch bands on the sampler leaving the hemstitched bands until last. Use two strands for the long-legged cross stitch, rice stitch, adapted double cross stitch and large crosses. Use Madeira No.22 gold thread as supplied. Using Method 2 (page 111) and referring to the chart, withdraw four fabric threads for each hemstitch band. Add the hemstitch to the top and bottom band and somersault stitch to the middle one. I completed the design with a border of four-sided stitch and a hemstitch edge cut to the stitching (see page 119 for instructions).

Working a Hemstitch Square

The Corner Flowers and Hemstitch Square project is an ideal one to stitch if you haven't yet created a hemstitch square. The threads remaining in the centre of this square have been wrapped and decorated with eight dove's eye stitches. The central detail (right) from the picture, shows how attractive the finished effect is.

1 Using two strands of DMC 712 (Anchor 926), work a square of simple hemstitch, following the chart and taking care to count each side carefully. As you turn a corner, count the last stitch on one row as the first on the next – otherwise you will end up with the wrong number of threads. Finish off carefully underneath the hemstitches on the wrong side of the stitching.

2 You can now cut the fabric threads. To ensure that you cut the correct ones it's helpful to run a line of tacking (basting) threads through the square (as shown by the blue dashed lines in the diagram below). Count to the centre of the hemmed area and snip alternate pairs. Carefully unravel the cut threads from the middle to the hemstitched edge, leaving a two-thread border at the sides. When each side is unravelled, tack (baste) these threads out of the way on the back of the work or they will get in the way.

3 To decorate the remaining threads, wrap each pair with one strand of DMC 712 (Anchor 926) adding dove's eye stitches as you wrap. To complete the square, use two strands of DMC 712 (Anchor 926) to work one row of satin stitch all around the square – as shown by the red stitches in the diagram below. Remove the tacking and cut away loose fabric whiskers.

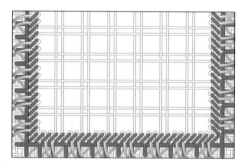

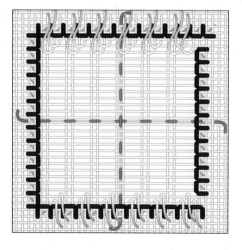

CORNER FLOWERS AND HEMSTITCH SQUARE

Stitch count: 25h x 25w   **Design size**: 4.5cm (1¾in) square
Fabric: Zweigart Cashel linen 28-count shade   **Needle**: Tapestry size 24   **Chart**: Page 201

Work the cross stitch over two linen threads, using two strands of stranded cotton (floss). Now use two strands of DMC 712 (Anchor 926) to work a square of hemstitch – see opposite for instructions. Once all stitching is complete, mount and frame your picture. The addition of a contrast fabric beneath the embroidery will show the hemstitch square to best advantage.

Stitch Perfect – DRAWN THREAD EMBROIDERY

❖ Always study the chart well and count the site very carefully so you know exactly how many threads need to be cut.

❖ Work slowly and methodically when cutting and re-weaving threads. Take it in small stages, use a fabric you can see clearly and work in a good light.

❖ If you are new to drawn thread work and a little nervous, work a line of tacking (basting) threads over and under two threads of the linen prior to thread withdrawal.

❖ If working on a wide band, work roughly from the centre of the band when cutting and re-weaving threads. If working on a narrow band, remove the fabric threads from the edge of the band to leave longer fabric ends to re-weave.

❖ When working hemstitch bands, try to avoid running out of thread halfway across as it is difficult to hide where you start the new threads.

❖ Work the hemstitches as indicated on the chart you are following, taking care to count two threads carefully.

ROSE AND VIOLET SAMPLER

Stitch count: 128h x 66w
Design size: 23 x 12cm (9 x 4¾in) excluding folded hem
Fabric: Zweigart Cashel linen 28-count
Needle: Tapestry size 24 and 22
Chart: Pages 188–189

This exquisite band sampler has a satisfying mixture of pulled thread and drawn thread techniques for you to try and includes a decorative folded hem (see overleaf). Work the sampler from the top down. Work the counted stitches in two strands of stranded cotton (floss) referring to the chart for the numbers of fabric threads involved and the Stitch Library for stitch instructions. Work backstitch with one strand. Work the various hemstitch bands with two strands of DMC 712 (Anchor 926), with the optional use of Mill Hill beads as embellishment. Use Method 1 (page 111) for the thread withdrawal and refer to the diagrams in this section as needed. Wrapped bars and dove's eyes decorate the hemstitch square (see page 114 for hemstitch square instructions).

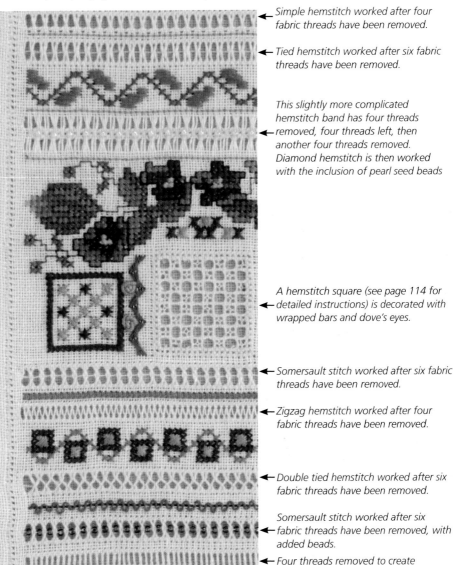

← *Simple hemstitch worked after four fabric threads have been removed.*

← *Tied hemstitch worked after six fabric threads have been removed.*

← *This slightly more complicated hemstitch band has four threads removed, four threads left, then another four threads removed. Diamond hemstitch is then worked with the inclusion of pearl seed beads*

← *A hemstitch square (see page 114 for detailed instructions) is decorated with wrapped bars and dove's eyes.*

← *Somersault stitch worked after six fabric threads have been removed.*

← *Zigzag hemstitch worked after four fabric threads have been removed.*

← *Double tied hemstitch worked after six fabric threads have been removed.*

← *Somersault stitch worked after six fabric threads have been removed, with added beads.*

← *Four threads removed to create ladder hemstitch.*

Folded Hems

When using a folded hem as a border around a piece of stitching, you can decide on the margin you prefer. You can see an example of a narrow margin from the close-up photograph of the Rose and Violet Sampler, right and the Beautiful Band sampler, below.

The steps below and opposite describe how to create a simple folded hem. If you wish you can make a folded hem even more complicated by withdrawing extra fabric threads from around the edge of the project, so that the hem is still the same width but there is room to add decorative hemstitching in the gap.

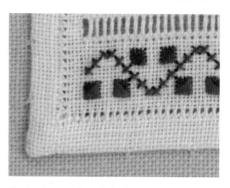

The detail picture above shows the narrow folded hem border on the Rose and Violet Sampler (shown in full on page 116), which finishes the project off beautifully. The Beautiful Band sampler (see page 136) also has a folded hem border on all sides.

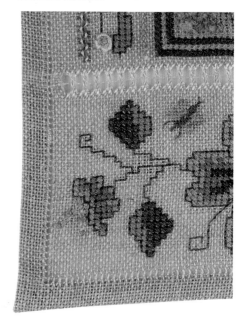

Jane's Tip

When scoring fabric prior to folding a hem, try using a glossy magazine cover for an excellent working surface.

Scoring Fabric

To form a perfect fold when stitching a hem, it is essential to score the fabric so that your hem will follow the fabric threads.

1 Place the fabric on a clean, flat surface (not French polished) and place the needle in a line of threads that will form the fold.

2 Carefully pull the fabric not the needle, which will create a score mark on the fabric making turning the material simple. This score line will need pressing with a steam iron to remove!

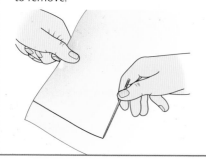

Jane's Tip

When planning a folded hem use a little spray starch whilst pressing the embroidery (on the back of area to be scored) and this will help the folding and rolling of the fabric edges.

CREATING A FOLDED HEM

1 From the middle of the long side of the stitching count five threads out from the edge of the stitching and cut the sixth thread. Carefully unravel this thread back to the corner and re-weave it into the margin. Repeat on all four sides. Now lay the fabric wrong side up on a hard surface and count out from the missing thread to the ninth and tenth threads.

2 Place a tapestry needle between these threads and pull the fabric (not the needle) to score a line that will form a crease – this will form the fold at the edge of the work (see box opposite for how to score fabric). Repeat on all four sides.

3 Score the fabric again, nine threads further out (line 2 on the diagram). Score another line seven threads out and cut the fabric carefully following this line of threads.

4 Fold the fabric piece at the corners and cut as shown in the diagram. Now fold in all the edges, mitring the corners.

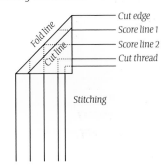

Fold line
Cut line
Cut edge
Score line 1
Score line 2
Cut thread
Stitching

5 Using an away waste knot start, hemstitch the folded edge in place. At the corners, stitch the mitres with invisible stitching up the seam.

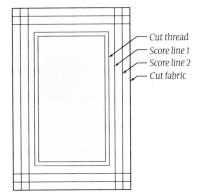

Cut thread
Score line 1
Score line 2
Cut fabric

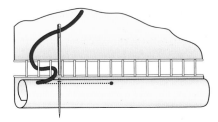

HEMSTITCH EDGING

It is possible to work a row of hemstitch as shown in the diagram below and then cut the excess fabric away without the fabric fraying. This is an ideal way to create bookmarks if you do not have linen or Aida band. This stitch may be worked on Aida fabric, as you can see from the needlecase on page 40, and can be effective when worked in a contrasting colour if you want to create a more striking effect.

If you are nervous of the result, stitch as shown in the diagram but work each stitch twice, thus forming an even stronger edge. You can see

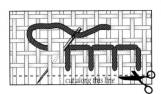

cut along this line

this type of cut edge used here on the Heart and Stork Sachet. If the project is going to require regular washing I prefer to use the folded hem described above.

ADAPTING AND DESIGNING CROSS STITCH

This section is an introduction to creating your own cross stitch designs. One easy way to start is to adapt an existing cross stitch kit, perhaps by changing some of the colours used, replacing a motif with something else or using different stitches. Once you start to think outside the box, it is easier to move on to designing from scratch – and you will find plenty of advice here. See also Stitching from a Kit on page 21.

USING PURCHASED KITS

There can be no better introduction to cross stitch than working one of the many small kits available. However, there is no reason why the more experienced embroiderer should not enjoy these too. They are still the cheapest way to collect the essentials to complete a project, and they can provide the perfect opportunity to develop simple designing techniques using the chart from the kit as a starting point. A counted needlework kit will contain the fabric and threads for the project, sometimes with the addition of special threads, charms or beads.

It is possible, with just a little imagination, to create many new designs from the original provided, and the joy of counted embroidery is that there is no printing on the fabric so you can decide where and how you want to make changes. Generally, people buy ready-made kits partly for convenience and partly to avoid making design decisions. This section will start you thinking of ways to change and personalize kits – the beginning of designing for yourself.

ADAPTING A KIT

There are many ways that you can adapt a cross stitch kit – here are a few suggestions.

◆ Consider adding names and dates to the finished piece to make it unique. To add wording, draw the letters on to a sheet of graph paper, mark the centre and then stitch in position.

◆ Look at the picture of the kit design and try a simple change of colour. For example, you may prefer a blue and silver border rather than pink and gold.

◆ Make a copy of the original chart and write notes on this. Keep the notes simple, e.g., 'French knots here' or 'change these cross stitches to seed beads' – the colours and details can come as you stitch.

◆ Keep a record of what colour was used for each change so that you can ensure that both sides of the design match, if this is crucial.

◆ Avoid adding too many different colours to a pattern: instead use different shades of the same colour.

JANE'S TIP
Keep your store of threads organized and labelled so that when you are ready to give full vent to your artistic bent you will have all you need to work your own design.

DESIGNING A SAMPLER

There are many books devoted to sampler design so this section can only give you some basic tips on how to start designing your own work. A sampler usually features certain elements: the Stork Birth Sampler on page 125 is a straightforward cross stitch design (with a little backstitch), which contains the following basic elements.

◆ A border around the design, which may be wide or narrow, single or double.

◆ An alphabet, sometimes an upper case and a lower case one, and perhaps numbers too.

◆ A selection of motifs or patterns within the border, which may be single or mirror image and may reflect a specific theme.

◆ Some initials or a name and a date, either of the stitcher or the intended recipient of the stitched piece.

DESIGN CONTENT

When designing for the first time, whether on the computer or using graph paper and coloured pencils, the idea may seem daunting but try dealing with it in small, bite-sized pieces. You will need to make fairly basic decisions before you start work and considering the following points should help.

Do some research: Is the design for a family member or special friend and is it a secret? Ask older or more distant relatives for family details. If planning a local design to include maps or plans, use libraries to collect information. Make lists of the receiver's hobbies and favourite pastimes to help you decide what motifs or theme to use.

Choose the motifs: Don't be afraid to experiment with using different motifs as trial and error often achieve the most successful results. Use a master chart on which you can temporarily stick motifs to judge the overall effect. When selecting a house motif, relate the size and style of the house to any figures included and adjust the choices of flowers and trees to suit the overall plan. Aim for a balance between the motifs and the overall design size.

Decide on style: Are you designing a traditional piece or one with a more modern feel? This will affect what motifs you choose and how you combine them, particularly for a traditional sampler, where it is important to select motifs of the right style and weight. An extreme example would be adding a Ferrari car to a traditional border and stylized trees and flowers!

Choose the stitches: Are you planning to work the design entirely in cross stitch or use additional stitches as well? Some stitches are not as successful on Aida as on evenweave.

Select the fabric: The following factors are important when choosing fabric. If the design is very traditional (and also includes lots of three-quarter cross stitches), it might suit an evenweave rather than an Aida fabric. You may also want to work some lettering over one fabric thread (for longer verses). If your design is a large one you may need to work it on a higher stitch count, i.e., an 18-count Aida, which would result in a smaller finished size. If working on a finer fabric though, consider your eyesight and the amount of time you have to complete the stitching.

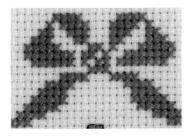

Decide on size: What size do you want your work to be? A sampler can be any size or shape, generally determined by how much time you have and if you have a deadline.

Think about borders: When designing a large sampler, deep, strong borders work better than narrow, rather mean ones. Use simple narrow borders around smaller projects.

Choose lettering: Is the design intended to be read like a verse or a prayer? If so, keep the style simple or the text may be difficult to read. A large alphabet may be better on its own rather than part of a mixed sampler.

Consider the making up: What is the end use of your piece of stitching? A sampler doesn't have to be a picture – a small design might look well as a card or bag. You may have to allow more fabric for some making up techniques.

Sign and date your work: Why not write a paragraph about the design, its date and how it came to be, plus your own details to put inside the back of the frame? Alternatively, draw a label to stick on the back, with details such as: Designed and stitched by . . . Completed and presented on . . .

COMPUTER-AIDED DESIGN

Since I started using a computer to help with my cross stitch design, people (not stitchers) have asked me what I do with the spare time! When designing a lovely, complicated border I can spend time perfecting the pattern repeat rather than copying or tracing mirror images. I do not use a scanner to produce cross stitch patterns because I would be breaking any number of copyright laws, and I can always tell when a design is scanned, so I use a computer to remove the drudgery out of designing. The computer replaces the pen, paper, scissors, correction fluid and eraser but does not 'produce' designs by magic. You still need to draw the images on the screen and position the coloured squares.

DESIGN DEVELOPMENT

I use my own computer programme to design all my counted embroidery (see page 220) and I have included some pictures of the computer screen opposite so you can see the development of a cross stitch chart. The programme enables you to create different counted stitches, draw Hardanger, pulled and drawn thread embroidery in addition to cross stitch and canvaswork charts. You can, of course, scan in your own photographs and import them into the programme to create cross stitch charts for your own use. It is possible to draw in backstitch, copy and paste, flip, reverse and mirror image your motifs. In addition you can create text in cross stitch and look at the chart in black and white symbols, colour and in a combination of both (see page 11).

Some charting software programmes (including my own), allow you to see what a design would look like if worked on different types of fabrics and different colours. Here, this little violet is shown on green Aida, mauve linen and white stitching paper.

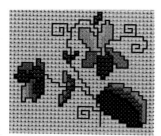 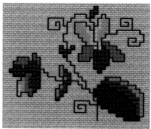 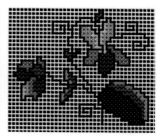

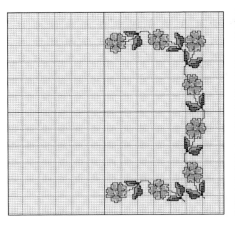

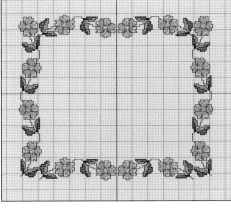

At this stage, I have designed the right-hand side of the border for the Forget-Me-Not Wedding Sampler (stitching instructions on page 128).

Here, the border for the sampler has been completed by copying the right side, pasting it and flipping the image to create a mirror half.

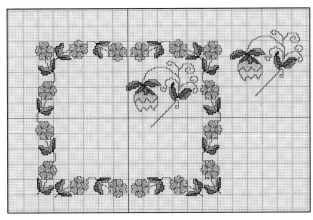

At this point in the designing process one of the main flower motifs has been drawn outside the border, and then copied and pasted into position within the design area.

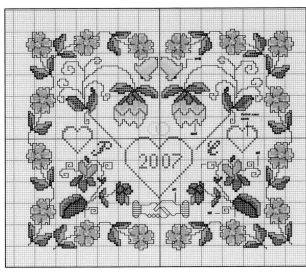

Other elements of the design are created and added in a similar way until at last the chart is complete and ready for stitching to begin.

CELEBRATION SAMPLERS

This section has a bonus collection of four large samplers – a birth sampler, a wedding sampler, a festive sampler and a traditional band sampler. These designs are perfect to stitch for special celebrations and can either be stitched as shown or adapted and personalized to suit events and occasions in your life. Colours can be changed, messages added and motifs substituted. You can also use smaller parts from the charts to create quick-stitch projects, such as the sachet and cards shown. Full stitching instructions are given for each of the four designs and their charts are also contained within this section.

STORK BIRTH SAMPLER

A birth sampler is often the starting point for a new cross stitcher. Whether a new mum or doting grandparent, many stitchers have discovered cross stitch by working a celebratory sampler and this project would be ideal. Worked on Aida fabric, it is simple to stitch, has very few fractional stitches and grows quickly. The design was stitched on a soft peachy-pink fabric but you use blue or a brighter candy pink.

Stitch count: 121h x 91w
Design size: 22 x 16.5cm (8¾ x 6½in)
Fabric: Zweigart 14-count Aida shade 406
Needle: Tapestry size 24
Chart: Overleaf

1 Prepare your fabric for work and stitch over one block of Aida, using two strands of stranded cotton (floss) for cross stitch and then one strand for backstitch.
2 Use the alphabet and the numbers to personalize the design, adding initials and a date. Plan the letters and numbers on graph paper first, to ensure they fit the space.
3 When all the stitching is complete, mount and frame your sampler.

HEART AND STORK SACHET

Stitch count: 38h x 33w
Design size: 7 x 6cm (2¾ x 2½in)
Fabric: Zweigart Cashel 28-count washed unbleached linen
Needle: Tapestry size 24

This little sachet uses motifs from the Stork Birth Sampler but you could make up your own combination, and change the colours too if you wish. Use two strands of stranded cotton for cross stitch and one for backstitch. The design was made into a sachet (see page 213) with the top edge hemstitched and trimmed to the stitching (see page 119). Fill with scented pot-pourri or perhaps a little christening gift and tie with a ribbon.

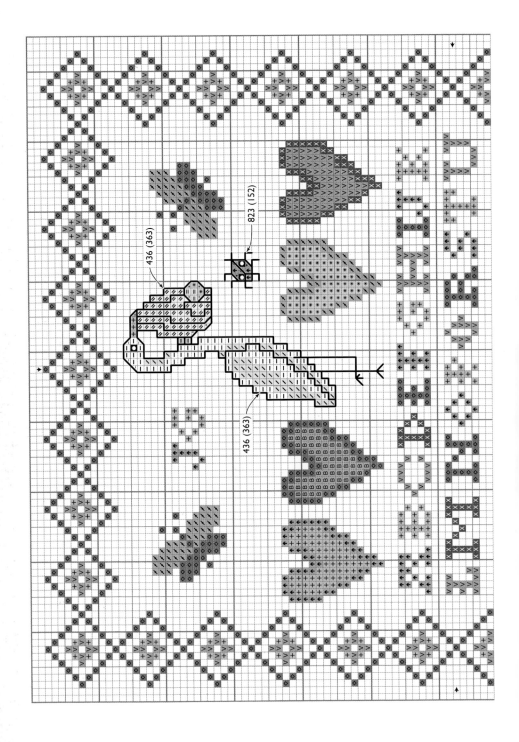

823 (152)

436 (363)

436 (363)

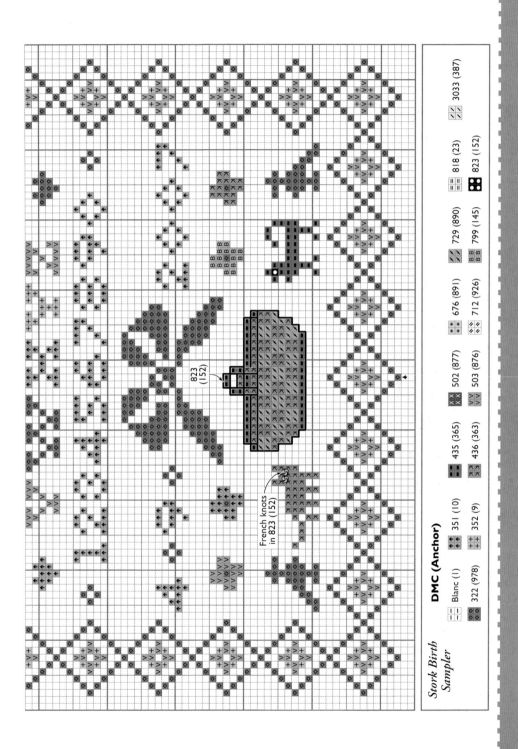

Stork Birth Sampler

DMC (Anchor)

Blanc (1)	322 (978)	351 (10)	352 (9)	435 (365)	436 (363)	502 (877)
503 (876)	676 (891)	712 (926)	729 (890)	799 (145)	818 (23)	823 (152)
3033 (387)						

823 (152)

French knots in 823 (152)

FORGET-ME-NOT WEDDING SAMPLER

This pretty sampler could be adapted for a wedding or anniversary, perhaps altering the colour of the hearts to suit the occasion. I have worked some pulled satin stitches in the two heart motifs to add interest and texture but if you prefer not to work these then the design could be stitched on a 14-count Aida. The illustrations on page 123 show this chart being developed by computer software.

Stitch count: 103h x 128w
(excluding alphabet)
Design size: 18.5 x 23cm (7¼ x 9in)
Fabric: Zweigart Cashel 28-count linen, shade 224
Needle: Tapestry size 24
Chart: Overleaf

1 Prepare fabric for work and stitch over two threads of linen, using two strands of stranded cotton (floss) for cross stitch and one for backstitch. Work pulled satin stitch with two strands of DMC 712 (Anchor 926).
2 Use the alphabet and numbers on page 205 to personalize the design, adding initials and a date. Plan the letters and numbers on graph paper first, to ensure they fit.
3 When all the stitching is complete, mount and frame your sampler.

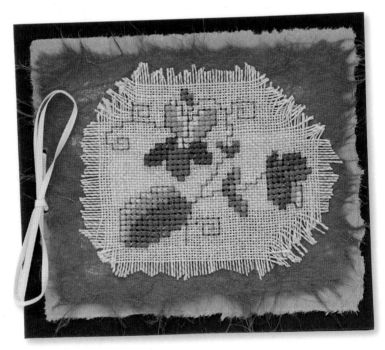

VINTAGE VIOLA CARD

Stitch count: 29h x 35w   **Design size:** 5.5 x 6.5cm (2¼ x 2¾in)
Fabric: Zweigart Dublin 26-count washed unbleached linen   **Needle:** Tapestry size 24

This pretty motif was taken from the Forget-Me-Not Wedding Sampler. Stitch using two strands of stranded cotton for cross stitch and one for backstitch. Prepare as a tattered patch, mount on handmade paper and card and trim with a narrow ribbon. See page 215 for making cards. This motif is shown on different coloured computer-generated fabrics on page 122.

3740 (872)

501 (878)

3834 (100)

Pulled
satin stitch
in 712 (926)

200.

501 (878)

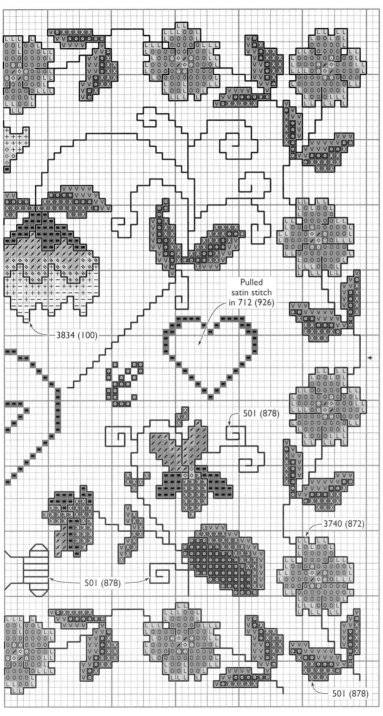

Pulled
satin stitch
in 712 (926)

3834 (100)

501 (878)

3740 (872)

501 (878)

501 (878)

*Forget-Me-Not
Wedding
Sampler*

**DMC
(Anchor)**

	351 (10)
	352 (9)
	353 (8)
	501 (878)
	502 (877)
	503 (876)
	676 (891)
	677 (361)
	712 (926)
	3740 (872)
	3834 (100)
	3838 (177)
	3839 (176)
	3840 (120)

Use the alphabet
and numbers on
page 205 to
personalize the
design

HOLLY AND HELLEBORE GARLAND

This festive design makes a lovely sampler to be brought out each year to herald the arrival of Christmas. Instead of working the alphabet you could use the charted letters to create a greeting – perhaps 'Happy Christmas to One and All'.

Stitch count: 105h x 125w
Design size: 19 x 23cm (7½ x 9in)
Fabric: Zweigart Cashel 28-count linen shade 638
Needle: Gold-plated tapestry size 24
Chart: Overleaf

HELLEBORE CARD

Stitch count: 22h x 35w
Design size: 4 x 6.5cm (1½ x 2½in)
Fabric: Zweigart 14-count Star Aida
Needle: Tapestry size 24

Another motif taken from the Holly and Hellebore Garland. Stitch over one block of Aida, using two strands of stranded cotton (floss) for cross stitch and one for backstitch. Add French knots in two strands, with two twists around the needle. Prepare the design as a patch, mount it on handmade card and trim with silk ribbon. See page 215 for making up cards.

1 *Prepare your fabric for work and stitch over two threads of linen (or one block of 14-count Aida), using two strands of stranded cotton (floss) for cross stitch and French knots, and one strand for backstitch. There are some tweeded cross stitches in the cottage – use one strand of each colour together in the needle (see page 17). Work eyelets in Madeira No.22 gold thread.*
2 *Use the alphabet to change the initials or personalize the design in some other way.*
3 *When all the stitching is complete, mount and frame your sampler.*

POINSETTIA GIFT TAG

Stitch count: 12h x 16w
Design size: 2 x 3cm (¾ x 1⅛in)
Fabric: Zweigart linen Aida with Lurex 14-count
Needle: Tapestry size 24

This motif was taken from the Holly and Hellebore Garland. Stitch over one block of Aida, using two strands of stranded cotton (floss) for cross stitch and one for backstitch. Fray the patch and make up as a folded gift tag trimmed with metallic thread. See page 215 for making up cards.

934 (852)

Eyelets in gold thread

840 (1084)

3830 (5975)

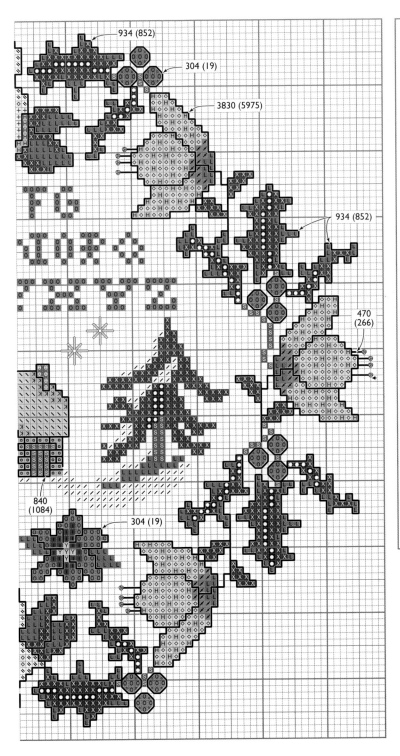

934 (852)

304 (19)

3830 (5975)

934 (852)

470 (266)

840 (1084)

304 (19)

Holly and Hellebore Garland

DMC (Anchor)

⁄⁄	Blanc (1)
▨	223 (1027)
HH	224 (895)
◇◇	225 (894)
▦	304 (19)
✕✕	437 (362)
LL	470 (266)
00	666 (46)
◈◈	712 (926)
YY	725 (305)
◥◥	738 (361)
SS	840 (1084)
▦	934 (852)
✕✕	937 (268)
++	3072 (397)
◉◉	3830 (5975)
••	758 (9575) + 3830 (5975)
◔◔	French knots in 470 (266)
✳	Eyelets in Madeira No.22 gold

135

BEAUTIFUL BAND SAMPLER

Band samplers were originally stitched as learning and remembering tools long before pen and paper were used to record stitches and techniques. A stitcher would copy a row of a stitch or pattern on to a narrow piece of linen and then roll the fabric up and keep it as a reference work.

As a self-confessed addict of band samplers I always find a way of including one in my books. This exquisite sampler is not difficult to stitch as all the techniques are explained within this book, but I would not recommend it as a project for a beginner! Work this project on evenweave as some of the stitches cannot be constructed on Aida – see the extensive Stitch Library or relevant techniques within the body of the book. This design is also a treasury of small motifs that could be used in smaller projects for quick gifts and cards.

Stitch count: 60w x 259h   **Design size:** 11.5 x 50.5cm (4½ x 20in)   **Fabric:** Zweigart 26-count Dublin linen washed unbleached   **Needle:** Gold plated size 26

Press the fabric to remove creases and oversew the edges to prevent fraying (particularly important if finishing the project with a folded hem). Start at the top of the sampler, leaving at least 6.5cm (2½in) at the top of the fabric. The chart occurs over six pages, with the key on each spread. You will find the design easier to work if you colour photocopy the parts and carefully tape them together.

BAND 1

Work the cross stitch motifs using two strands of stranded cotton (floss) and two strands of Caron Waterlilies silk. Use one strand for backstitch. Once you have established the width of the sampler, work a line of tacking (basting) stitches down each side (under and over two fabric threads) to help keep you in position as you work down the project. This also helps when removing

fabric threads in preparation for working the various hemstitch bands. See also page 111.

Use two strands of stranded cotton for half Rhodes stitch, braided cross stitch, crossed cushion stitch, threaded herringbone, double cross stitch and rice stitch, combining the latter with one strand of gold metallic thread. Use three strands of Caron Waterlilies for the large Rhodes stitch.

Band 2

Work the vertical satin stitch bands in three strands of Caron Waterlilies (don't pull stitches too tight – they should lie smoothly side by side). For the double tied hemstitch, remove six threads (see page 111) and then work two rows of hemstitch with two strands of 712 (926) across either side of the fabric ladder. Use one strand to work the double tied hemstitch.

Band 3

Use two strands of stranded cotton for the cross stitch and one for backstitch. Use two strands to work the red berry motifs in detached buttonhole stitch and then outline in counted chain stitch. Use one strand to backstitch outline the area for braid stitch and then work the braid stitch with one strand of De Haviland Flower Thread. Couch a strand of metallic gold in place with one strand of stranded cotton. Work satin stitch with two strands, in two shades of pink. Work two rows of Montenegrin stitch with two strands of stranded cotton prior to removing and re-weaving four fabric threads. Work hemstitch on one side of the ladder, grouping the fabric threads in fours.

Band 4

Use two strands of stranded cotton for cross stitch, French knots and four-sided stitch and one strand for backstitch. Work the hemstitch square (see page 114) with two strands of 712 (926). Fill with wrapped bars and dove's eyes with one strand. Remove and re-weave four fabric threads, leave four, and remove and re-weave another four before working the diamond hemstitch in two strands, adding beads as you go. Work a line of backstitch with gold metallic.

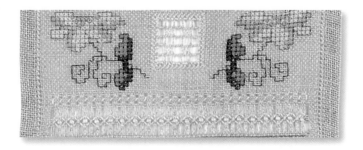

BAND 5

Use two strands of stranded cotton for cross stitch, half Rhodes stitch, queen stitch, eyelets, Algerian eyes, French knots, four-sided stitch, hemstitch and needlelace petals (the needlelace is shown in a detail beside the chart). Work tied hemstitch after removing and re-weaving six fabric threads.

BAND 6

Use two strands of stranded cotton for cross stitch, long-legged cross stitch and threaded herringbone (with one strand of Caron Waterlilies). Use one strand of Caron Waterlilies for Pekinese stitch, bullion roses, half cross stitch and French knots. Use one strand of Madeira Lana wool for velvet stitch in the 'pond' and one strand of stranded cotton for half cross stitch background. Remove and re-weave six fabric threads and work somersault stitch with two strands of 712 (926).

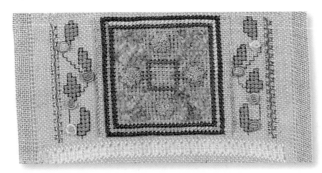

BAND 7

Use two strands of stranded cotton for cross stitch, counted chain stitch and bullions. Use one strand of Caron thread for French knots. Use one strand for backstitch. Work the insects in tent stitch, with one strand over just one fabric thread.

Finish the sampler with a folded and stitched hem (see page 118). Remove all tacking. Alternatively, mount and frame your sampler.

Beautiful Band Sampler

DMC (Anchor)

▦	315 (1019)	▦	930 (1035)	
✕✕	316 (1017)	▧▧	931 (1034)	
⊤⊤	470 (255)	○○	932 (1033)	
▵▵	471 (265)	++	3041 (871)	
＊＊	676 (891)	⁄⁄	3042 (870)	
GG	729 (890)	✕✕	3051 (845)	
∣∣	778 (361)			

	Caron Waterlilies Far Horizon	◈	Queen stitch in 3687 (68)
▦	De Haviland Green Flower Thread	⊔⊔	All hemstitching in 712 (926)
▦	Velvet stitch in Madeira Lana Wool 3396	⊛⊛	Mill Hill antique glass beads 03021 pearl
▦	Half cross in one strand of 932 (1033)		

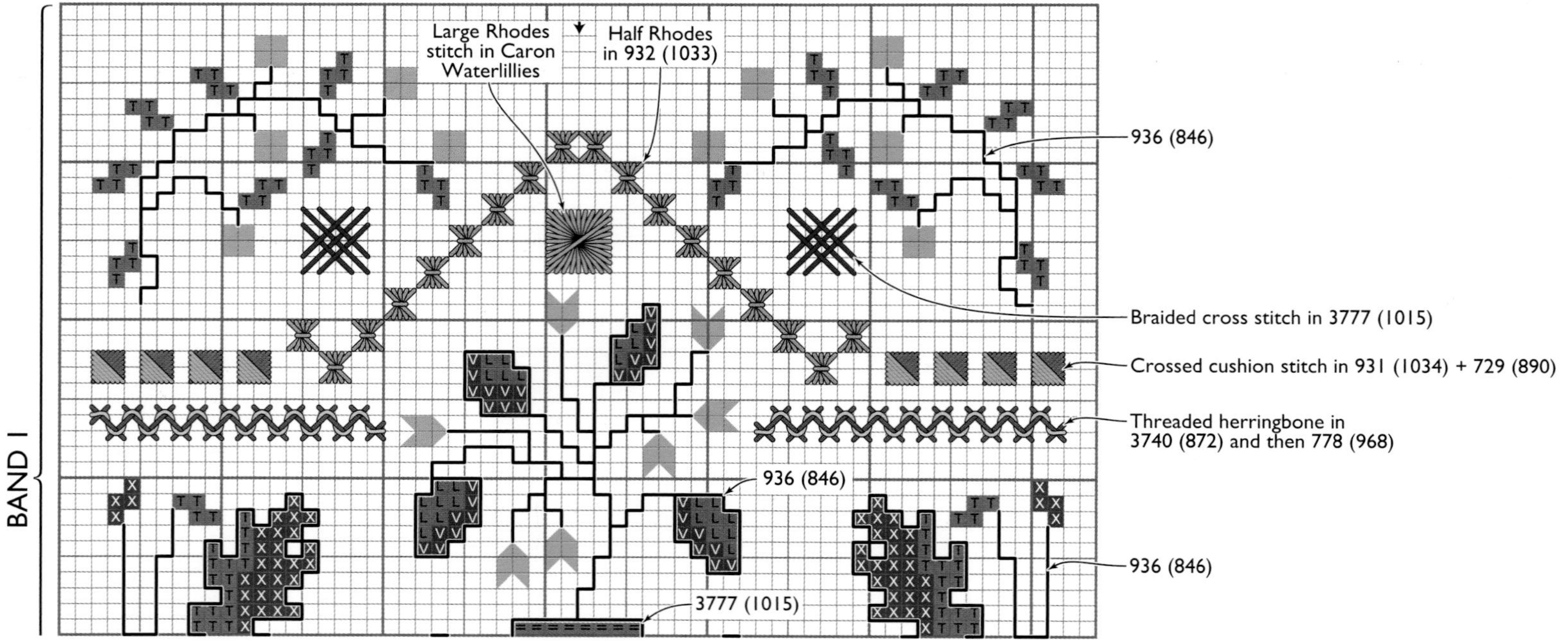

▦▦	3346 (267)		
∟∟	3347 (266)		
CC	3721 (896)		
▲▲	3740 (872)		
≈≈	3772 (1007)		
✕✕	3777 (1015)		
←←	3778 (1013)		

→ Half Rhodes in 932 (1033)

Large Rhodes stitch in Caron Waterlillies

936 (846)

Braided cross stitch in 3777 (1015)

Crossed cushion stitch in 931 (1034) + 729 (890)

Threaded herringbone in 3740 (872) and then 778 (968)

936 (846)

936 (846)

3777 (1015)

BAND I

140

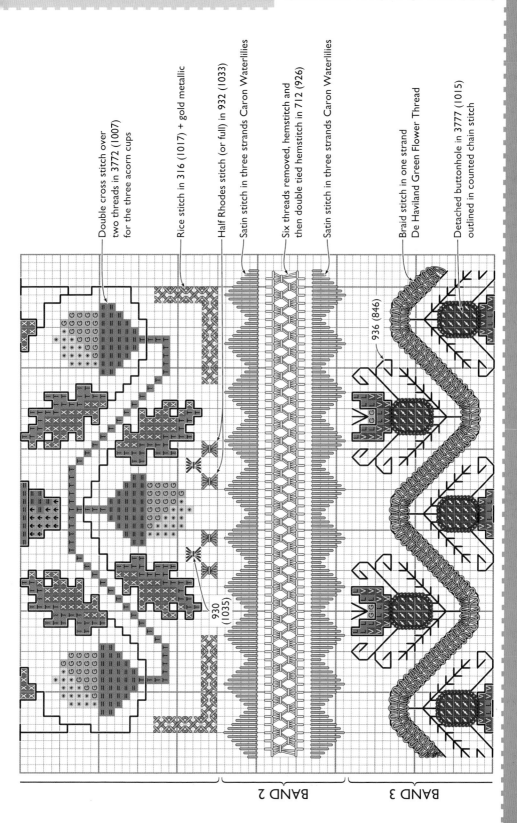

Double cross stitch over two threads in 3772 (1007) for the three acorn cups

Rice stitch in 316 (1017) + gold metallic

Half Rhodes stitch (or full) in 932 (1033)

Satin stitch in three strands Caron Waterlilies

Six threads removed, hemstitch and then double tied hemstitch in 712 (926)

Satin stitch in three strands Caron Waterlilies

Braid stitch in one strand De Haviland Green Flower Thread

Detached buttonhole in 3777 (1015) outlined in counted chain stitch

936 (846)

930 (1035)

BAND 2

BAND 3

Beautiful Band Sampler

DMC (Anchor)

315 (1019)
316 (1017)
470 (255)
471 (265)
676 (891)
729 (890)
778 (361)

930 (1035)
931 (1034)
932 (1033)
3041 (871)
3042 (870)
3051 (845)

3346 (267)
3347 (266)
3721 (896)
3740 (872)
3772 (1007)
3777 (1015)
3778 (1013)

Caron Waterlilies Far Horizon

De Haviland Green Flower Thread

Velvet stitch in Madeira Lana Wool 3396

Half cross in one strand of 932 (1033)

Queen stitch in 3687 (68)

All hemstitching in 712 (926)

Mill Hill antique glass beads 03021 pearl

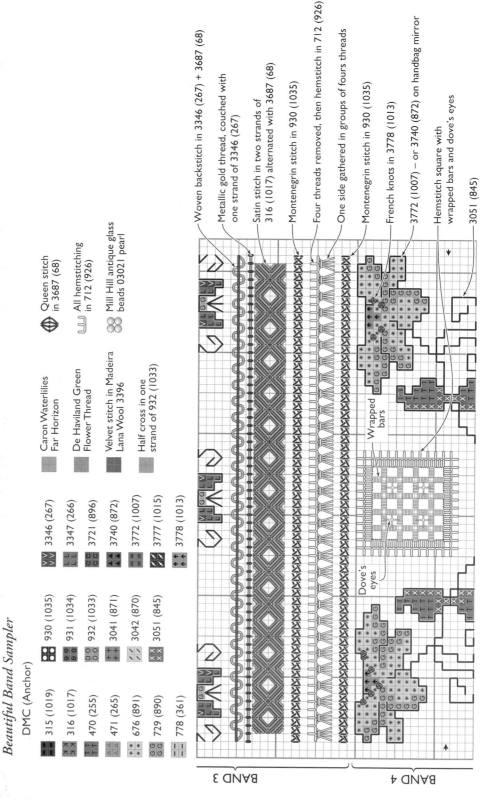

Woven backstitch in 3346 (267) + 3687 (68)

Metallic gold thread, couched with one strand of 3346 (267)

Satin stitch in two strands of 316 (1017) alternated with 3687 (68)

Montenegrin stitch in 930 (1035)

Four threads removed, then hemstitch in 712 (926)

One side gathered in groups of fours threads

Montenegrin stitch in 930 (1035)

French knots in 3778 (1013)

3772 (1007) – or 3740 (872) on handbag mirror

Hemstitch square with wrapped bars and dove's eyes

3051 (845)

Wrapped bars

Dove's eyes

BAND 3

BAND 4

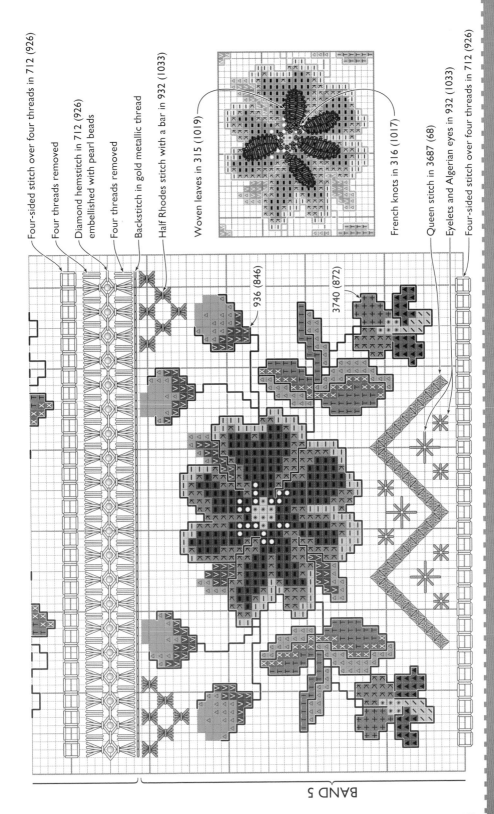

Four-sided stitch over four threads in 712 (926)

Four threads removed

Diamond hemstitch in 712 (926) embellished with pearl beads

Four threads removed

Backstitch in gold metallic thread

Half Rhodes stitch with a bar in 932 (1033)

Woven leaves in 315 (1019)

French knots in 316 (1017)

Queen stitch in 3687 (68)

Eyelets and Algerian eyes in 932 (1033)

Four-sided stitch over four threads in 712 (926)

936 (846)

3740 (872)

BAND 5

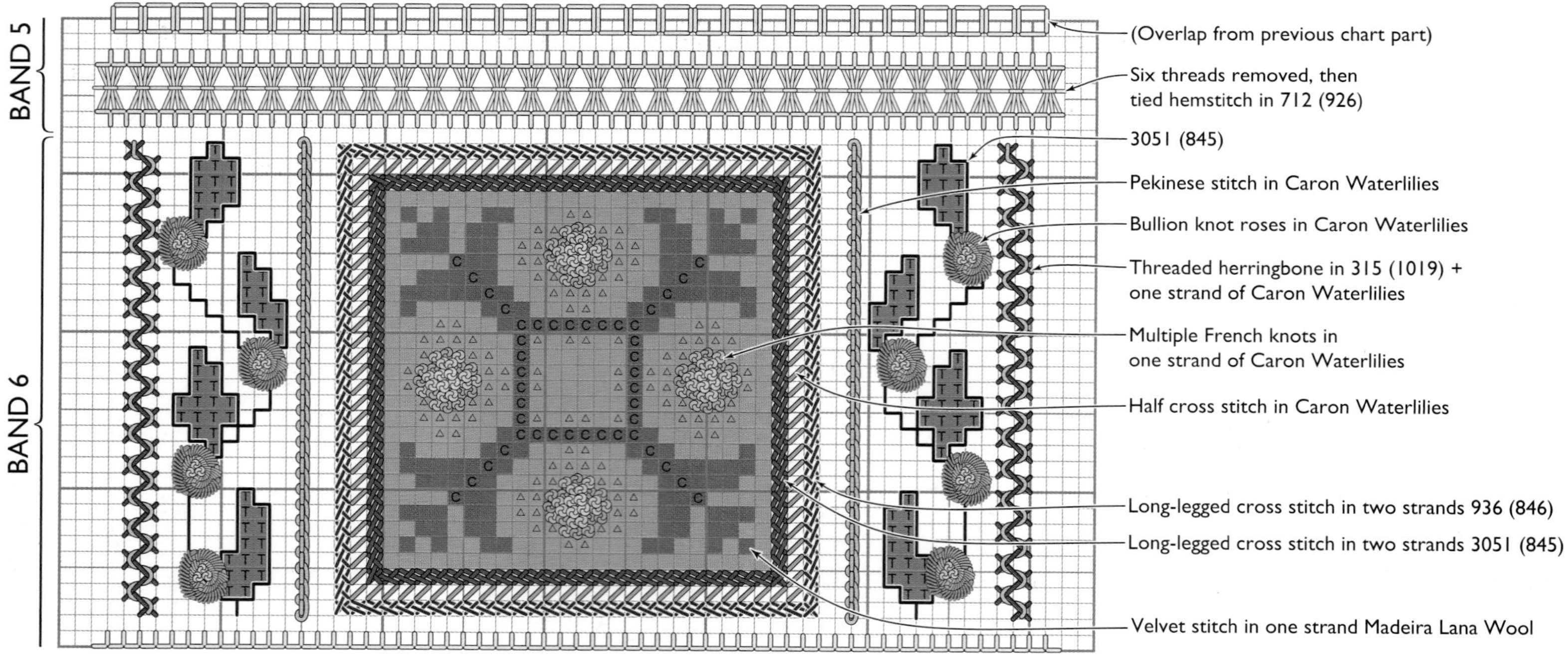

(Overlap from previous chart part)

Six threads removed, then tied hemstitch in 712 (926)

3051 (845)

Pekinese stitch in Caron Waterlilies

Bullion knot roses in Caron Waterlilies

Threaded herringbone in 315 (1019) + one strand of Caron Waterlilies

Multiple French knots in one strand of Caron Waterlilies

Half cross stitch in Caron Waterlilies

Long-legged cross stitch in two strands 936 (846)

Long-legged cross stitch in two strands 3051 (845)

Velvet stitch in one strand Madeira Lana Wool

BAND 5

BAND 6

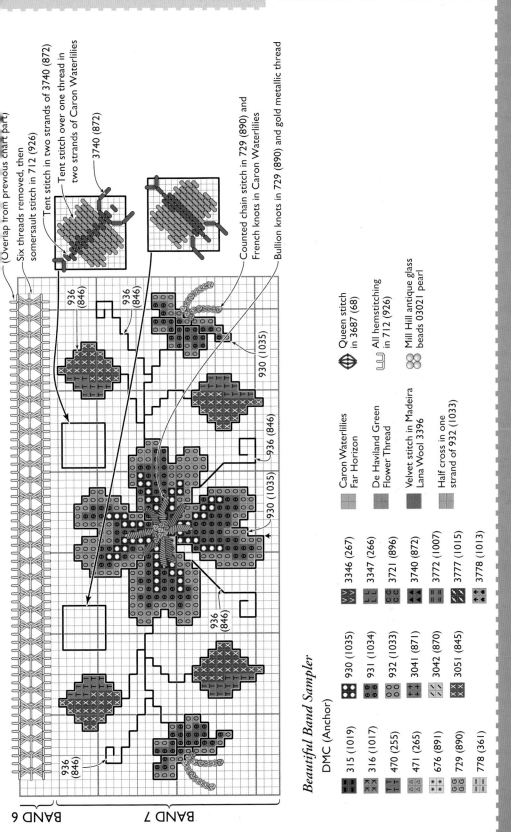

(Overlap from previous chart part)

Six threads removed, then somersault stitch in 712 (926)

Tent stitch over one thread in two strands of Caron Waterlilies

3740 (872)

Tent stitch in two strands of 3740 (872)

Counted chain stitch in 729 (890) and French knots in Caron Waterlilies

Bullion knots in 729 (890) and gold metallic thread

936 (846)

936 (846)

930 (1035)

936 (846)

930 (1035)

936 (846)

936 (846)

BAND 6

BAND 7

Beautiful Band Sampler
DMC (Anchor)

- 315 (1019)
- 316 (1017)
- 470 (255)
- 471 (265)
- 676 (891)
- 729 (890)
- 778 (361)
- 930 (1035)
- 931 (1034)
- 932 (1033)
- 3041 (871)
- 3042 (870)
- 3051 (845)
- 3346 (267)
- 3347 (266)
- 3721 (896)
- 3740 (872)
- 3772 (1007)
- 3777 (1015)
- 3778 (1013)

Caron Waterlilies Far Horizon

De Haviland Green Flower Thread

Velvet stitch in Madeira Lana Wool 3396

Half cross in one strand of 932 (1033)

Queen stitch in 3687 (68)

All hemstitching in 712 (926)

Mill Hill antique glass beads 03021 pearl

145

STITCH LIBRARY

This is a very personal library of stitches collected over more than 20 years of my own enjoyment of counted thread embroidery. The term 'counted thread' can strike terror in the heart of the cross stitcher but it is only the generic name for the type of embroidery that we do. It just means working from a chart rather than the design being printed on the fabric.

I continue to be an avid cross stitcher but having discovered all these lovely stitches I can't resist using them! Many of the stitches in this collection can be worked on Aida fabric but some need the additional threads available on evenweave. This will become easier to grasp as you look at the diagrams. The clear stitch diagrams will lead you through the construction of the stitches in easy stages. Some of the diagrams are numbered to indicate that there are several steps to working the stitch. Remember that the construction of a stitch remains the same but may be worked over a variety of fabric threads so it is important to check the chart each time.

The stitches are alphabetical and are also indexed. If the stitch you require is not included in this section you will find it within the relevant chapter of the book; for example, Kloster blocks are in the Hardanger section.

ALGERIAN EYE

This pretty, star-shaped stitch is a pulled stitch, which means that when formed correctly holes are pulled in the fabric. It usually occupies the space taken by four cross stitches and is an ideal stitch to combine with cross stitch as it can add a delicate lacy appearance without the anxiety of cutting threads. Algerian eye can be worked over two or four threads of evenweave as shown and is more successful worked on evenweave than Aida. (See also eyelet variations on page 153.)

> ### JANE'S TIP
> When trying new stitches, I use a piece of 20-count Cork linen so I can master the stitch on a large-count material before working it on my project. There is no point learning a new stitch and fighting your eyesight at the same time.

1 Start to the left of a vertical thread and work from left to right around each stitch in an clockwise direction (or vice versa but keeping each stitch the same).

2 Always work the stitch by passing the needle down through the central hole, pulling quite firmly so that a small hole is formed in the centre. Take care that trailing threads do not cover this hole as you progress to the next stitch.

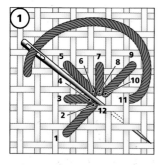

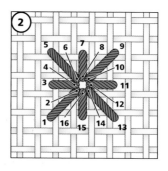

BACKSTITCH – SEE PAGE 25

BRAID STITCH

This very decorative stitch seen on early band samplers was often stitched using metallic threads. The stitch may be formed filling an area surrounded by cross stitch or be worked after marking the fabric with a backstitch line, which gives a framework to create the stitch.

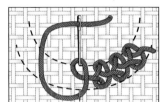

1 Work the backstitch line on the chart using one strand of stranded cotton (floss). On the back of the embroidery, at the right-hand end of the band, form a loop start through the back of the backstitch just completed and bring the needle to the front of the work at the bottom of the backstitched line. Pass the thread across to the left and hold in place with your thumb.

2 Pass the needle under the held thread towards you and twist to the left so that it is pointing in the opposite direction. The needle should now have the thread twisted around it.

3 Now pass the needle through the top backstitch and out again through the bottom row. Wrap the thread around the point of the needle and pull through. Work across the backstitch band keeping the stitches as even as you can.

BRAIDED CROSS STITCH

This is a very decorative stitch that can be worked over a number of fabric threads and is effective when worked in one or two colours. The secret is to work the stitch in one direction at a time and then weave the second set of stitches through the first.

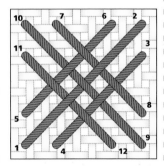

   Following the number sequence in the diagram, work one long stitch from bottom left to top right. Work two further stitches facing the same direction. Now complete the stitch by working from right to left, weaving in and out of the first set of long stitches.

BULLION STITCH

This unusual stitch, also called a knot or bar, is not a counted stitch but is useful as it adds a three-dimensional texture to a design. It can be formed in straight lines, be adapted to make a raised bar, and can also be made to curve for petal shapes and for building up roses (see overleaf). Bullion bars are easier to form using a gold-plated needle. Don't panic when you reach the end – careful teasing with a needle will rescue any apparent disaster.

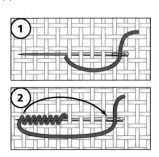

1 Begin the stitch by working an incomplete backstitch, leaving the needle in the fabric. It is vital that the point of the needle exits from the hole where it started.

2 With the needle still in the fabric, wind the thread around the needle as many times as necessary to make the coil the length of the incomplete backstitch. Hold the needle and coil of thread firmly against the fabric, then gently pull the needle through the coil and fabric. To finish the stitch turn the coil back on itself and push the needle through the fabric at the rear of the backstitch.

Bullion Rose

Working bullion stitch this way can create roses or cabbages or cauliflowers, depending on the colours you choose!

1 First work a few French knots.

2 Now work a bullion bar, adding extra winds to the needle to force the bar to bend. Begin to build up the rose, adding more tightly curved bullions around the first two.

3 A completed bullion rose can have as many curved bullions as you like. The final diagram here shows six, with the colour changed to a deeper shade on the final two.

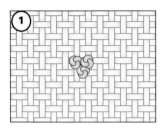

Buttonhole Stitch

This very old stitch is very simple to work and extremely versatile. See also buttonhole edging on page 104.

Start with an away waste knot and follow the number sequence in the diagram. Buttonhole stitches are usually worked closely together but may be spaced more widely according to the pattern you are working.

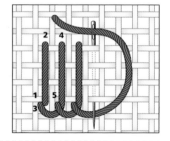

Coil Stitch

This pulled stitch is simple but very pretty and is most effective when worked in the same colour as the fabric and pulled fairly firmly.

Beginning at 1, work three satin stitches over the required number of horizontal fabric threads (in this case four). Leave a gap of the same number of vertical fabric threads. Repeat to the end. Take a small stitch into the back of the last cluster of each row to secure it. Work the next row staggered midway between the stitches of the pervious row, as shown.

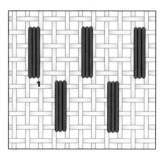

Couching

This is not a counted stitch as such but can be very effective, particularly on a band sampler. Couching is often worked with a metallic thread laid on the fabric, held down by small vertical stitches. Start by bringing the laid thread up through the fabric and laying it across the fabric. Using the couching thread, work small vertical stitches, as shown. When working on linen, I try to come up and go down the same holes in the fabric to avoid long stitches spoiling the effect.

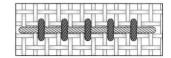

COUNTED CHAIN STITCH

This stitch is very versatile as it may be used on Aida or evenweave fabric, as part of a pattern or to join sections of stitching together. It can be used as an outline stitch or worked in close rows when filling in a pattern. If using counted chain stitch to join sections of stitching you normally use the same colour thread for the join but you could use a contrasting colour.

1 To work chain stitch on evenweave, start to the left of a vertical thread, bringing the needle up through the fabric and down through the same hole, forming a loop on the surface. Pass the point of the needle under two threads and up to the surface forming another loop. Each new stitch thus anchors the previous stitch.

2 If chain stitch is worked as a border, then the last stitch will anchor the first. If not, the last stitch may be anchored with a small stitch over one thread, as shown in the second diagram.

CROSS STITCH – SEE PAGE 23

THREE-QUARTER CROSS STITCH – SEE PAGE 24

CROSS STITCH VARIATIONS

Basic cross stitch can be altered in various ways to produce interesting new stitches. Try some of the variations shown here and overleaf. The diagrams are shown in two colours as the stitches look most effective this way.

DOUBLE CROSS STITCH

Double cross stitch, also known as Smyrna or Leviathan stitch, may be worked over two or four threads of an evenweave fabric or over two blocks of Aida, to create a series of bold crosses or 'stars'. Tiny double cross stitches may be formed over two threads of evenweave but they are difficult to work on one block of Aida.

ADAPTED DOUBLE CROSS STITCH

This stitch can be worked vertically or diagonally but is more difficult on Aida as the second stage of the stitch needs to be carefully placed. To keep all double cross stitches uniform make sure that the direction of the stitches within them is the same. Adapted double cross stitch looks particularly effective when the second stage of the stitch is added in metallic thread.

Work the stitch in the same way as double cross stitch but with the first large cross over twice as many threads as the second smaller cross.

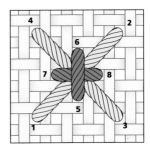

VERTICAL DOUBLE CROSS STITCH

This stitch is worked in a similar way to double cross stitch and can also be worked in two colours, or with the second stage worked in metallic thread.

BOXED VERTICAL CROSS STITCH

For this cross stitch variation, work a vertical cross stitch and then add four smaller stitches at the top, bottom and both sides to create a box-like appearance.

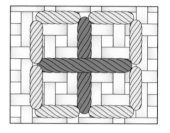

TACKED CROSS STITCH

Work a cross stitch over four evenweave threads or two blocks of Aida, and then add a single stitch across the centre of the cross over two threads or one block.

CUSHION STITCH

This is really an adaptation of satin stitch and is very straightforward. It is most effective when worked in small even squares and reversing the stitch direction as shown here. You may find this stitch easier to form using an embroidery frame.

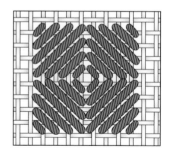

CROSSED CUSHION STITCH

Crossed cushion stitch is formed by working the satin stitch square and then crossing the stitch in the other direction in a different colour thread covering half the base stitch completely. Again these can be most effective when the direction of the stitch is reversed.

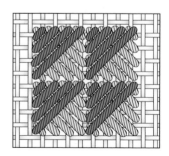

DETACHED BUTTONHOLE STITCH

This stitch can be used to fill shapes. The stitches should lie closely together but are shown widely spaced in the second diagram below to explain the stitch more clearly. The rows are worked to and fro, with the first and last stitches of each row worked into the fabric, to anchor all the buttonhole stitches.

1 Begin by outlining the motif in backstitch, then work two long stitches across the width of the shape. Work the first row of buttonhole stitch (see page 148) over this satin stitch line.

2 When you come to the end of the row, reverse direction and work the next row into the previous row, with the stitches close together. Continue working to and fro, reducing the length of the rows to follow the shape being filled.

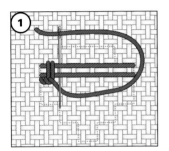
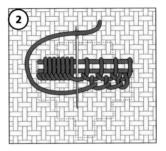

DIAMOND HEMSTITCH

This is an attractive hemstitch variation (see simple hemstitch page 112), which can be formed over two, four or other combinations of threads. Withdraw threads either side of a solid fabric area (see withdrawing and re-weaving page 111) and then work the hemstitch in two journeys. The stitches will form diamond shapes on the front of the work and if pulled firmly will create small holes in the solid fabric area. This stitch is formed on the front of the fabric, so if you find yourself with the needle on the back you know something is wrong!

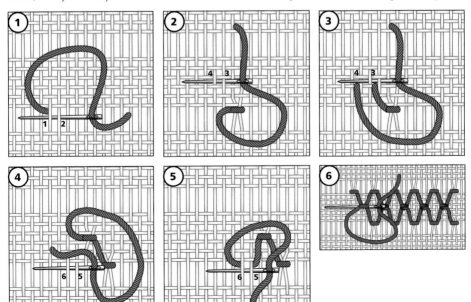

DOUBLE FAGGOT STITCH

This stitch is used almost exclusively as a pulled stitch and it is intended to create a decorative, lacy effect on the fabric. As with all pulled stitches, it is better formed on linen. The stitch creates textured areas in a design and can be worked as a border or in a regular pattern for filling in larger areas. The effect created looks particularly good if worked in thread the same colour as the fabric.

1 Bring the thread through the fabric at position 1, then insert the needle at 2 (four threads to the right) and bring through at 1 again.

2 Re-insert the needle at 2, then bring it through at 3 (four threads down and four to the left). Pull stitches firmly to achieve the open effect.

3 Insert the needle at 1 (four threads up) and bring it through at 3 again.

4 Re-insert the needle at 1, then bring it through at 4 (four threads down and four to the left).

5 Continue in this way, following the number sequence to the end of the row. Complete the last stitch 7–8 by re-inserting the needle at 6 and bringing it out at 8 (four threads down and four to the right).

6 Turn the work around to work the last row. Bring the thread through at 8, insert the needle at 7 and bring through at 8 again. Turn the work and repeat the procedure to create four sides to each stitch.

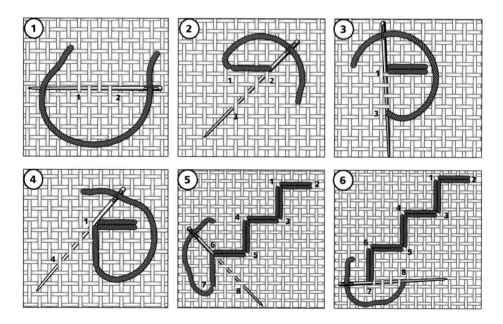

DOUBLE RUNNING STITCH (HOLBEIN STITCH) – SEE PAGE 80

DOVE'S EYE STITCH – SEE PAGE 102

CORNER DOVE'S EYE – SEE PAGE 103

EYELET VARIATIONS

There are a number of eyelet stitch variations, some of which are shown in the diagrams here. You can choose the shape you like and work it over more or less threads to create larger or smaller eyelets.

The rules are the same for all eyelets. As with Algerian eye you need to work the stitch in the correct order and in one direction to ensure that the hole created is uniform and as round as possible. When following the number sequence on the diagrams always work the stitch by passing the needle down through the central hole each time, and take care that trailing threads do not cover this hole as you progress to the next stitch.

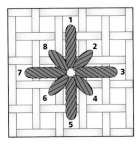  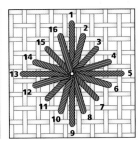

FLY STITCH

This is a versatile looped stitch that can be used singly or worked in rows as a border or filling.

1 Bring the needle out at position 1 and hold down the thread. Insert the needle a little to the right at 2 and then out at 3, halfway between 1 and 2 but lower.

2 Keeping the thread under the needle, pull the thread through. Insert the needle at 4 to make a small tying stitch in the centre – this stitch can be longer if desired.

3 If working a row of fly stitch, continue on to make the next stitch. The stitch can also be worked in vertical rows, as shown in the final diagram, and in this case the tying stitches should butt up together. The stitch width can also be altered.

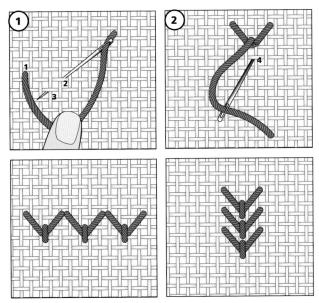

FOUR-SIDED STITCH

This is traditionally worked as a pulled stitch to create a lacy effect without the removal of fabric threads. It can also be used as a hemstitch when threads are to be cut or removed. The secret of creating a perfect four-sided stitch is to make sure that your needle travels in the correct direction on the back of the stitch. The stitches on the front should be vertical or horizontal but diagonal on the back. It is this tension that forms the small holes as the stitch is worked. The stitch is not recommended for Aida fabric.

1 Begin to the left of a vertical thread and work a horizontal straight stitch across four threads (or the number indicated on the chart), passing the needle diagonally across four threads at the back of the work.

2 Bring the needle up and form a vertical straight stitch, again passing the needle diagonally across four threads at the back of the work.

3 Bring the needle up and form another vertical straight stitch, again passing the needle diagonally across four threads at the back.

4 Work a horizontal straight stitch to form the last side of the square but this time pass the needle across diagonally to begin the next stitch.

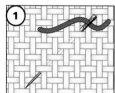 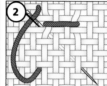 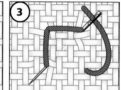 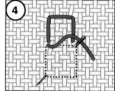

FRENCH KNOT – SEE PAGE 26

GATHERED RIBBON ROSE – SEE PAGE 88

GOBELIN STITCH

Gobelin stitch is a straight stitch often used as a filling stitch as it can mimic the appearance of a woven tapestry. The stitch can be worked to form regular shapes or in encroaching rows to create softer shapes. It can also be worked as long stitches in zigzag rows to form a Florentine pattern or flame stitch. When worked this way it is often known as bargello and is used as a hard-wearing stitch for upholstery. Gobelin stitch can be worked in stranded cotton or in crewel or tapestry wool and should not be pulled too tight.

1 Work a long, straight stitch over the number of threads indicated on the chart and follow the number sequence in the diagrams. The stitch shouldn't pull or distort the fabric.

2 Leaving a space for the second row, work along the row, positioning the needle to return to fill the gaps.

3 Continuing to follow the number sequence, work the second row of stitches, which should encroach on the first row.

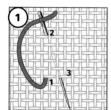 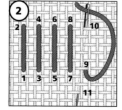 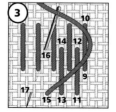

GREEK CROSS STITCH

This pulled stitch looks very ordinary on its own but creates wonderful patterns when worked on groups. The pattern created will vary depending on the relative position of each stitch. The stitch needs to be pulled fairly firmly to create the correct effect.

1 Bring the needle and thread through at position 1, go down at 2 (four threads up and four to the right) then up at 3 (four threads down), keeping the thread under the needle.

2 Pull the thread through then put the needle down at 4 (four threads to the right) and up at 3 as shown (four threads to left), keeping the thread under the needle.

3 Pull the thread through then put the needle down at 5 (four threads down) and up at 3 as shown (four threads up), keeping the thread under the needle.

4 Pull the thread through and secure the cross by inserting the needle at 3 to overlap the first and last stitches.

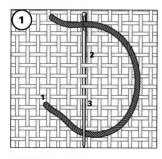
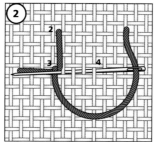
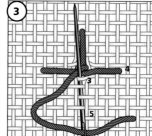
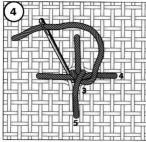
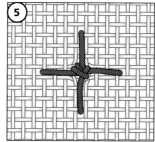

HEMSTITCH – SEE PAGE 112

HEMSTITCH EDGING – SEE PAGE 119

HEMSTITCH RECTANGLE – SEE PAGE 114

HERRINGBONE STITCH

This stitch is also known as plaited stitch, catch stitch, fishnet stitch and witch stitch. It is a simple and decorative stitch often used on band samplers and makes a fine companion to cross stitch. It looks particularly pretty when combined with stitches like long-legged cross stitch. It can also be whipped with a second colour (see also threaded herringbone below). It is shown here worked over four evenweave threads diagonally and under two horizontally. It can be worked over two threads and under one to make it smaller, or over and under more threads to make it larger.

Work the stitch by starting to the left of a vertical thread, across the number of threads indicated on the chart, following the number sequence in the diagram.

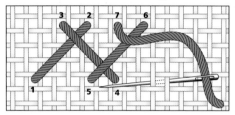

THREADED HERRINGBONE STITCH

This version of herringbone is usually worked in two different colours. Work herringbone as normal and then weave the second colour through the foundation stitches, without piercing the fabric. The length of these woven stitches can vary to create different effects.

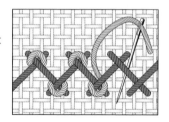

HONEYCOMB STITCH

As its name suggests, this stitch creates a honeycomb effect, which is more pronounced when the thread colour contrasts with the fabric colour.

1 Bring the needle out at 1, insert it at 2, two threads to the right, and bring it out at 3, two threads down. Insert the needle at 2 and bring it out at 3 again.

2 Continue as shown, going down at 4, out at 5, in at 4 again and back out at 5, in at 6 and so on.

3 To work the second row position the stitches as shown, working the connecting stitches into the same holes. Repeat these two rows to fill an area.

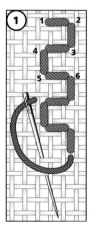
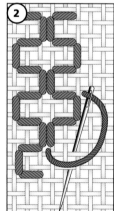

LONG-LEGGED CROSS STITCH

This stitch, also known as long-armed Slav stitch and Portuguese stitch, seems very uninteresting when first seen but looks wonderful when worked in rows because it forms a plaited effect, which is ideal for borders or for the outside edges of pieces to be made up as a pincushion or scissor keeper. It can also be worked on Aida across two blocks and upwards over one. The stitch may also be used to join sections – see below.

1 To work the stitch on evenweave, begin to the left of a vertical thread. Following the number sequence, insert the needle four threads forward and two up in a long diagonal 'leg'.

2 Insert the needle two threads upwards and two backwards diagonally to make the short leg.

3 If working a row, continue making stitches across the fabric, following the number sequence.

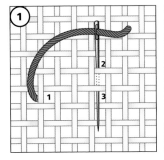
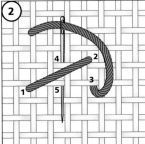
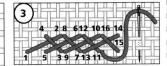

LONG-LEGGED CROSS STITCH AS A JOINING STITCH

This stitch is easy to do when working on canvas but can also be stitched on Aida or linen effectively. To join two pieces of work, the sections to be joined need to be folded along a row of threads and then stitched, picking up threads from either side of the gap.

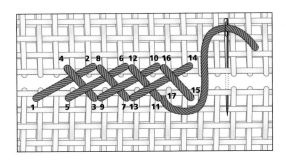

Montenegrin Stitch

This unusual stitch looks similar to long-legged cross stitch but is constructed in a different way and includes an extra vertical leg, which gives it a richer, fuller appearance. It forms an embossed braid on the front of the stitching and makes a fine, raised edge for folding. It is shown worked on evenweave but can also be worked on Aida fabric by moving two blocks forwards and one block up.

1 Start to the left of an evenweave thread, and following the number sequence in the diagram, work a long diagonal leg by moving four threads forwards and two threads up. Bring the needle two threads back and two threads down to emerge at position 3.

2 Insert the needle two threads backwards diagonally to make the short leg at 4. Bring the needle back up at 5 and down at 6 to form the final vertical leg.

3 Repeat Montenegrin stitch to form the pattern shown in the final diagram.

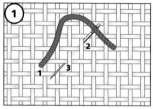 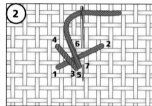 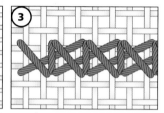

Needleweaving – see page 101

Corner Needleweaving – see page 101

Pekinese Stitch

This looped stitch is worked over a line of backstitch and may use two different types of thread and two colours. To explain the stitch more clearly, the loops are shown loosely worked in the diagram below but can be pulled tighter to achieve different effects.

Work a line of backstitch the width of the area to be stitched. Take the interlaced thread from left to right, passing it beneath the second backstitch, and then looping to pass beneath the third and so on. The fabric is not pierced by the interlaced thread.

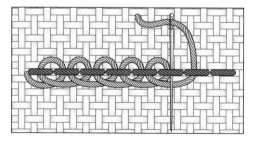

Picots – see page 104

QUEEN STITCH

This is an ancient pulled stitch made of four parts, which forms little dimples in the embroidery by pulling small holes in the fabric. It is also known as Rococo stitch. Although this stitch looks fairly unexciting on its own it is gorgeous when worked as a group. As it is a fairly labour-intensive stitch it is best used in small areas. Following the instructions and diagrams, work the stitch over a square of four threads in four stages. This stitch is traditionally worked from right to left, but if you find this difficult to count, try working the two middle parts first followed by the outer ones.

1 Work one long stitch over four threads of the fabric, which is then moved two threads to the right by the needle coming up at position 3 and a small stitch worked across one thread.

2 Repeat the long stitch from the same position as in Fig 1, but this time bending the stitch over one thread only.

3 Repeat the long stitch from the same position as in Fig 1, but bend the long stitch to the left, re-entering the fabric in the centre position.

4 The last stage of the stitch is completed to form a lantern shape. Note how the top and bottom hole is shared by each stage of the stitch so forming the distinctive little dimples.

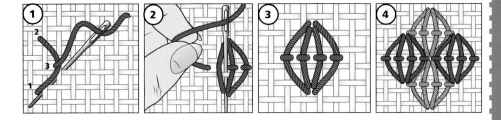

REVERSIBLE CROSS STITCH

This stitch is truly reversible, although it has the addition of a vertical line at the end of a row which cannot be avoided. The stitch is quite time consuming as each row is worked four times but it is very useful for bookmarks and table linen. The vertical line created at the end of rows can appear as the backstitch outline if you plan your route carefully.

1 The first journey is across two threads on the front, working diagonally across the back of the next two threads, missing the stitch on the front.

2 The return journey covers the first diagonal threads on the front and back of the work.

3 The third journey fills in the missed stitches back and front.

4 The final journey completes the row.

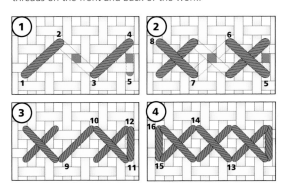

Rhodes Stitch

Rhodes stitch produces a solid, slightly raised, three-dimensional effect, almost like a series of studs on the fabric. The diagrams below illustrate one version but the size of the stitch can be altered – refer to the chart to see how many threads are in each stitch. This stitch doesn't work well on Aida fabric. (See also half Rhodes stitch with a bar, below.)

1 Begin to the left of a vertical evenweave thread, working each stitch over squares of two, four or more threads.

2 Following the number sequence, build up the stitch, working in an anticlockwise direction around the square.

3 A complete Rhodes stitch will have a raised central area. Maintain the same sequence for every stitch to produce a uniform effect.

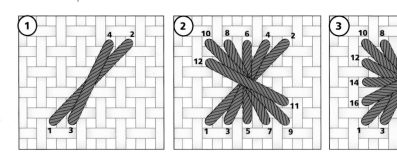

Half Rhodes Stitch with Bar

This is an adaptation of Rhodes stitch, producing a decorative stitch shaped rather like a sheaf of corn, with a straight bar across the centre to tie the threads together. Buttonhole stitches could be added to the bar.

1 Work over squares of two, four, six or eight threads of evenweave fabric, in a slanting, anticlockwise direction.

2 Complete the half Rhodes stitch and maintain the same sequence for every stitch to create a uniform effect.

3 To finish, add a single straight stitch across the centre, holding the threads firmly.

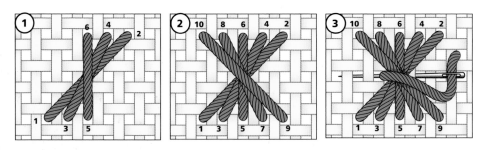

Ribbon Stitch – see page 89

RICE STITCH

Rice stitch is a cross stitch with an additional stitch worked over each 'leg' or corner of the cross. It can be worked in two stages: a row of normal cross stitches, followed by the additional stitches as a second row. This makes it ideal for working in two colours, which can create very pretty effects. When using two colours, work all large crosses first, followed by the additional stitches in the second colour. Rice stitch is worked over an even number of threads, usually over four threads of an evenweave fabric but it can also be worked to occupy the space of four blocks of Aida. Do not pull the stitch and form holes around the edge.

1 Start to the left of a vertical thread, working a half cross stitch across four evenweave threads, then returning to complete the cross.

2 Add the additional stitches across the legs in a second colour. These are traditionally worked as a backstitch into the central side hole in each case.

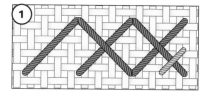 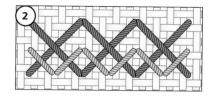

SATIN STITCH

This is a long, smooth stitch, also known as damask stitch, which covers the fabric and is often used to fill in shapes. When worked in a glossy thread like stranded cotton (floss), the stitches have a velvety sheen and can look very effective when worked in blocks facing in different directions. Avoid using very long lengths of thread as this will suffer by being pulled through the fabric too many times. You could experiment with the number of strands of thread used, to vary the effect – many strands can give an almost padded look.

Follow the number sequence in the diagram, laying flat stitches neatly side by side. Don't pull too tightly, unless working pulled satin stitch –see below.

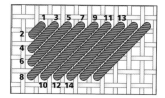 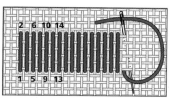

PULLED SATIN STITCH

Working pulled satin stitch is a very different matter to working normal satin stitch as the intention is to make some seriously large holes in the fabric and create a lacy appearance. Pulled thread embroidery is better formed on linen fabric as the stitches once pulled will stay pulled! The stitch may be worked horizontally, vertically or diagonally, in boxes, groups or offset, and over various numbers of fabric threads (keeping the pattern consistent).

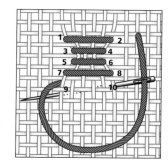

SOMERSAULT STITCH

This stitch is formed on the vertical threads that remain after hemstitching and thread withdrawal.

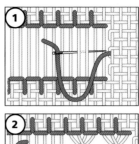

1 Begin the stitch after thread withdrawal and two rows of hemstitch have been completed. Using the hemstitch thread, bring the needle up at the side centre of the hemstitched frame (you will need to snick through the back of the fabric to do this). Count four fabric threads and insert the needle under two threads and up between the two pairs, so the needle is positioned over the second pair of threads. Don't pull the needle through the work yet.

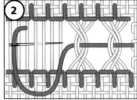

2 Without removing the needle from these threads, twist the needle until it faces the other way. The threads will twist automatically as you do this. Pinch your fingers together over this stitch and gently pull the needle through, keeping the thread horizontal and taut. Repeat this process down the row, fastening off into the fabric edge.

BEADED SOMERSAULT STITCH

This is worked in the same way as somersault stitch above but slipping a bead on in between each stitch.

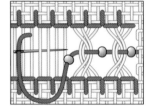

SPIDER'S WEB STITCH – SEE PAGE 103

STEM STITCH

Stem stitch is another surface embroidery stitch I have borrowed with success. The secret is to form the stitch in the same manner for the whole project, carefully counting the threads each time. Using spare fabric, experiment with turning gentle corners to perfect your technique. The stitch is most effective on evenweave fabric.

1 Follow the number sequence in the diagram, working a straight stitch across four threads on evenweave, passing the needle back two threads.

2 Make the next stitch by holding the thread over and below the previous stitch and working across four threads again.

3 Repeat the stitching sequence so each stitch is formed in the same manner, checking that each new stitch is on the same side, to create the rope-like effect required.

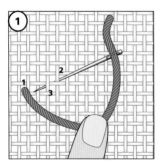
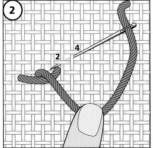
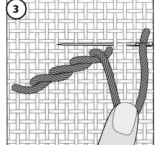

TENT STITCH

Tent stitch is best known as a canvaswork stitch and is sometimes called continental tent stitch. It has long slanting stitches on the back and even, full stitches on the front. It is the long slanting stitches on the back that cause the distortion of the canvas which is characteristic of this stitch. Tent stitch is sometimes mistaken for half cross stitch but it uses a third more wool than half cross stitch and creates a much thicker and harder-wearing stitch, which makes it ideal for furnishings. This stitch could be used for the little butterflies in the Butterflies and Buddleia picture on page 27.

Tent stitch is a diagonal stitch formed by the needle being taken under the stitches from right to left, supporting the stitches and forming a fuller stitch. Ensure that you don't use tent stitch in one direction and half cross stitch in the other.

Tent stitch used in a sparkly Christmas decoration (see pages 45 and 61).

DIAGONAL TENT STITCH

The alternative name for diagonal tent stitch is basketweave stitch because of the woven effect produced on the reverse.

The stitches are worked diagonally across the canvas threads, so they distort the canvas less than ordinary tent stitch. You could use straight lines of tent stitch for working a design and then complete the background in diagonal tent stitch.

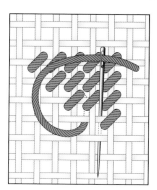

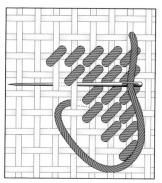

THREADED BACKSTITCH

This pretty embellishment to backstitch is very simple to work. It is sometimes called woven backstitch or embellished backstitch. Work backstitch, as shown on page 25 and then take the second thread colour and weave it in and out of each backstitch, creating smooth S-shaped loops. The pattern lines can be straight, as shown, or in any pattern you choose.

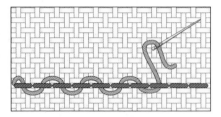

TIED HEMSTITCH

This pretty hemstitch variation is created by hemstitching two rows, withdrawing the intervening threads and then simply using the needle to tie groups of threads together.

Begin by stitching two rows of simple hemstitch, spaced four threads apart (or as indicated on the chart). Take the needle and thread over a group of eight threads (or as the chart), knotting them around. The secret of perfection is to ensure that the tying thread is as straight as possible.

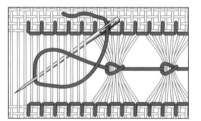

DOUBLE TIED HEMSTITCH

Remove at least six fabric threads prior to working ladder hemstitch as shown on page 112. To create the tied effect use one strand of stranded cotton and, coming from the side of the band, tie the first four fabric threads together (or the number indicated on the chart). Slide down these threads and tie these four with the next four. Slide up these four threads and tie these to the next four, and so on.

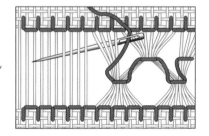

TIPSY STITCH

This is my variation on Rhodes stitch, which produces an interesting 'tipsy' slant to your stitching. The stitch can be worked over a variety of fabric threads. Follow the number sequence in the diagram.

Velvet Stitch

This stitch, also known as plush or Turkey stitch, was commonly used by Victorian embroiderers who worked in wools: after completing an area of velvet stitch, the loops were cut and sometimes actually sculpted to great effect.

This stitch is basically a cross stitch with an extra loop in it, left long to create a pile on the fabric. The loops can be left as they are or can all be cut to the same length. Work in rows from bottom to top and left to right.

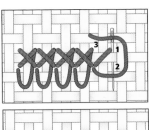

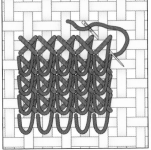

Woven or Needlelace Flowers

Needlelace flowers are not a modern idea – some samplers from the 17th century included pretty flower petals created this way. Practise on spare fabric before starting your sampler.

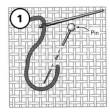

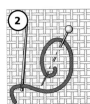

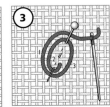

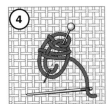

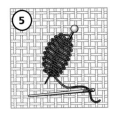

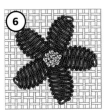

Wrapped Bars – see page 102

Zigzag Hemstitch

This is formed in almost the same way as ladder hemstitch (page 112). Cut the horizontal threads (see chart for how many) and then re-weave them as shown. Work one row of hemstitch, as for ladder hemstitch, and then work the second row but offset the stitches by one fabric thread to create a zigzag effect.

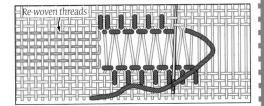

Re-woven threads

CHART LIBRARY

I have used a variety of projects in the book to illustrate a stitching technique or unusual type of thread and most of the charts can be found in this section of the book.

◆ The charts are in colour with a black or white symbol to aid colour identification. Refer to Following a Chart on page 10.

◆ The DMC range of stranded cotton (floss) was used to stitch the projects, with Anchor alternatives given in brackets (although accurate colour matches may not always be possible).

◆ Some of the designs are charted over two pages: there is no overlap, so just continue the stitching. For your own use you could colour photocopy the parts and tape them together.

◆ The chart keys give the page reference where you can find the stitching instructions captions and pictures of the projects.

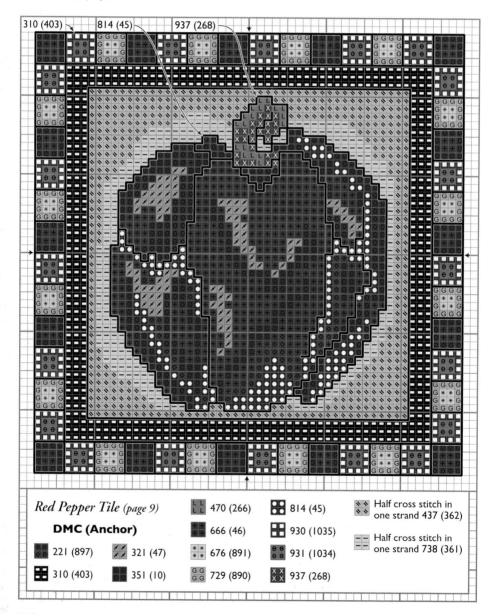

Red Pepper Tile (*page 9*)

DMC (Anchor)

	LL / LL 470 (266)		814 (45)		Half cross stitch in one strand 437 (362)
	666 (46)		930 (1035)		
221 (897)	// 321 (47)	** / ** 676 (891)	931 (1034)		Half cross stitch in one strand 738 (361)
310 (403)	351 (10)	GG / GG 729 (890)	XX / XX 937 (268)		

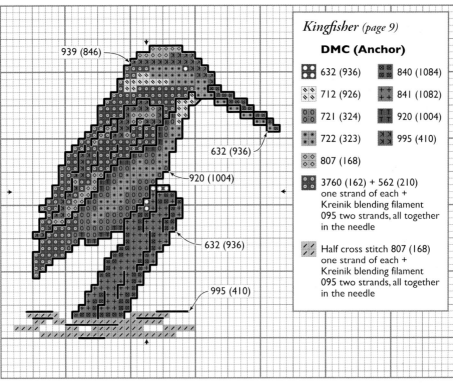

Kingfisher *(page 9)*

DMC (Anchor)

632 (936)   840 (1084)

712 (926)   841 (1082)

721 (324)   920 (1004)

722 (323)   995 (410)

807 (168)

3760 (162) + 562 (210)
one strand of each +
Kreinik blending filament
095 two strands, all together
in the needle

Half cross stitch 807 (168)
one strand of each +
Kreinik blending filament
095 two strands, all together
in the needle

939 (846)
632 (936)
920 (1004)
632 (936)
995 (410)

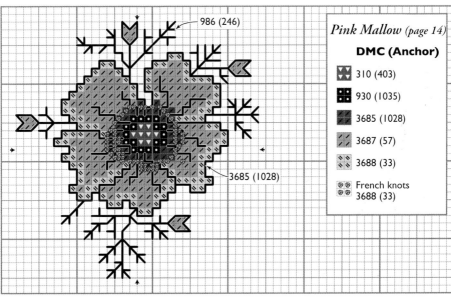

Pink Mallow *(page 14)*

DMC (Anchor)

310 (403)

930 (1035)

3685 (1028)

3687 (57)

3688 (33)

French knots
3688 (33)

986 (246)
3685 (1028)

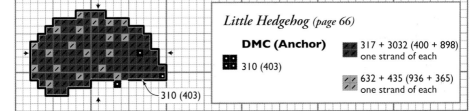

Little Hedgehog *(page 66)*

DMC (Anchor)

310 (403)

317 + 3032 (400 + 898)
one strand of each

632 + 435 (936 + 365)
one strand of each

310 (403)

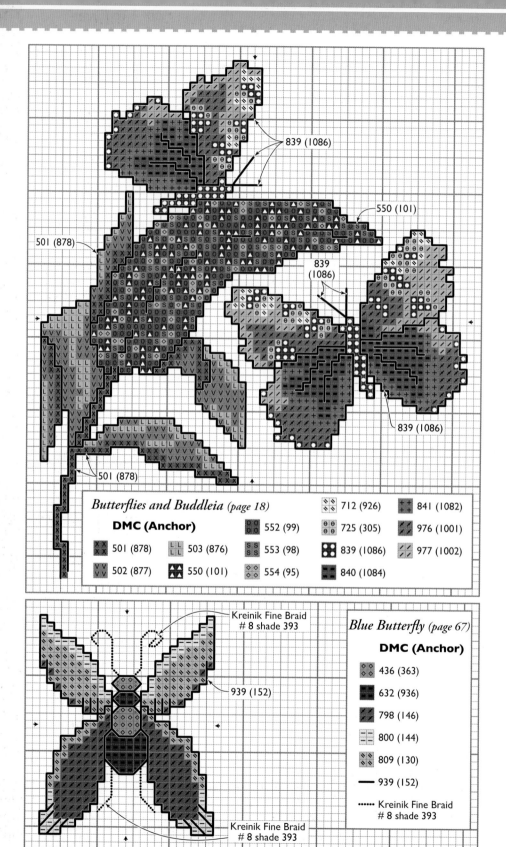

Butterflies and Buddleia *(page 18)*

DMC (Anchor)

XX 501 (878)	**LL** 503 (876)	**SS** 553 (98)	**++** 841 (1082)
VV 502 (877)	**▲▲** 550 (101)	**◇◇** 554 (95)	**//** 976 (1001)
	◦◦ 552 (99)	**θθ** 725 (305)	**//** 977 (1002)
		θθ 712 (926)	**⊞** 839 (1086)
			⊟ 840 (1084)

Labels in chart: 839 (1086), 550 (101), 501 (878), 839 (1086), 839 (1086), 501 (878)

Blue Butterfly *(page 67)*

DMC (Anchor)

◇◇	436 (363)
■	632 (936)
//	798 (146)
==	800 (144)
◊◊	809 (130)
—	939 (152)
•••••	Kreinik Fine Braid #8 shade 393

Labels in chart: Kreinik Fine Braid #8 shade 393, 939 (152), Kreinik Fine Braid #8 shade 393

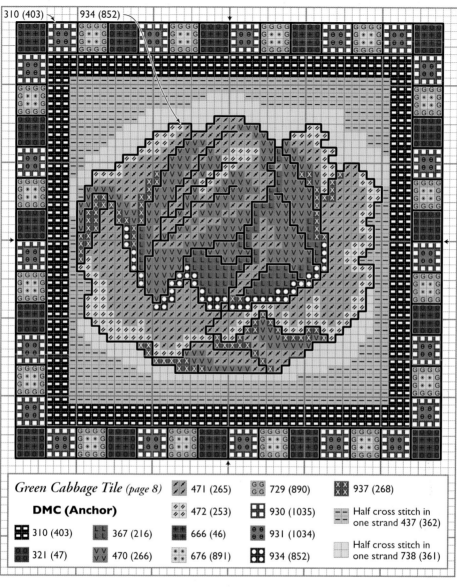

310 (403)   934 (852)

Green Cabbage Tile *(page 8)*

DMC (Anchor)

310 (403)	367 (216)	470 (266)
321 (47)		

- 471 (265)
- 472 (253)
- 729 (890)
- 930 (1035)
- 666 (46)
- 676 (891)
- 931 (1034)
- 934 (852)
- 937 (268)
- Half cross stitch in one strand 437 (362)
- Half cross stitch in one strand 738 (361)

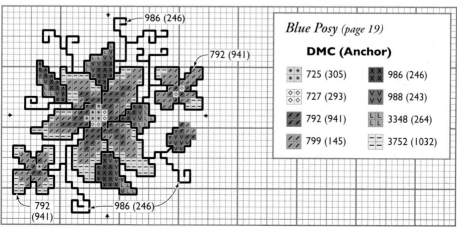

986 (246)

792 (941)

792 (941)

986 (246)

Blue Posy *(page 19)*

DMC (Anchor)

725 (305)	986 (246)
727 (293)	988 (243)
792 (941)	3348 (264)
799 (145)	3752 (1032)

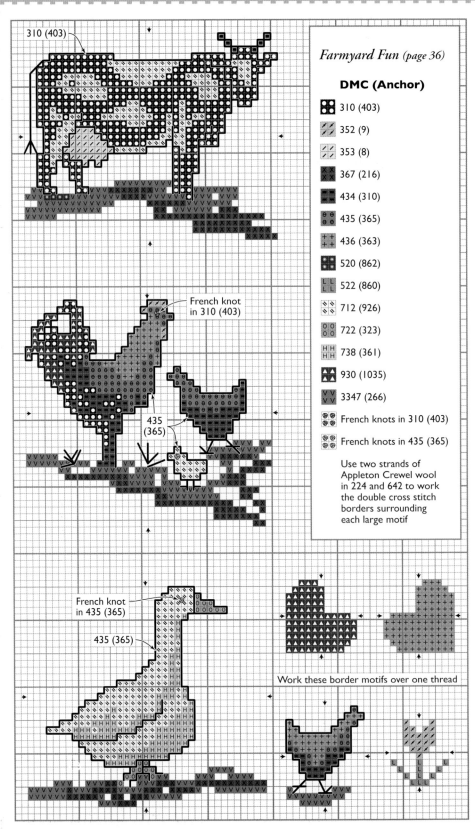

310 (403)

Farmyard Fun (page 36)

DMC (Anchor)

- 310 (403)
- 352 (9)
- 353 (8)
- 367 (216)
- 434 (310)
- 435 (365)
- 436 (363)
- 520 (862)
- 522 (860)
- 712 (926)
- 722 (323)
- 738 (361)
- 930 (1035)
- 3347 (266)
- French knots in 310 (403)
- French knots in 435 (365)

Use two strands of Appleton Crewel wool in 224 and 642 to work the double cross stitch borders surrounding each large motif

French knot in 310 (403)

435 (365)

Work these border motifs over one thread

French knot in 435 (365)

435 (365)

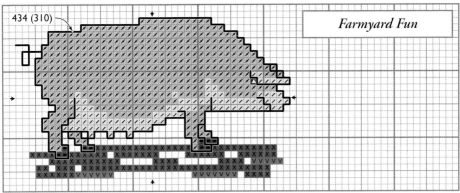

434 (310)

Farmyard Fun

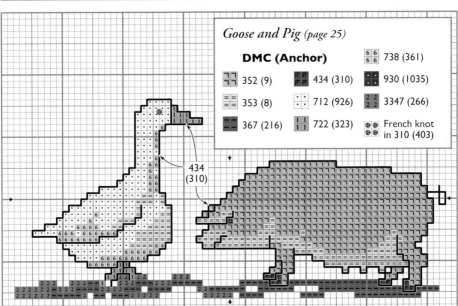

Goose and Pig (page 25)

DMC (Anchor)

352 (9)	434 (310)	738 (361)	
353 (8)	712 (926)	930 (1035)	
367 (216)	722 (323)	3347 (266)	
		French knot in 310 (403)	

434 (310)

434 (310)

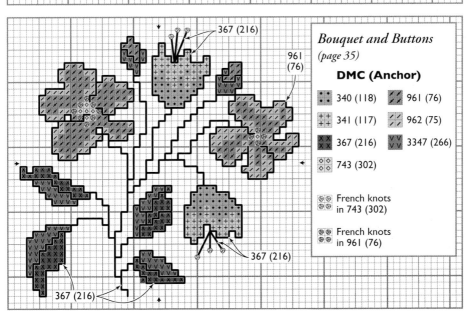

367 (216)

961 (76)

367 (216)

367 (216)

Bouquet and Buttons (page 35)

DMC (Anchor)

340 (118)	961 (76)
341 (117)	962 (75)
367 (216)	3347 (266)
743 (302)	

French knots in 743 (302)

French knots in 961 (76)

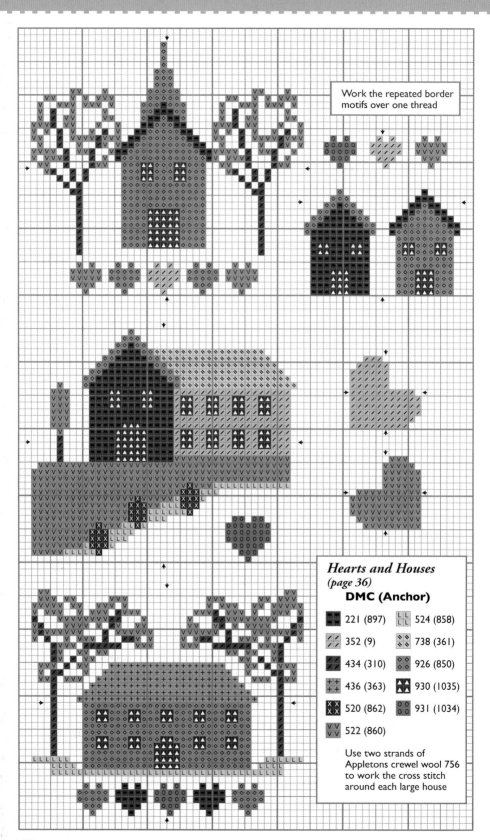

Work the repeated border motifs over one thread

Hearts and Houses
(page 36)

DMC (Anchor)

■	221 (897)	L L / L L	524 (858)
/ /	352 (9)	§ § / § §	738 (361)
▨	434 (310)	◇ ◇	926 (850)
+ + / + +	436 (363)	▲ ▲	930 (1035)
X X / X X	520 (862)	0 0 / 0 0	931 (1034)
V V / V V	522 (860)		

Use two strands of Appletons crewel wool 756 to work the cross stitch around each large house

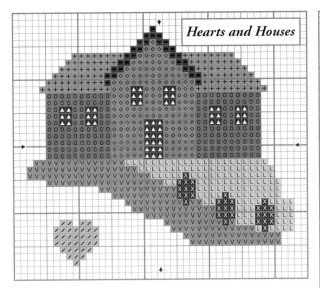

Hearts and Houses

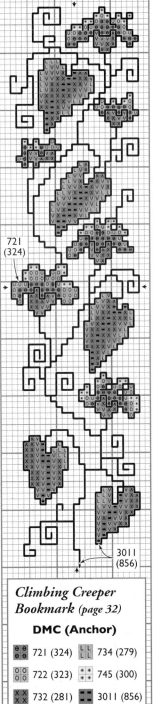

721 (324)

3011 (856)

Climbing Creeper Bookmark (page 32)

DMC (Anchor)

721 (324)		734 (279)
722 (323)		745 (300)
732 (281)		3011 (856)
733 (280)		

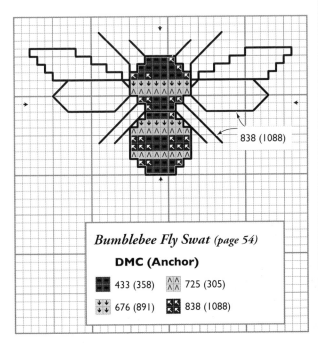

838 (1088)

Bumblebee Fly Swat (page 54)

DMC (Anchor)

433 (358)		725 (305)
676 (891)		838 (1088)

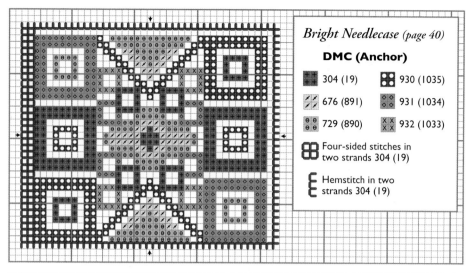

Bright Needlecase (page 40)

DMC (Anchor)

- 304 (19)
- 676 (891)
- 729 (890)
- 930 (1035)
- 931 (1034)
- 932 (1033)

Four-sided stitches in two strands 304 (19)

Hemstitch in two strands 304 (19)

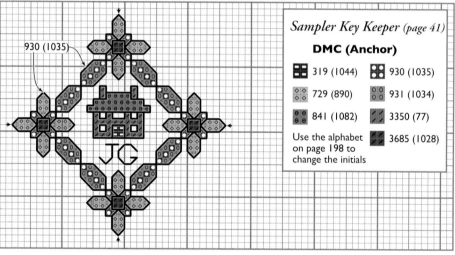

930 (1035)

Sampler Key Keeper (page 41)

DMC (Anchor)

- 319 (1044)
- 729 (890)
- 841 (1082)
- 930 (1035)
- 931 (1034)
- 3350 (77)
- 3685 (1028)

Use the alphabet on page 198 to change the initials

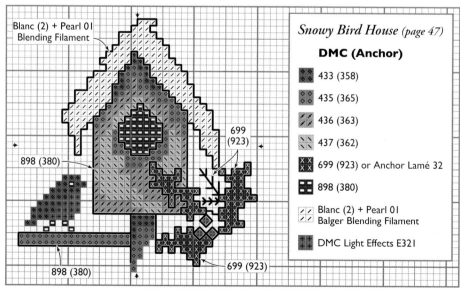

Blanc (2) + Pearl 01 Blending Filament

899 (923)

898 (380)

898 (380)

699 (923)

Snowy Bird House (page 47)

DMC (Anchor)

- 433 (358)
- 435 (365)
- 436 (363)
- 437 (362)
- 699 (923) or Anchor Lamé 32
- 898 (380)
- Blanc (2) + Pearl 01 Balger Blending Filament
- DMC Light Effects E321

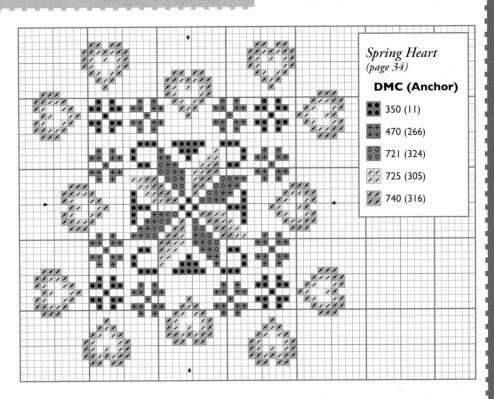

Spring Heart
(page 34)

DMC (Anchor)

- 350 (11)
- 470 (266)
- 721 (324)
- 725 (305)
- 740 (316)

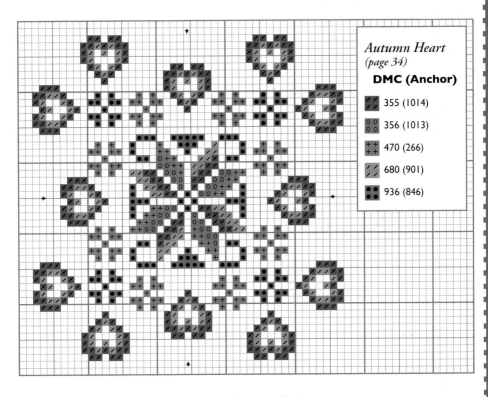

Autumn Heart
(page 34)

DMC (Anchor)

- 355 (1014)
- 356 (1013)
- 470 (266)
- 680 (901)
- 936 (846)

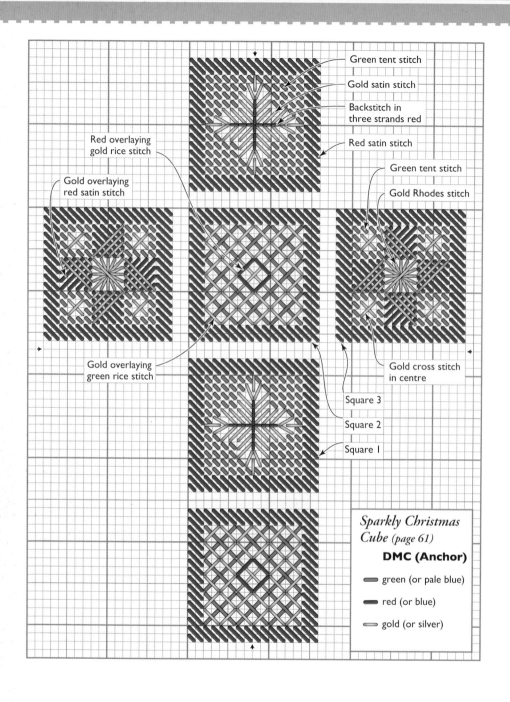

Green tent stitch

Gold satin stitch

Backstitch in three strands red

Red overlaying gold rice stitch

Gold overlaying red satin stitch

Red satin stitch

Green tent stitch

Gold Rhodes stitch

Gold overlaying green rice stitch

Gold cross stitch in centre

Square 3

Square 2

Square 1

Sparkly Christmas Cube (page 61)

DMC (Anchor)

- green (or pale blue)
- red (or blue)
- gold (or silver)

Peach Blossom Card (page 86)

DMC (Anchor)

937 (268)

French knots in 2mm YLI silk ribbon in pale peach and dark rose

Gathered ribbon stitch in 7mm YLI silk ribbon in pale peach

✕ Button position

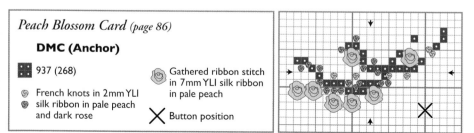

3012 (855)
3777 (1015)
3012 (855)
930 (1035)
3012 (855)
3012 (855)
3011 (856)
3777 (1015)
3012 (855)
3011 (856)

Willow Tree Sampler (page 55)

DMC (Anchor)

315 (1019)	356 (1013)	
316 (1017)	676 (891)	

841 (1082)
930 (1035)
931 (1034)
3011 (856)

3012 (855)
3013 (853)
3777 (1015)
3830 (5975)

French knots in 3011 (856)
French knots in 3012 (855)

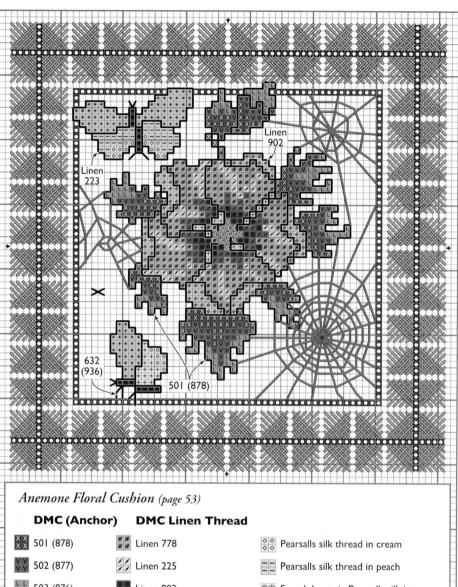

Anemone Floral Cushion (*page 53*)

DMC (Anchor)

- 501 (878)
- 502 (877)
- 503 (876)
- 632 (936)
- 772 (259)
- 930 (1035)
- 945 (881)

DMC Linen Thread

- Linen 778
- Linen 225
- Linen 902
- Linen 223
- ✕ Dragonfly charm
- Work cobwebs with one strand of Kreinik Blending Filament 034 confetti

- Pearsalls silk thread in cream
- Pearsalls silk thread in peach
- French knots in Pearsalls silk in cream
- Crossed cushion stitch in one strand of De Haviland Tudor Twist (antique peacock and purple)

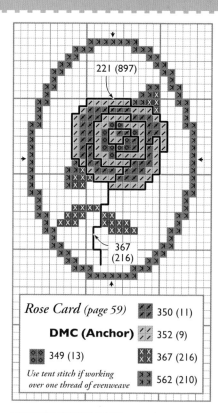

221 (897)

367 (216)

Rose Card *(page 59)*

DMC (Anchor)

349 (13)

Use tent stitch if working over one thread of evenweave

350 (11)

352 (9)

367 (216)

562 (210)

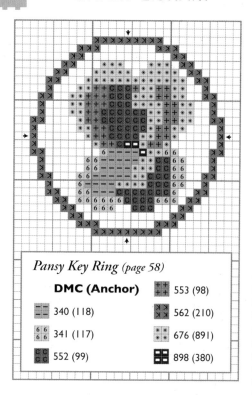

Pansy Key Ring *(page 58)*

DMC (Anchor)

== 340 (118)

6 6 / 6 6 341 (117)

C C / C C 552 (99)

++ / ++ 553 (98)

562 (210)

** / ** 676 (891)

898 (380)

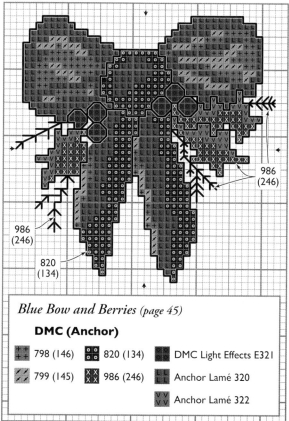

986 (246)

986 (246)

820 (134)

Blue Bow and Berries *(page 45)*

DMC (Anchor)

++ 798 (146)

// 799 (145)

820 (134)

XX 986 (246)

LL Anchor Lamé 320

VV Anchor Lamé 322

DMC Light Effects E321

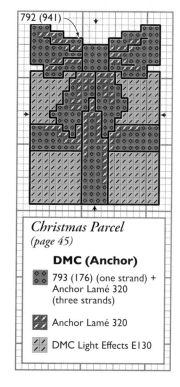

792 (941)

Christmas Parcel
(page 45)

DMC (Anchor)

793 (176) (one strand) + Anchor Lamé 320 (three strands)

Anchor Lamé 320

DMC Light Effects E130

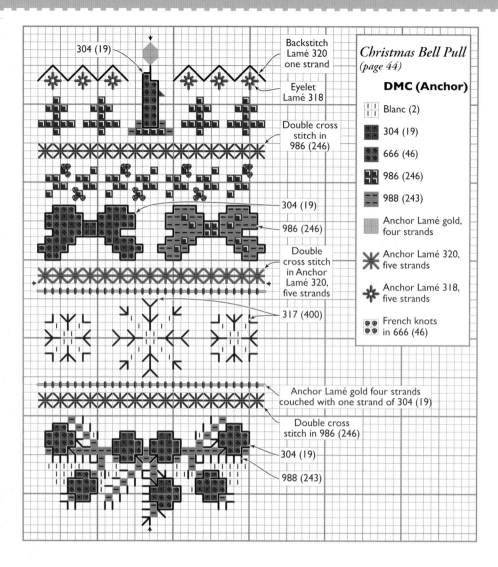

304 (19)

Backstitch
Lamé 320
one strand

Eyelet
Lamé 318

Double cross
stitch in
986 (246)

304 (19)

986 (246)

Double
cross stitch
in Anchor
Lamé 320,
five strands

317 (400)

Anchor Lamé gold four strands
couched with one strand of 304 (19)

Double cross
stitch in 986 (246)

304 (19)

988 (243)

Christmas Bell Pull
(page 44)

DMC (Anchor)

Blanc (2)

304 (19)

666 (46)

986 (246)

988 (243)

Anchor Lamé gold,
four strands

Anchor Lamé 320,
five strands

Anchor Lamé 318,
five strands

French knots
in 666 (46)

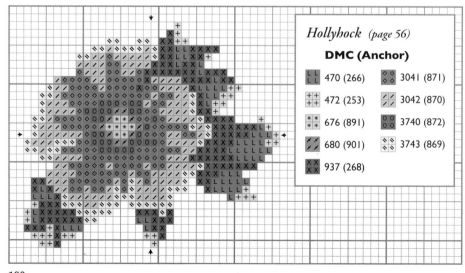

Hollyhock (page 56)

DMC (Anchor)

470 (266)	3041 (871)
472 (253)	3042 (870)
676 (891)	3740 (872)
680 (901)	3743 (869)
937 (268)	

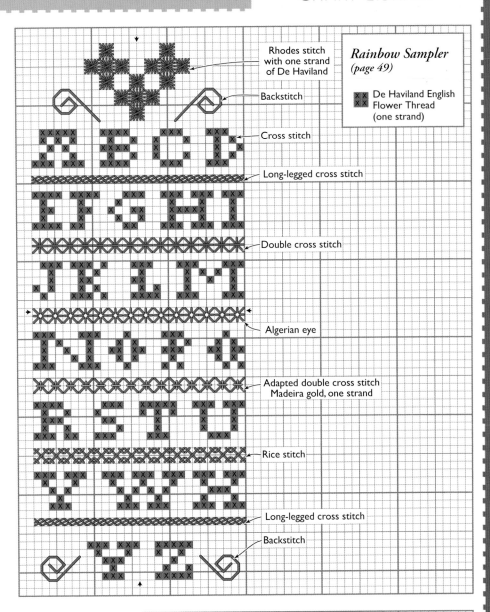

Rhodes stitch with one strand of De Haviland

Backstitch

Rainbow Sampler
(page 49)

De Haviland English Flower Thread (one strand)

Cross stitch

Long-legged cross stitch

Double cross stitch

Algerian eye

Adapted double cross stitch Madeira gold, one strand

Rice stitch

Long-legged cross stitch

Backstitch

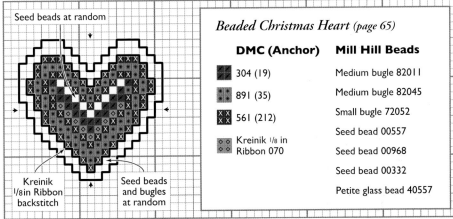

Seed beads at random

Kreinik 1/8in Ribbon backstitch

Seed beads and bugles at random

Beaded Christmas Heart *(page 65)*

DMC (Anchor)	Mill Hill Beads
304 (19)	Medium bugle 82011
891 (35)	Medium bugle 82045
561 (212)	Small bugle 72052
Kreinik 1/8 in Ribbon 070	Seed bead 00557
	Seed bead 00968
	Seed bead 00332
	Petite glass bead 40557

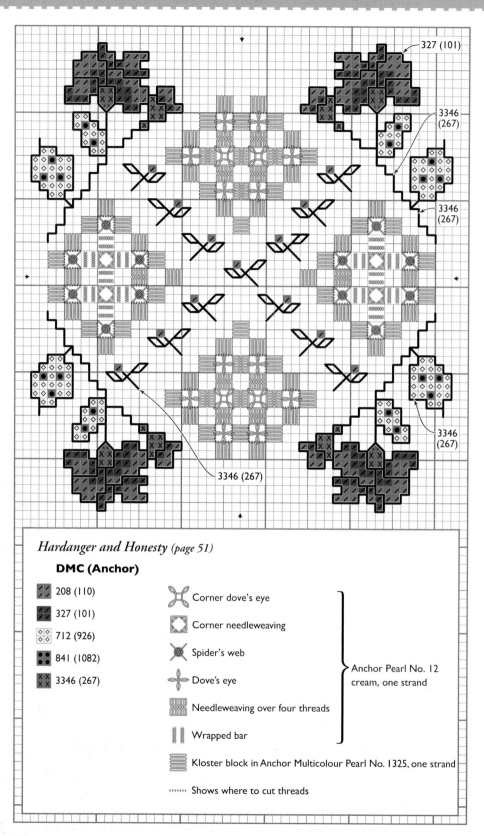

Hardanger and Honesty (page 51)

DMC (Anchor)

- 208 (110)
- 327 (101)
- 712 (926)
- 841 (1082)
- 3346 (267)

Corner dove's eye

Corner needleweaving

Spider's web

Dove's eye

Needleweaving over four threads

Wrapped bar

Anchor Pearl No. 12 cream, one strand

Kloster block in Anchor Multicolour Pearl No. 1325, one strand

······ Shows where to cut threads

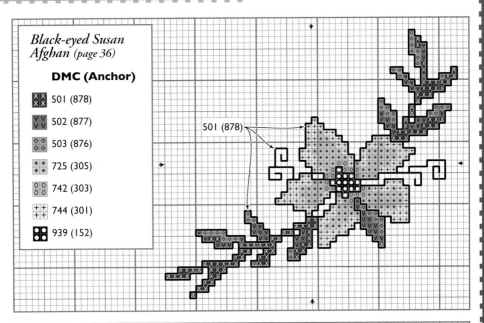

Black-eyed Susan Afghan *(page 36)*

DMC (Anchor)

- ⊠⊠ 501 (878)
- VV 502 (877)
- ◇◇ 503 (876)
- ** 725 (305)
- 00 742 (303)
- ++ 744 (301)
- ●● 939 (152)

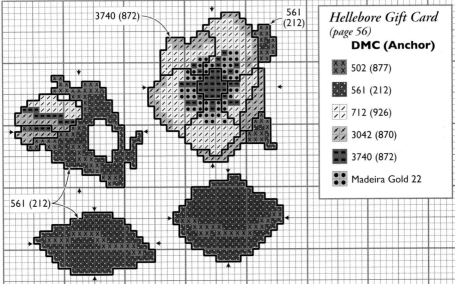

3740 (872)

561 (212)

561 (212)

Hellebore Gift Card *(page 56)*

DMC (Anchor)

- ⊠⊠ 502 (877)
- ∷ 561 (212)
- // 712 (926)
- // 3042 (870)
- ▬▬ 3740 (872)
- ●● Madeira Gold 22

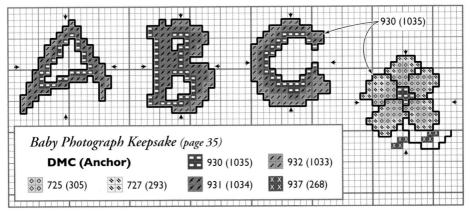

930 (1035)

Baby Photograph Keepsake *(page 35)*

DMC (Anchor)

◇◇ 725 (305)	▬▬ 930 (1035)	// 932 (1033)	
§§ 727 (293)	// 931 (1034)	⊠⊠ 937 (268)	

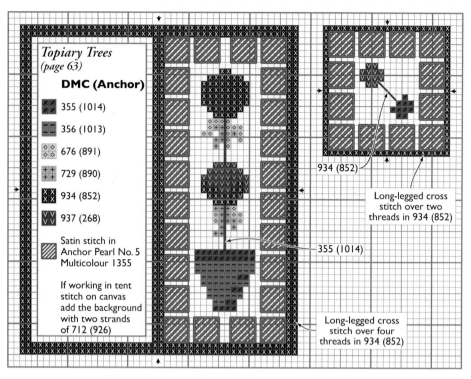

Topiary Trees
(page 63)

DMC (Anchor)

- 355 (1014)
- 356 (1013)
- 676 (891)
- 729 (890)
- 934 (852)
- 937 (268)
- Satin stitch in Anchor Pearl No. 5 Multicolour 1355

If working in tent stitch on canvas add the background with two strands of 712 (926)

934 (852)

Long-legged cross stitch over two threads in 934 (852)

355 (1014)

Long-legged cross stitch over four threads in 934 (852)

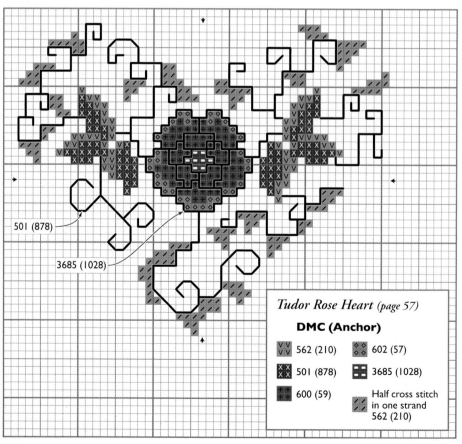

501 (878)

3685 (1028)

Tudor Rose Heart *(page 57)*

DMC (Anchor)

- 562 (210)
- 501 (878)
- 600 (59)
- 602 (57)
- 3685 (1028)
- Half cross stitch in one strand 562 (210)

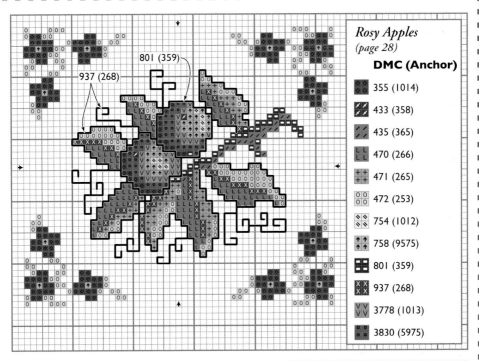

Rosy Apples
(page 28)

DMC (Anchor)

- 355 (1014)
- 433 (358)
- 435 (365)
- 470 (266)
- 471 (265)
- 472 (253)
- 754 (1012)
- 758 (9575)
- 801 (359)
- 937 (268)
- 3778 (1013)
- 3830 (5975)

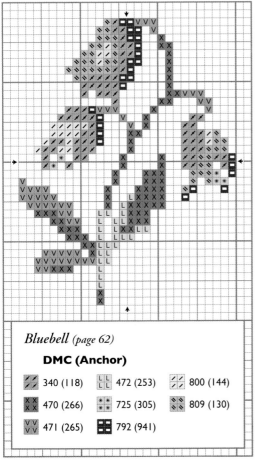

Bluebell *(page 62)*

DMC (Anchor)

- 340 (118)
- 472 (253)
- 800 (144)
- 470 (266)
- 725 (305)
- 809 (130)
- 471 (265)
- 792 (941)

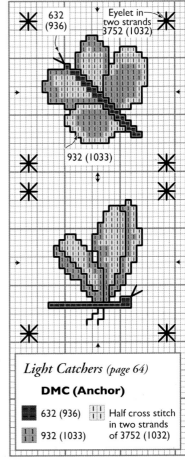

Light Catchers *(page 64)*

DMC (Anchor)

- 632 (936)
- 932 (1033)
- Half cross stitch in two strands of 3752 (1032)

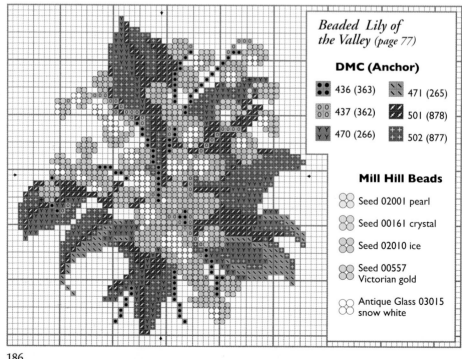

Beaded Iris Chatelaine *(page 75)*

Mill Hill Beads

- Seed 02015 sea blue
- Seed 02024 heather mauve
- Seed 00151 ash mauve
- Seed 00330 copper
- Seed 02010 ice
- Seed 00332 emerald
- Seed 00167 Christmas green
- Seed 02008 sea breeze
- Frosted seed 62031 gold

Fold line

Beaded Lily of the Valley *(page 77)*

DMC (Anchor)

- 436 (363)
- 437 (362)
- 470 (266)
- 471 (265)
- 501 (878)
- 502 (877)

Mill Hill Beads

- Seed 02001 pearl
- Seed 00161 crystal
- Seed 02010 ice
- Seed 00557 Victorian gold
- Antique Glass 03015 snow white

562 (210)

Flowerpot Button Darn (page 85)

DMC (Anchor)

XX XX 561 (212)	▬▬	561 (212)
VV VV 562 (210)	▬▬	729 (890)
◇◇ ◇◇ 676 (891)	▬▬	3350 (77)
++ ++ 729 (890)	✕	Button position
3350 (77)		
3731 (76)		

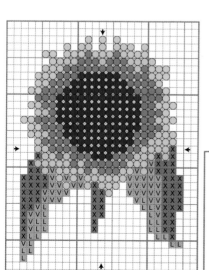

Sunflower Card (page 76)

DMC (Anchor)	**Mill Hill Beads**
XX XX 3346 (267)	⬤ Seed 02011 Victorian gold
VV VV 3347 (266)	⬤ Seed 00330 copper
LL LL 3348 (264)	⬤ Seed 00557 gold

187

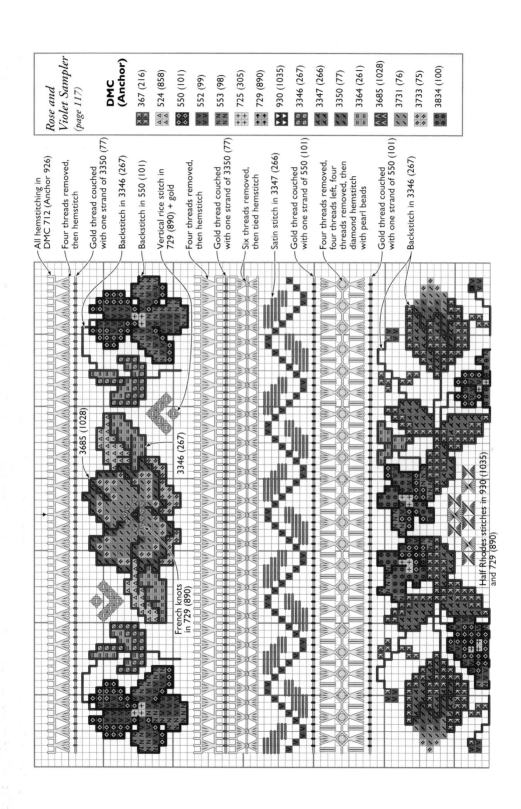

Rose and
Violet Sampler
(page 117)

DMC (Anchor)

367 (216)	
524 (858)	
550 (101)	
552 (99)	
553 (98)	
725 (305)	
729 (890)	
930 (1035)	
3346 (267)	
3347 (266)	
3350 (77)	
3364 (261)	
3685 (1028)	
3731 (76)	
3733 (75)	
3834 (100)	

All hemstitching in
DMC 712 (Anchor 926)

Four threads removed,
then hemstitch

Gold thread couched
with one strand of 3350 (77)

Backstitch in 3346 (267)

Backstitch in 550 (101)

Vertical rice stitch in
729 (890) + gold

Four threads removed,
then hemstitch

Gold thread couched
with one strand of 3350 (77)

Six threads removed,
then tied hemstitch

Satin stitch in 3347 (266)

Gold thread couched
with one strand of 550 (101)

Four threads removed,
four threads left, four
threads removed, then
diamond hemstitch
with pearl beads

Gold thread couched
with one strand of 550 (101)

Backstitch in 3346 (267)

3685 (1028)

3346 (267)

French knots
in 729 (890)

Half Rhodes stitches in 930 (1035)
and 729 (890)

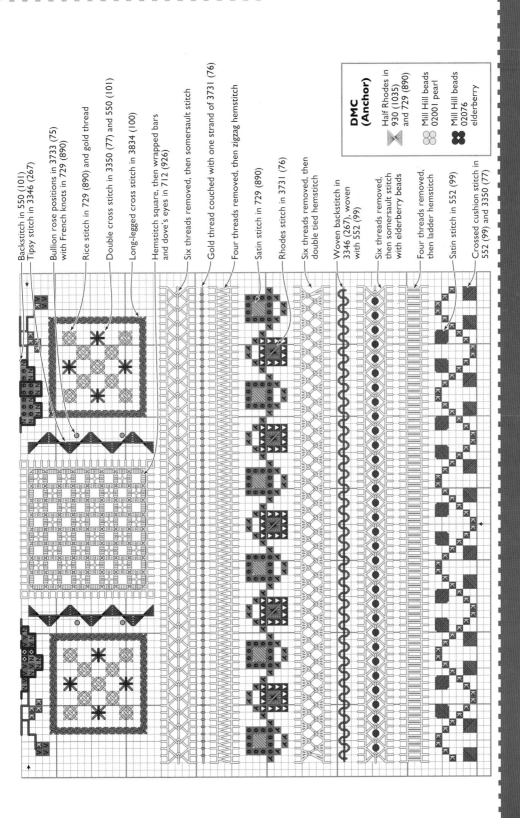

Backstitch in 550 (101)
Tipsy stitch in 3346 (267)

Bullion rose positions in 3733 (75)
with French knots in 729 (890)

Rice stitch in 729 (890) and gold thread

Double cross stitch in 3350 (77) and 550 (101)

Long-legged cross stitch in 3834 (100)

Hemstitch square, then wrapped bars
and dove's eyes in 712 (926)

Six threads removed, then somersault stitch

Gold thread couched with one strand of 3731 (76)

Four threads removed, then zigzag hemstitch

Satin stitch in 729 (890)

Rhodes stitch in 3731 (76)

Six threads removed, then
double tied hemstitch

Woven backstitch in
3346 (267), woven
with 552 (99)

Six threads removed,
then somersault stitch
with elderberry beads

Four threads removed,
then ladder hemstitch

Satin stitch in 552 (99)

Crossed cushion stitch in
552 (99) and 3350 (77)

DMC (Anchor)

Half Rhodes in 930 (1035) and 729 (890)

Mill Hill beads 02001 pearl

Mill Hill beads 02076 elderberry

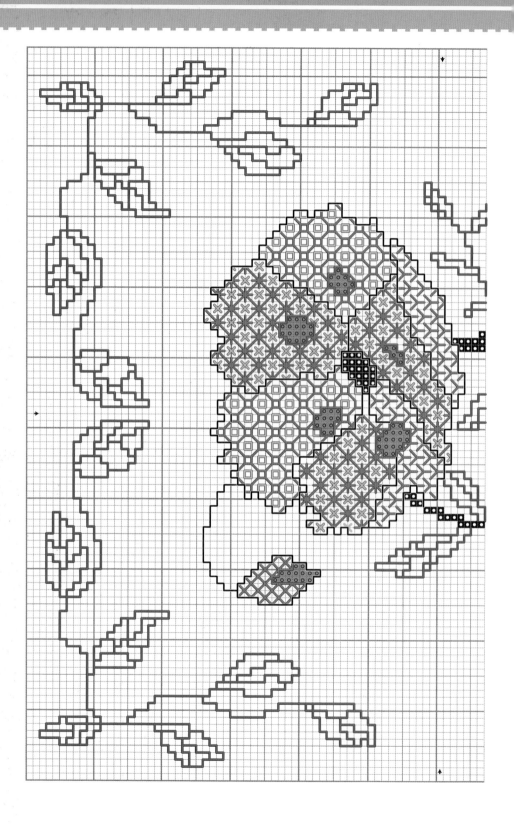

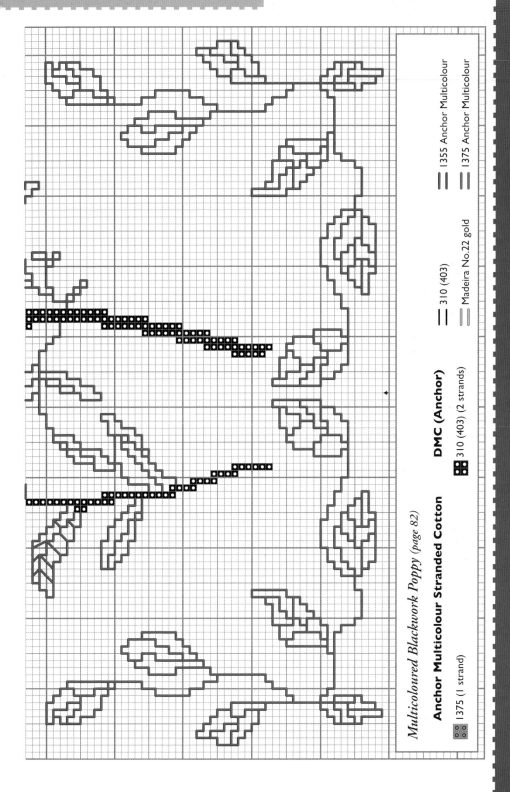

Multicoloured Blackwork Poppy (page 82)

Anchor Multicolour Stranded Cotton

DMC (Anchor)

▨ 1375 (1 strand)	▨ 310 (403) (2 strands)

═ 1355 Anchor Multicolour	═ 310 (403)
═ 1375 Anchor Multicolour	═ Madeira No.22 gold

Hardanger Diamond *(page 105)*

Kloster blocks DMC Perlé No.8 ecru

Buttonhole edging DMC Perlé No.8 ecru

Filling stitches in DMC Perlé No.12 ecru

Needleweaving

Needleweaving with picots

Corner needleweaving

Eyelets

Dove's eyes

Corner dove's eyes

Spider's webs

Wrapped bars

----- Red dotted lines show where to cut threads

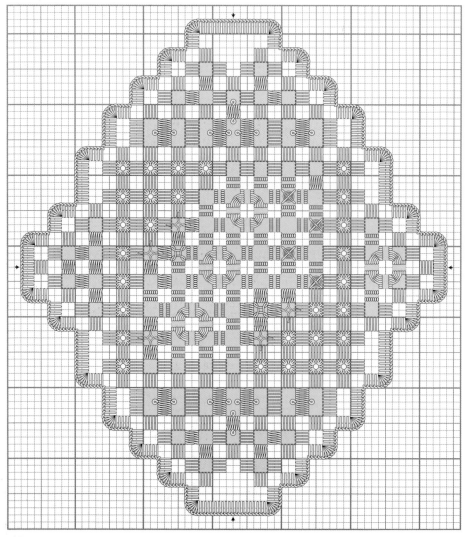

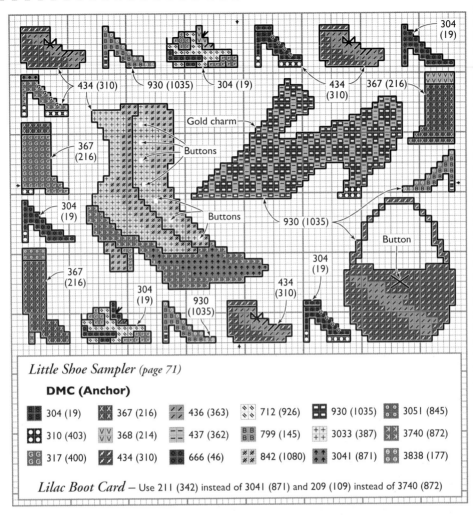

Little Shoe Sampler *(page 71)*

DMC (Anchor)

304 (19)	367 (216)	436 (363)	712 (926)	930 (1035)	3051 (845)
310 (403)	368 (214)	437 (362)	799 (145)	3033 (387)	3740 (872)
317 (400)	434 (310)	666 (46)	842 (1080)	3041 (871)	3838 (177)

Lilac Boot Card – Use 211 (342) instead of 3041 (871) and 209 (109) instead of 3740 (872)

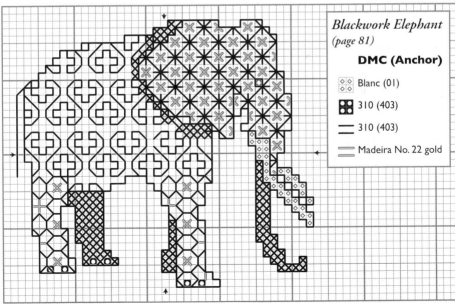

Blackwork Elephant
(page 81)

DMC (Anchor)

Blanc (01)

310 (403)

310 (403)

Madeira No. 22 gold

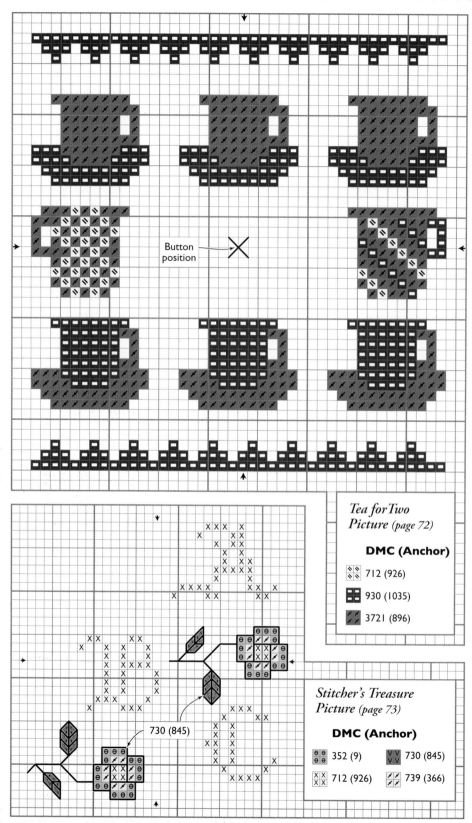

Button position

Tea for Two
Picture (page 72)

DMC (Anchor)

712 (926)

930 (1035)

3721 (896)

Stitcher's Treasure
Picture (page 73)

DMC (Anchor)

352 (9)   730 (845)

712 (926)   739 (366)

730 (845)

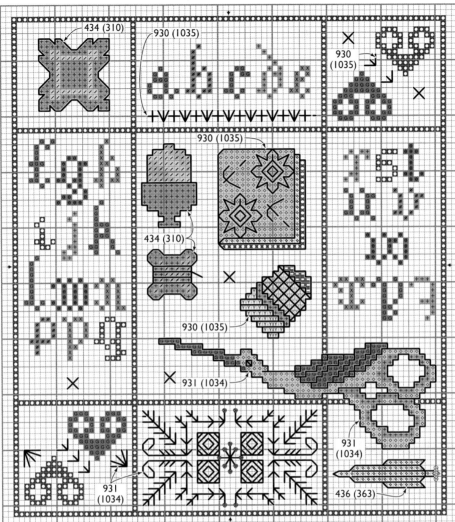

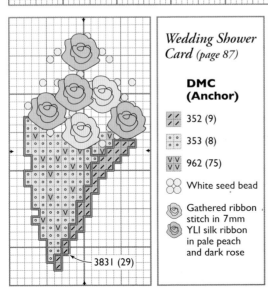

Wedding Shower Card (page 87)

DMC (Anchor)

- 352 (9)
- 353 (8)
- 962 (75)
- White seed bead
- Gathered ribbon stitch in 7mm YLI silk ribbon in pale peach and dark rose

3831 (29)

Stork Scissor Sampler (page 69)

DMC (Anchor)

- 315 (1019)
- 316 (1017)
- 434 (310)
- 436 (363)
- 437 (362)
- 522 (860)
- 676 (891)
- 677 (301)
- 712 (926)
- 738 (361)
- 930 (1035)
- 931 (1034)
- 3721 (896)

French knots

- 712 (926)
- 930 (1035)

✕ Positions of charms

Queen Stitch Sampler (page 91)

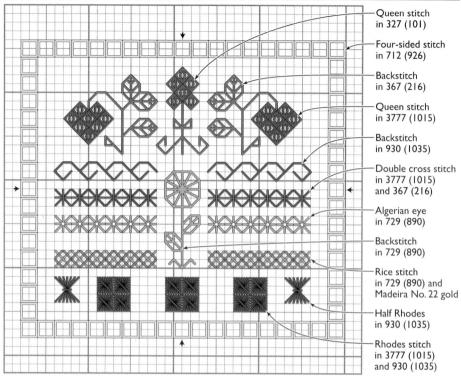

Queen stitch
in 327 (101)

Four-sided stitch
in 712 (926)

Backstitch
in 367 (216)

Queen stitch
in 3777 (1015)

Backstitch
in 930 (1035)

Double cross stitch
in 3777 (1015)
and 367 (216)

Algerian eye
in 729 (890)

Backstitch
in 729 (890)

Rice stitch
in 729 (890) and
Madeira No. 22 gold

Half Rhodes
in 930 (1035)

Rhodes stitch
in 3777 (1015)
and 930 (1035)

Tiny Band Sampler (page 91)
DMC (Anchor)

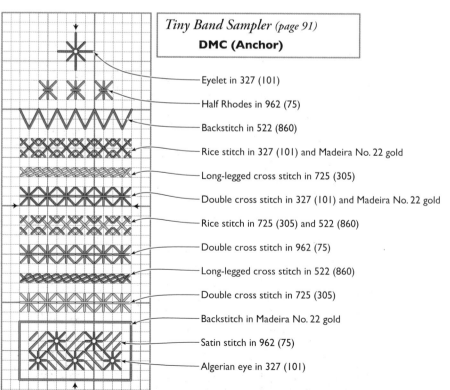

Eyelet in 327 (101)

Half Rhodes in 962 (75)

Backstitch in 522 (860)

Rice stitch in 327 (101) and Madeira No. 22 gold

Long-legged cross stitch in 725 (305)

Double cross stitch in 327 (101) and Madeira No. 22 gold

Rice stitch in 725 (305) and 522 (860)

Double cross stitch in 962 (75)

Long-legged cross stitch in 522 (860)

Double cross stitch in 725 (305)

Backstitch in Madeira No. 22 gold

Satin stitch in 962 (75)

Algerian eye in 327 (101)

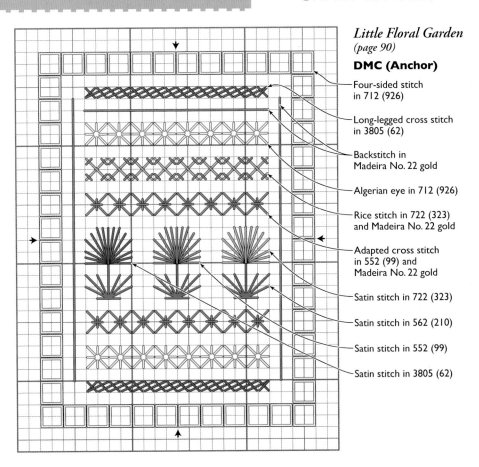

Little Floral Garden
(page 90)

DMC (Anchor)

Four-sided stitch
in 712 (926)

Long-legged cross stitch
in 3805 (62)

Backstitch in
Madeira No. 22 gold

Algerian eye in 712 (926)

Rice stitch in 722 (323)
and Madeira No. 22 gold

Adapted cross stitch
in 552 (99) and
Madeira No. 22 gold

Satin stitch in 722 (323)

Satin stitch in 562 (210)

Satin stitch in 552 (99)

Satin stitch in 3805 (62)

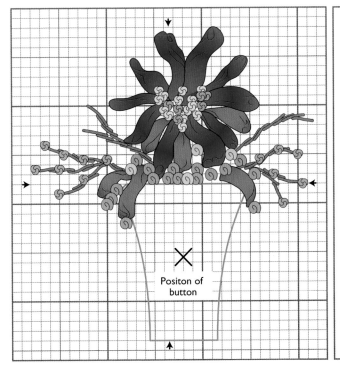

Positon of
button

Blue Ribbon Flower Card *(page 86)*

 Ribbon stitch in bright blue 7mm silk ribbon

 Ribbon stitch in pale olive 7mm silk ribbon

French knots in rose pink and pale pink 2mm silk ribbon

French knots in DMC (Anchor) stranded cotton 745 (300) and 3821 (305)

 Stem stitch in DMC (Anchor) stranded cotton 3346 (267)

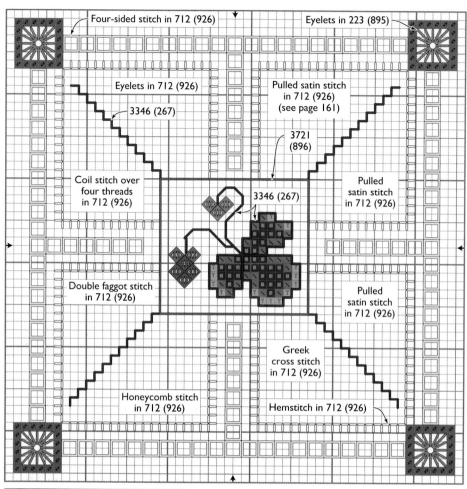

Four-sided stitch in 712 (926)

Eyelets in 223 (895)

Eyelets in 712 (926)

3346 (267)

Pulled satin stitch in 712 (926) (see page 161)

3721 (896)

Coil stitch over four threads in 712 (926)

3346 (267)

Pulled satin stitch in 712 (926)

Double faggot stitch in 712 (926)

Pulled satin stitch in 712 (926)

Greek cross stitch in 712 (926)

Honeycomb stitch in 712 (926)

Hemstitch in 712 (926)

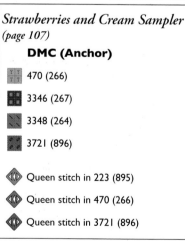

Strawberries and Cream Sampler
(page 107)

DMC (Anchor)

470 (266)

3346 (267)

3348 (264)

3721 (896)

Queen stitch in 223 (895)

Queen stitch in 470 (266)

Queen stitch in 3721 (896)

Use this alphabet to change the initials on the key keeper on page 41 (chart on page 174).

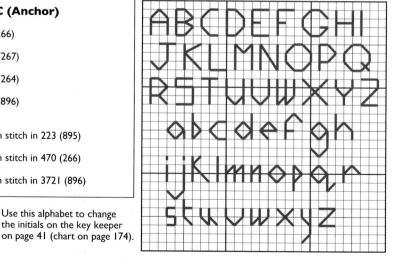

ABCDEFGHI
JKLMNOPQ
RSTUVWXYZ
abcdefgh
ijklmnopqr
stuvwxyz

Mini Cream Sampler *(page 108)*

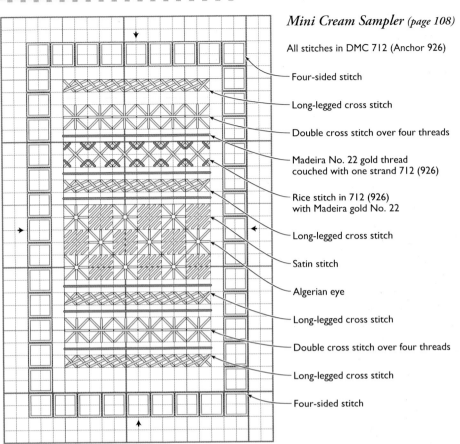

All stitches in DMC 712 (Anchor 926)

— Four-sided stitch

— Long-legged cross stitch

— Double cross stitch over four threads

— Madeira No. 22 gold thread couched with one strand 712 (926)

— Rice stitch in 712 (926) with Madeira gold No. 22

— Long-legged cross stitch

— Satin stitch

— Algerian eye

— Long-legged cross stitch

— Double cross stitch over four threads

— Long-legged cross stitch

— Four-sided stitch

Lacy Flower Face *(page 109)*

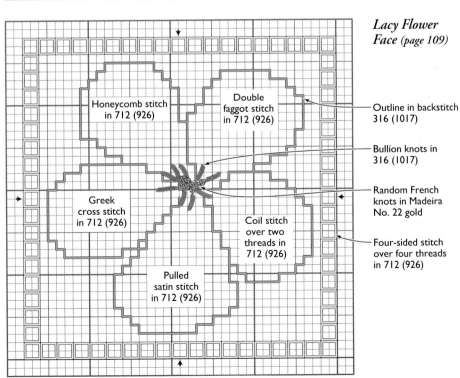

Honeycomb stitch in 712 (926)

Double faggot stitch in 712 (926)

Greek cross stitch in 712 (926)

Coil stitch over two threads in 712 (926)

Pulled satin stitch in 712 (926)

— Outline in backstitch 316 (1017)

— Bullion knots in 316 (1017)

— Random French knots in Madeira No. 22 gold

— Four-sided stitch over four threads in 712 (926)

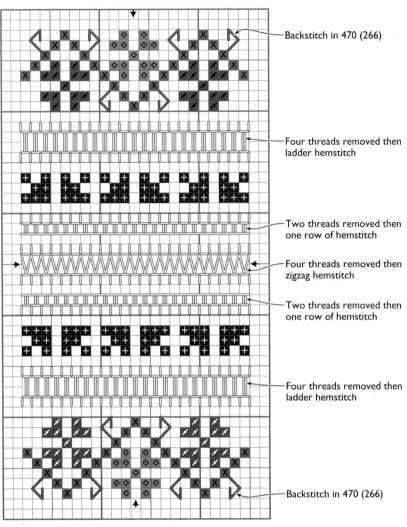

Backstitch in 470 (266)

Four threads removed then ladder hemstitch

Two threads removed then one row of hemstitch

Four threads removed then zigzag hemstitch

Two threads removed then one row of hemstitch

Four threads removed then ladder hemstitch

Backstitch in 470 (266)

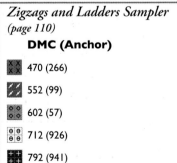

Zigzags and Ladders Sampler
(page 110)

DMC (Anchor)

470 (266)

552 (99)

602 (57)

712 (926)

792 (941)

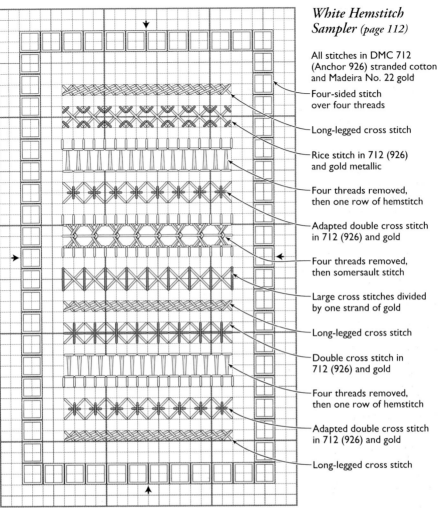

White Hemstitch Sampler *(page 112)*

All stitches in DMC 712 (Anchor 926) stranded cotton and Madeira No. 22 gold

Four-sided stitch over four threads

Long-legged cross stitch

Rice stitch in 712 (926) and gold metallic

Four threads removed, then one row of hemstitch

Adapted double cross stitch in 712 (926) and gold

Four threads removed, then somersault stitch

Large cross stitches divided by one strand of gold

Long-legged cross stitch

Double cross stitch in 712 (926) and gold

Four threads removed, then one row of hemstitch

Adapted double cross stitch in 712 (926) and gold

Long-legged cross stitch

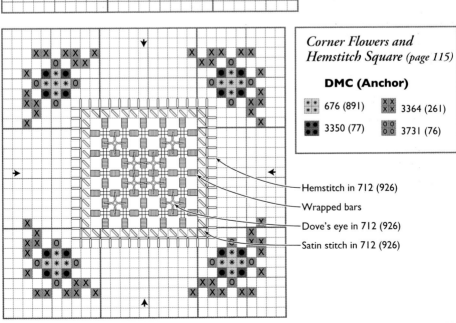

Corner Flowers and Hemstitch Square *(page 115)*

DMC (Anchor)

✳✳	676 (891)	✕✕	3364 (261)
●●	3350 (77)	○○	3731 (76)

Hemstitch in 712 (926)

Wrapped bars

Dove's eye in 712 (926)

Satin stitch in 712 (926)

201

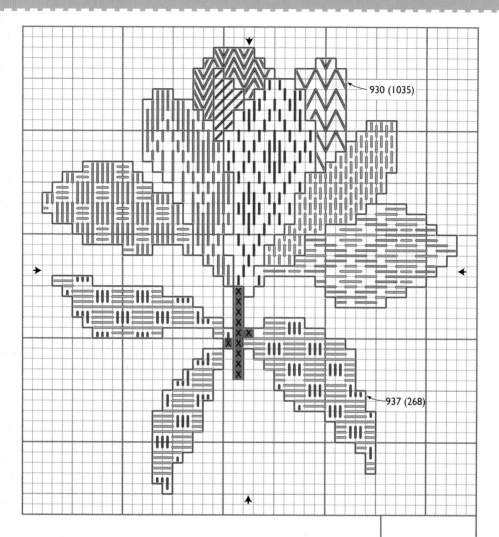

930 (1035)

937 (268)

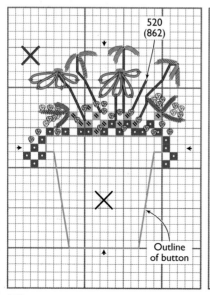

520
(862)

Outline
of button

Summer Flower Card *(page 68)*

DMC (Anchor)

- 520 (862)
- 522 (860)

French knots
- 783 (307)
- 3731 (76)
- 3821 (305)

Bullion knots
- 522 (860)
- 3733 (75)
- 3821 (305)

Lazy daisy stitches
- 792 (177)

✕ Position of button

✕ Position of charm

Pattern Darn Flower *(page 85)*

DMC (Anchor)

- 470 (266)
- 304 (19)
- 470 (266)
- 729 (890)
- 930 (1035)
- 931 (1034)
- 937 (268)
- 3041 (871)
- 3830 (5975)

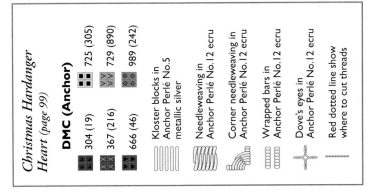

Christmas Hardanger Heart *(page 99)*

DMC (Anchor)

- 304 (19)
- 367 (216)
- 666 (46)
- 725 (305)
- 729 (890)
- 989 (242)

- Kloster blocks in Anchor Perlé No.5 metallic silver
- Needleweaving in Anchor Perlé No.12 ecru
- Corner needleweaving in Anchor Perlé No.12 ecru
- Wrapped bars in Anchor Perlé No.12 ecru
- Dove's eyes in Anchor Perlé No.12 ecru
- Red dotted line show where to cut threads

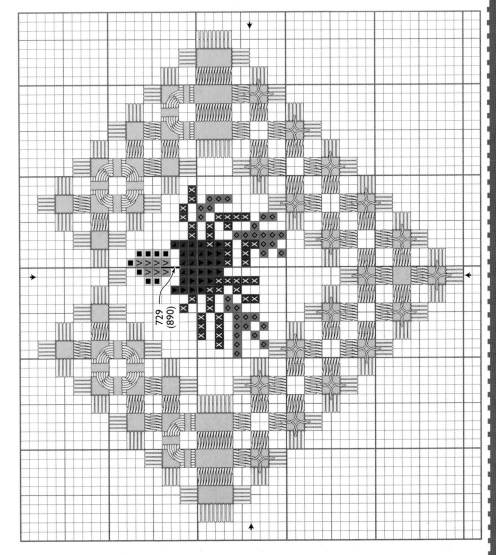

729 (890)

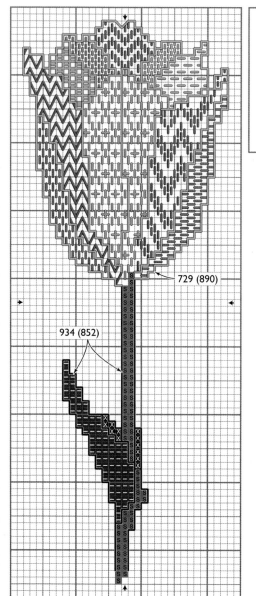

470 (266)	221 (897)	931 (1034)
934 (852)	327 (101)	934 (852)
937 (268)	470 (266)	3740 (872)
	729 (890)	

729 (890)

934 (852)

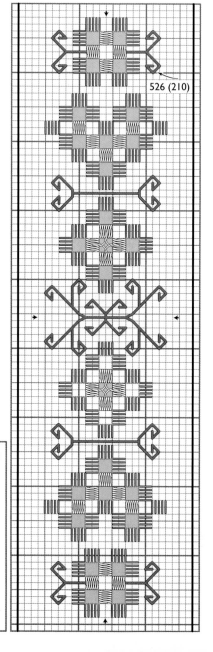

526 (210)

||||| Kloster blocks Anchor Perlé No.8 multicolour 1375

Dove's eyes Anchor Perlé No.12 ecru

Needleweaving Anchor Perlé No.12 ecru

— Hemstitched edge Anchor Perlé No.12 ecru

...... Red dotted lines show where to cut threads

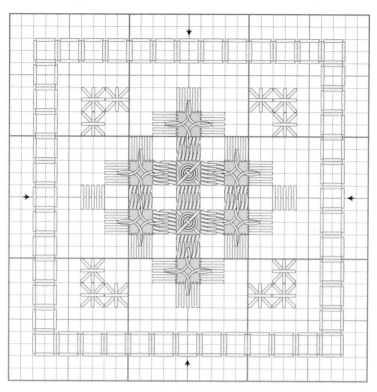

Mini Hardanger Sampler *(page 100)*

Kloster blocks in
DMC Perlé No.5 cream

Needleweaving in
DMC Perlé No.8 cream

Dove's eyes in
DMC Perlé No.8 cream

Spider's webs in
DMC Perlé No.8 cream

Double cross stitch in
DMC Perlé No.5 cream

Four-sided stitch in
DMC Perlé No.8 cream

Red dotted line show
where to cut threads

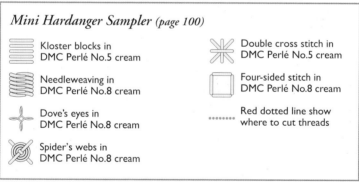

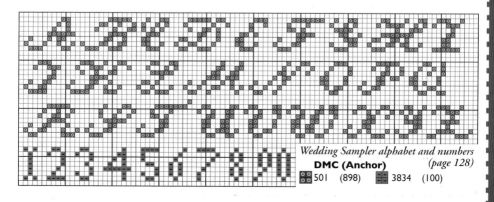

Wedding Sampler alphabet and numbers
(page 128)
DMC (Anchor)
501 (898)   3834 (100)

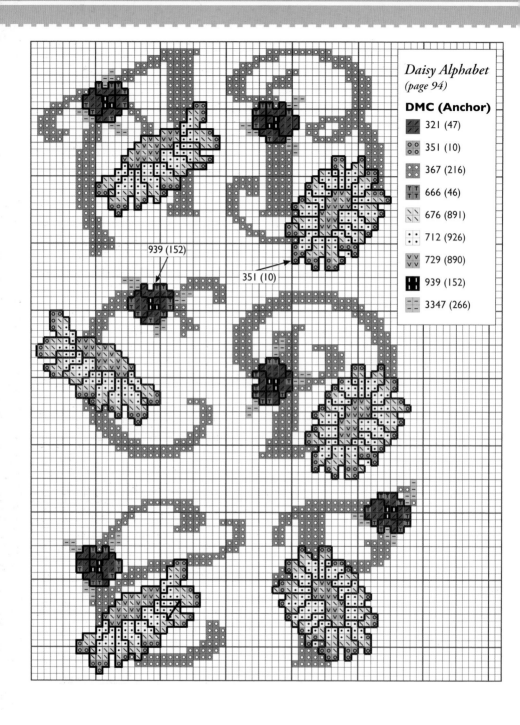

Daisy Alphabet
(page 94)

DMC (Anchor)

◢	321 (47)
o o	351 (10)
⊡	367 (216)
T T / T T	666 (46)
\ \ / \ \	676 (891)
: :	712 (926)
V V / V V	729 (890)
⊞	939 (152)
= =	3347 (266)

939 (152)

351 (10)

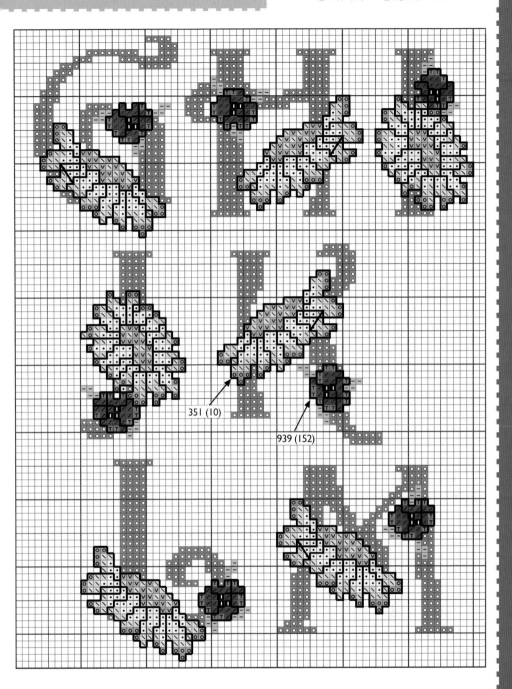

351 (10)

939 (152)

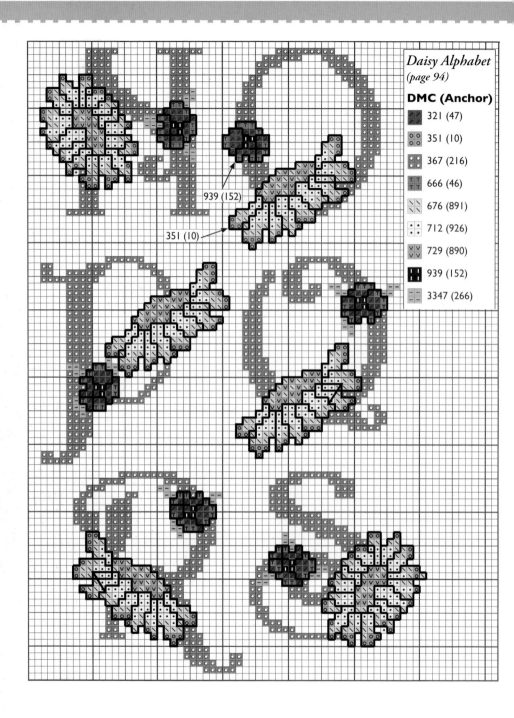

Daisy Alphabet
(page 94)

DMC (Anchor)

- 321 (47)
- 351 (10)
- 367 (216)
- 666 (46)
- 676 (891)
- 712 (926)
- 729 (890)
- 939 (152)
- 3347 (266)

939 (152)

351 (10)

939 (152)

351 (10)

FINISHING AND MAKING UP

Embroidery designs can be made up into a wonderful selection of objects, both practical and decorative and how they are made up or completed makes a great deal of difference to the look of the finished piece. This section describes some of the basic finishing techniques used in the book and suggests ways of displaying your embroidery. If you are unable to find any items mentioned – don't panic! – there are always alternatives on the market. Experiment!

WASHING AND IRONING YOUR WORK

If it becomes necessary to wash your embroidery, hand wash the stitching in bleach-free soap, rinse well and remove excess water by squeezing gently in a soft, clean towel. Allow the piece to dry naturally.

To iron a piece of embroidery, first cover the ironing board with four layers of thick white towel and press the work from the wrong side, using the steam setting if your iron has one. Take extra care when ironing work containing buttons and charms and avoid ironing metallic threads.

JANE'S TIP

If disaster strikes and you do get a difficult mark on the fabric there are now specialist bleaches for stain removal, which can save the situation – something to be kept for real emergencies. Apply with a cotton bud and a very good light.

STRETCHING AND MOUNTING

Professional framing can be very expensive, but we all feel that our larger projects deserve the professional touch. It is a great shame when, after spending hundreds of hours stitching a precious piece of cross stitch, the finished piece is just poked in an unsuitable frame without any further attention. By following the method explained below for padded mounting, you will be able to produce a very good result and have the pleasure of knowing that you completed the whole project on your own. The advantage of a padded mounting for embroidery is that any slightly 'lumpy bits' on the back of your work will be pushed into the padding rather than appear as raised areas on the front of the embroidery.

◆ Take time to make sure that you have centred the work carefully and that the edges are really straight, otherwise it will show when you put the completed piece in the frame.

◆ Pad all your completed pieces even cards as the padding raises the embroidery, which displays it to better effect.

◆ Use foamcore board, which consists of two layers of thin card with a layer of polystyrene between. This construction makes it easy to cut the board and to pin into the edge as the pins are actually inserted into the polystyrene. You will probably have to buy foamcore board at an artists' supply store rather than a needlework shop.

You will need: 3mm foamcore board, or acid-free mounting board; double-sided adhesive tape, or strong thread for lacing; polyester wadding (batting) for padding and glass- or plastic-headed pins.

1 Using a sharp craft knife, cut a piece of foamcore to fit your frame (cut round the piece of glass that fits the frame).
2 Attach a piece of wadding (batting) to the foamcore board using strips of double-sided adhesive tape, then trim the wadding to exactly the same size as the foamcore.
3 Position your embroidery on top of the padding and centre it carefully in relation to the padded board. Fix the embroidery in position by pinning through the fabric into the edges of the board (see Fig 1). Start in

the middle of each side and pin towards the corners. Make sure your pins follow a line of Aida holes or a thread of linen so that your edges will be really straight. Adjust the fabric's position until you are completely confident that it is centred and straight.
4 Turn the work over and, leaving the pins in place, trim the excess fabric to about 5cm (2in) all round and fold it to the back.
5 Fix the edges of fabric in place using either double-sided tape or by lacing across the back using strong thread (see Fig 2). As the pins remain in place, it is still possible at this stage to adjust the position of the fabric and replace the tape or tighten the lacing. When you are completely satisfied with the result, remove the pins and assemble the work in its frame.

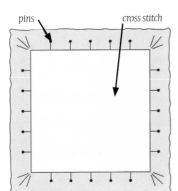

Fig 1 *Pinning out your embroidery.*

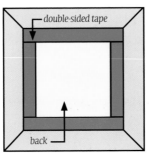 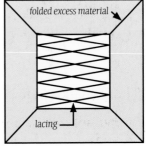

Fig 2 *Fixing the fabric in place by taping or lacing.*

FRAMING

Needlework generally looks better framed without glass. If you prefer to use glass with this method, you must ensure that the embroidery does not touch the underside of the glass. Insert very narrow strips of board (spacers) into the edges of the frame, between the glass and the mounted embroidery to hold them apart, before you assemble the frame. Always check that both sides of the glass are completely clean.
It is a good idea to line the back of the work with aluminium foil before adding the final backing board

to the back of the picture, to discourage small insects from finding their way in. When the frame is assembled, seal the back using gummed paper tape, gently pushing the tape into the rebate. The tape will shrink slightly as it dries thus sealing the picture.

Choosing a Frame

◆ When choosing a frame for a particular project, select the largest moulding you can afford and do not worry if the colour is not suitable. Ask the framer to make up the frame and a coloured or gold slip for you, but buy the frame, glass and so on in kit form (most framers do not mind!) and then decorate the frame yourself.

◆ You can use readily available products to decorate frames, for example car spray paint. There are dozens of colours but if you want more, try bicycle paints, which include even more colours!

◆ For subtle, matt shades, explore endless possibilities with emulsion paints from DIY shops, often available in tiny tester sizes, ideal for trial and error.

◆ Before you begin to paint a piece of moulding, take care to cover all nearby surfaces with paper or dust cloths, If the moulding is completely untreated, rub down gently with fine sand paper, clean with white spirit on a soft cloth and allow to dry completely before painting.

Stretching and Starching Canvas Work

It is the nature of canvas to distort especially when worked in tent stitch, so it is necessary to stretch and starch the needlework to restore a regular shape. You will be able to use the board and squared paper many times and will soon master the technique.

You will need: a flat, clean board (e.g., chipboard); squared paper (e.g., dressmaker's graph paper); hammer and 2.5cm (1in) long nails; cold water starch (e.g., wallpaper paste without preservatives or anti-fungal agent); masking tape and kitchen palette knife.

1 Cover the board with the squared paper and stick down with masking tape. Place the embroidery right side down on the paper. You should be able to see the squares on the paper through the unstitched canvas.

2 Start at one corner and begin nailing down the canvas about 5cm (2in) from the embroidery, hammering in the nails far enough to hold the fabric firmly. Following the line in the canvas, align the canvas with the squared paper, placing nails about 2.5cm (1in) apart (any further apart and the needlework may acquire a scalloped edge).

3 When you have completed the first side, go back to the corner and repeat for the side at right angles to it. Draw a pencil line on the canvas from the last nail on each side to cross at the opposite corner to one you started from. Work out where this should come in relation to the lines on the graph paper and pull the embroidery and nail the corner and the last two sides. If your stitching is very distorted it may help to dampen the embroidery.

4 When the last nail is in position the work should be completely square. Mix a small quantity of the starch to the consistency of soft butter and spread it evenly but sparingly with a knife over the canvas, avoiding the unstitched areas. Allow this to dry completely and then remove the nails to remove the work from the board. Not only will the work be completely square but the starch will have evened the tension so your stitches should look even better!

MAKING UP A CUBE

The cube decorations on pages 45 and 61 are quite simple to make up and can be stuffed with polyester stuffing, perhaps with some crushed cinnamon sticks inside for a festive aroma. You will need to make a length of twisted cord (see page 41) and a tassel (see page 218).

1 Press the embroidery carefully on the wrong side with plenty of steam and on a towel and gently pull the squares back into shape. Trim the bare canvas edges to 1.25cm (½in) and clip corners.

2 Fold in all the canvas edges leaving one thread of canvas exposed. You will be able to fold up the squares to make a cube. Now work long-legged cross stitch on all the empty canvas threads between the squares and on the joins of your box shape. Tuck in the cord and tassel at opposite corners and fill with polyester wadding just before you complete the last seam.

MAKING A BAG OR SACHET

A bag or sachet is easy to stitch, can be made in any size and has many different uses – holding small gifts, pot-pourri or wedding mementoes. A bag could be made entirely from Aida or an evenweave fabric, with the design embroidered directly on to the fabric, or it could be made from an ordinary dressmaking fabric with an embroidered panel sewn or fused on. The instructions that follow are for a sewn-on piece of embroidery – see page 216 for using fusible interfacing. You will need: sufficient fabric for the front and back of the bag; matching sewing thread and a length of cord or ribbon for a tie.

1 Cut out two rectangles of fabric according to the size you wish your bag to be, allowing for 6mm (¼in) seams. Stitch your piece of embroidery on to the front piece, perhaps fraying the edges of the fabric for a decorative effect.
2 With right sides of the bag rectangles together, pin and stitch both sides and the bottom of the bag, matching the edges for a neat finish. Press the side seams open.
3 To make the top of the bag, fold the top edge over to the wrong side by 6mm (¼in), press, then fold over again by another 4cm (1½in). Pin in place and sew two rows of stitching around the neck of the bag to form a casing for a tie. Turn the bag to the right side. Snip the side seam between the lines of parallel stitching, binding the cut edges with small

buttonhole stitches or over-stitching. (If preferred, you can make a bag like the one shown here, where the raw edge has been hemstitched and the ribbon is tied on the outside.)
4 To finish the bag with a tie, thread a piece of cord or ribbon through the channel and knot the ends to secure.

MAKING A BELL PULL

A bell pull is another useful way of displaying cross stitch. You could use one of the designs charted in the Chart Library or design one of your own. A simple rectangular shape is the easiest to make up but you could make one with a pointed bottom end if you prefer. First, decide on the size of your bell pull – the length of the bell pull hanging rod determines the width of the fabric you need, so buy the bell pull ends and rods before you start stitching. You could use rustic twigs or cinnamon sticks instead of commercial rods.

You will need: bell pull hanging rods and ends; cotton backing fabric; decorative braid and matching sewing thread.

1 Work your cross stitch design on to your stitching fabric.
2 Turn under the edges of your fabric so that your design is central. Fold your backing fabric to the same size and press the turnings.
3 Place the embroidered piece and the backing fabric wrong sides together (i.e., right sides outside) and pin. Slide the rods into position at the top and bottom, and add the bell pull ends, then slipstitch the fabric pieces together, adding decorative braid around the edges if desired.

MAKING A BOOKMARK

Bookmarks make quick gifts. You could make your own as described here or mount your work in a commercial bookmark, or use a band as shown here.

1 Decide on the size of your bookmark and stitch your design on to the fabric. Trim the fabric to within 1.25cm (½in) of the stitching all round.
2 Hem all the sides. If you want to create a shaped point at the bottom, don't hem the bottom but turn it under by about 6mm (¼in), making sure that none of the embroidery is included, and tack (baste). Find the seam centre point and bring the two corners together so they meet at the back then slipstitch these two edges together. A tassel at the point would finish the bookmark off nicely.

MOUNTING WORK IN CARDS AND TAGS

There are many card blanks available from needlecraft shops and mail-order companies or you can make your own using pretty papers, card and ribbon, as I have for the Vintage Viola Card shown below and the Lilac Boot Card on page 70.

MOUNTING INTO A DOUBLE-FOLD CARD

1 Open the folded card completely and check that the embroidered design fits in the opening.

2 Apply a thin coat of adhesive or double-sided adhesive tape to the inside of the opening (see Fig 3). Position the design carefully, checking the position of the stitching before pressing down firmly.

3 Fold the spare flap inside and stick in place with either double-sided adhesive tape or another thin application of adhesive. Leave to dry before closing and add ribbon trims as desired.

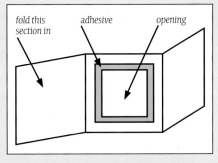

fold this section in   *adhesive*   *opening*

Fig 3 *Open out the card and apply double-sided tape around the aperture.*

MAKING HANDMADE CARDS

1 In all cases, cut the finished embroidery to the required size (allowing for fraying the edges if appropriate).

2 Select a coloured card to complement your embroidery threads and create a single-fold card and then embellish it with decorative paper.

3 Attach the embroidery to the card with double-sided adhesive tape and add trims or other embellishments as desired.

MAKING CARD PATCHES

One of the quickest methods of making a special card is to simply trim and fray the fabric around the project and stick the frayed patch on a piece of card using double-sided adhesive tape.

To make a tattered patch you need to use linen for the stitching as it frays more satisfactorily. Trim away the excess fabric and fray all four sides until you have the required size then gently tug at the corners to distort slightly.

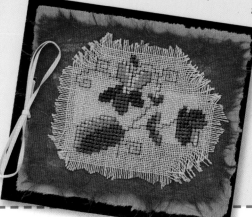

USING COMMERCIAL PRODUCTS

There are many items available today that have been specially designed to display embroidery, such as trays, stools, fire screens, mugs, boxes, mirrors, trinket pots and coasters. To mount work in these products, you generally only need to follow the manufacturer's instructions, but it helps to back the embroidered work with iron-on interfacing.

USING IRON-ON INTERFACING

Cross stitch embroidery can be stabilized with iron-on interfacing, which also helps prevent fraying when cutting the fabric. Double-sided interfacing can be used to fuse your embroidery to another fabric. Interfacing is available from needlework shops and good craft shops.

1 Cut a piece of interfacing a little larger than the finished design size (including any unworked fabric needed to fill an aperture or ready-made item).
2 Set the iron to the manufacturer's recommended heating (usually a medium setting). Do a test first on waste fabric and interfacing to make sure that they will bond without scorching the design.
3 Place the stitching face down on a towel and iron on the interfacing, trimming off excess.

MAKING CUSHIONS, PINCUSHIONS AND SCISSORS KEEPERS

Cross stitch embroidery can be made up into cushions, pincushions and scissors keepers following the same principles. Two pieces of fabric the same size and shape are joined together, with stuffing inserted into the centre. You could make a twisted cord (see page 41) and slipstitch this to the seam all round using matching thread. Tuck the raw edges inside the cover before slipstitching the gap closed or disguise the ends with a decorative button. Alternatively, use a ready-made cord for an edging. There are two main ways of joining the fabrics – using counted chain stitch or normal hand or machine sewing.

JOINING WITH COUNTED CHAIN STITCH

1 Place the two fabric sections wrong sides together and sew together using counted chain stitch (or long-legged cross stitch).
2 Insert the stuffing through an opening before the last side is completed. If a cord for scissors or to attach to a chatelaine is required, insert this immediately after stuffing and anchor it in place as the last side is stitched.

JOINING WITH HAND OR MACHINE SEWING

1 Pin the back and front pieces together, right sides facing.
2 Stitch the pieces together, by hand or machine, leaving an opening for turning through.
3 Turn right sides out, insert polyester filling and slipstitch the opening to close.

MAKING A PURSE

There are many designs in the book that could be stitched and made up into a purse. You will need: fabric to make the purse, lining fabric, thin wadding (batting) and bias binding to edge the flap. Alternatively, buy ready-made binding.

1 Decide what size the front flap is to be and stitch the flower design in the centre.
2 Cut a piece of fabric as wide as the stitched piece and at least twice the length. With right sides together stitch the embroidered section to the patterned fabric and press the seam flat. Use this long narrow shape as a template to cut wadding and lining fabric.
3 Sandwich the stitching, batting and lining together and tack in position. Trim the embroidered section to a gentle curve (draw around a plate). Using purchased or homemade bias binding, bind the short, straight edge of the purse (see page 219 for making and attaching binding).

4 Fold the purse into three, checking that the flap falls in the correct position, and tack in position. Starting at the bottom fold, bind up one side of the pocket, around the curve and down the other side. Trim the binding at the bottom edge, slipping the raw edges inside and slipstitching in place.

MAKING A PHOTOGRAPH CASE

A photograph case makes a lovely keepsake to hold some cute baby photos. You will need sufficient embroidery fabric to house the motifs and make up the case.

1 Stitch the motifs in the positions in Fig 4. Trim the embroidery fabric to the size required: a piece of fabric 18 x 30.5cm (7 x 12in) once folded will hold a 10 x 15cm (4 x 6in) photo.
2 Cut a piece of lining fabric 18 x 30.5cm (7 x 12in). Place the two pieces right sides together and sew together around each side, leaving a gap. Turn through to the right side, slipstitch the gap and press seams.
3 Fold the bottom of the case up by about 11.5cm (4½in) and pin the side seams together. Fold the flap over to check that the position. Using tiny stitches and matching sewing thread, join the two side seams together.

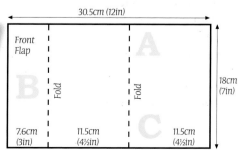

Fig 4 Position of the motifs on the case. Fold the fabric at the dashed lines to create the case.

217

Beaded Iris Chatelaine

Making up this chatelaine is quite simple. You will need: linen for the back, felt for the lining and Vilene stiffening.

1 Press your work on the wrong side, with at least two layers of towelling to cushion the beads.

2 Using the solid lines on the chart, tack the shape of your chatelaine on your linen. Cut out this shape leaving 1.25cm (½in) seam allowance around it.

3 Fold under this seam allowance and using the beaded shape as a pattern, cut Vilene to the same shape and then use the Vilene as a pattern to cut out the felt lining.

4 Tuck the Vilene stiffening in under the folded-in edges on the linen and use herringbone to stitch down the seam allowance, making sure that your stitches do not come through to the right side.

5 Make a twisted cord (see page 41).

6 Make a beaded tassel for the bottom of the chatelaine with five or six beaded lengths as follows. Thread a beading needle with one strand of stranded cotton and thread on one bead. Now thread both ends of the cotton through the needle so that one bead is trapped at the bottom. Thread more beads on to the needle. When you have enough beaded lengths tie them together at the top with a firm knot.

7 Place the felt lining over the turned-in edges including the knot of the tassel and the ends of the twisted cord and slipstitch in place.

8 Fold the whole thing so that the two long straight edges meet (right sides out) and slipstitch the two edges together.

Making a Tassel

Tassels are useful for adding a finishing touch to many projects, including cushions, cards and bookmarks. They can be made from various threads, usually from stranded cottons to match the cross stitch design, but you could also use metallic threads or tapestry wools.

1 Decide on the tassel length and cut a piece of stiff card this size. Wrap the thread around the card (Fig 5) to form the body of the tassel, to the thickness required.

2 Tie a thread around the top threads and then remove the tassel from the card. Cut across the threads at the bottom and tightly wrap a length of thread just below the loop at the top. Knot this and thread the ends through to join the other lengths. Trim the tassel ends if they are uneven.

3 To attach the tassel, use matching thread through the loop at the top.

A

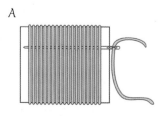

B

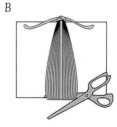

C

Fig 5 *Making a tassel.*

MAKING A MITRED CUSHION FRONT

A mitred front to a cushion or pillow gives it a professional touch and really sets off the embroidery. The Anemone Floral Cushion on page 53 uses pure silk fabric to great effect.

1 Measure the embroidery and decide on the size the finished cushion is to be. Allow 1.25cm (½in) seam allowances throughout. Subtract the embroidery measurement from the two finished measurements, divide by two and add on the two seam allowances. This gives the total width of the border pieces. The length of the border pieces is the finished measurement of the cushion cover plus two seam allowances.

2 Press the embroidery face down on several soft towels. Cut the linen to the required size plus two seam allowances.

3 Find the mid-point of each edge by folding and mark with a pin. Fold each border panel in half to find the centre point and mark with a pin. Pin the border panels to the embroidery, matching the centre points and leaving the edges free.

4 Machine stitch these seams around each side of the square. The seams should meet at the corners exactly at right angles. Fold the embroidery in half diagonally, wrong sides together, and mitre the corners by stitching a line from the corner of the embroidery to the corner of the border panels (see Fig 6). Trim excess fabric and clip corners. Repeat for the remaining corners.

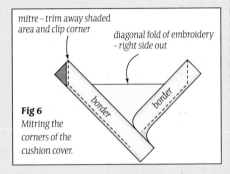

mitre - trim away shaded area and clip corner

diagonal fold of embroidery - right side out

Fig 6
Mitring the corners of the cushion cover.

MAKING BIAS BINDING

It is useful to be able to make your own bias binding as you will then be able to choose fabric that complements your project. Commercially made binding is available in various colours.

1 To make bias binding, cut strips of fabric 4cm (1½in) wide across the grain of the fabric and machine sew them together at a 45-degree angle to make the length needed (Fig 7A).

2 Attach the bias binding by hand or machine, first cutting the binding to the correct length. Pin the binding to the wrong side of the project, matching raw edges and then machine or hand stitch in place (Fig 7B). Now fold the binding to the right side and slipstitch neatly in position (Fig 7C). Press lightly to finish.

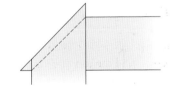

Fig 7A Joining bias strips at a 45-degree angle.

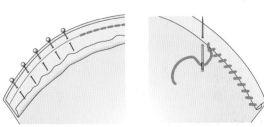

Fig 7B and C Pinning the binding to the front of the work, and then slipstitching the folded edge to the back of the work.

Bibliography

LOVE Janice, *Basics and Beyond* (Love 'n' Stitches, 1992)
O'STEEN Darlene, *The Proper Stitch* (Just Cross Stitch, 1994)
The New Anchor Book of Hardanger Embroidery (David & Charles, 2005)
The Anchor Book of Ribbon Embroidery (David & Charles, 1997)
The Anchor Book of Counted Thread Embroidery Stitches (David & Charles, 1987)
BISHOP, E. *A Collection of Beautiful Stitches* (Cross 'N' Patch, 2002)
DILLMONT, Therese *DMC Library: The Encyclopaedia of Needlework* (Bracken, reprinted 1987)
The Embroiderer's Guild *Making Samplers* (David & Charles, 1993)
McNEILL, Moyra *Pulled Thread Embroidery* (Dover Publications, 1999)
O'STEEN, D. *The Proper Stitch* (Symbol Of Excellence Publishers Inc, 1994)
SNOOK, Barbara *Embroidery Stitches* (Batsford, 1972)

Acknowledgments

Without the support of my family and my team at The Cross Stitch Guild it would be simply impossible to continue writing cross stitch books. To all the following with love and thanks:

Bill, my special husband, who has continued to accept the many hours spent apart, my late nights and bad temper, the household muddle and late meals. Sue Hawkins (CSG Technical Director) who is always at the end of a phone day and night, and for her friendship, which has even survived working together. This book would not have happened without her.

Daphne Cording who works with me, keeping kit production on target and me in my place and Judy Reynolds, my housekeeper superstar who keeps me sane.

A special thanks to all my stitchers, pattern checkers and testers – they have supported and encouraged me over the past twenty odd years and have made it possible for me to earn a living from my cross stitch passion: Susan Bridgens, Deborah Buglass, Elizabeth Burford, Lesley Clegg, Margaret Cornish, Neil Cuthbert, Jacqueline Davies, Elizabeth Edwards, Doreen Ely, Jean Fox, Ann Gerring, Kam Ghatoray, Joyce Halliday, Joan Hastewell, Jane Herbert, Janet Jarvis, Jane King, Margaret Locke, Margaret Pallant, Sue Smith, Suzanne Spencer, Jill Vaughan and Joan Winwood.

Vivienne Wells who is responsible for all things printed by the CSG and tries to keep me up to the task. To all the team at David & Charles for putting up with me, particularly Cheryl Brown who continues to have faith in me, and Linda Clements, who prevents me making silly mistakes and does not miss a thing! The design team who make such a lovely job of putting the pages together and Ethan Danielson who can read my writing and produces all the charts and excellent diagrams that make this book so special.

Thanks to all the generous suppliers of the materials and equipment required for this book, particularly Rainer Steimann of Zweigart for lovely fabrics, DMC Creative World and Coats Crafts UK for stranded cottons and metallic threads and Ian Lawson Smith for my wonderful cross stitch design programme.

JANE GREENOFF AND THE CROSS STITCH GUILD

The Cross Stitch Guild was formed in March 1996 and quickly became a worldwide organization with a committed and enthusiastic body of members – over 2,000 in the first six months of operation. As word spreads it is clear that many cross stitch and counted thread addicts around the world are delighted to have a Guild of their own. The CSG has received an extraordinary level of support from designers, retailers, manufacturers and stitchers. Guild members receive a full-colour magazine *Stitch That* with Jane Greenoff including free counted cross stitch designs and technical advice and information. The CSG also supplies cross stitch tours, weekends, cross stitch kits, gold-plated needles, stitchers' gifts, cross stitch design software and counted thread classes. Taster Membership and Full Membership is available all over the world and there is now a comprehensive website for members and non-members with discounted shopping.

www.thecrossstitchguild.com

For more information, to contact Jane or for the latest catalogue write to: CSG HQ, Pinks Barn, London Road, Fairford, Gloucestershire, GL7 4AR UK. Tel: from the UK 0800 328 9750; from overseas +44 1285 713799.

SUPPLIERS

UK

Coats Crafts UK
PO Box 22, Lingfield House, McMullen Road,
Darlington, County Durham DL1 1YQ
tel: 01325 394237 (consumer helpline)
www.coatscrafts.co.uk
For Anchor stranded cotton (floss) and other supplies.

Craft Creations Limited
1C Ingersoll House, Delamare Road, Cheshunt,
Herts EN8 9HD
tel: 01992 781900
www.craftcreations.com
For greetings card blanks and card-making accessories

Crafty Ribbons
3 Beechwood, Clump Farm Industrial Estate,
Tin Pot Lane, Blandford, Dorset DT11 7TD
tel: 01258 455889
www.craftyribbons.com
For ribbons, including YLI silk ribbons

DMC Creative World
Pullman Road, Wigston, Leicestershire
LE18 2DY
tel: 0116 281 1040
fax: 0116 281 3592
www.dmc/cw.com
*For a wide range of embroidery supplies and
DMC fabrics and threads*

Framecraft Miniatures Ltd
Unit 3, Isis House, Lindon Road, Brownhills, West
Midlands WS8 7BW
tel/fax (UK): 01543 360842
tel (international): 44 1543 453154
email: sales@framecraft.com
www.framecraft.com
*For Mill Hill beads, buttons, charms, wooden and
ceramic trinket pots, notebook covers, key rings,
handbag mirrors and many other pre-finished items
with cross stitch inserts*

Sue Hawkins
East Wing, Highfield House, Whitminster GL2 7PG
tel: 44 (0) 1452 740118
For upholstered embroidery frames

Heritage Stitchcraft
Redbrook Lane, Brereton, Rugeley, Staffordshire
WS15 1QU
tel: +44 (0) 1889 575256
email: enquiries@heritagestitchcraft.com
www.heritagestitchcraft.com
For Zweigart fabrics and other embroidery supplies

Willow Fabrics
95 Town Lane, Mobberley, Knutsford,
Cheshire WA16 7HH
tel freephone (UK): 0800 0567811
(elsewhere): #44 (0) 1565 87 2225
www.willowfabrics.com
*For embroidery fabrics, Madeira threads and
Kreinik metallics*

USA

Charles Craft Inc.
PO Box 1049, Laurenburg, NC 28353
tel: 910 844 3521
email: ccraft@carolina.net
www.charlescraft.com
Coats Crafts UK supply Charles Craft products in the UK

Kreinik Manufacturing Company Inc
3106 Timanus Lane, Suite 101
Baltimore, MD 21244
tel: 1800 537 2166
email: kreinik@kreinik.com www.kreinik.com
For metallic threads and blending filaments

Mill Hill, a division of Wichelt Imports Inc.
N162 Hwy 35, Stoddard WI 54658
tel: 608 788 4600
www.millhill.com
For Mill Hill beads and Framecraft products

Tokens & Trifles
Redefined Inc., PO Box 2243, Acton, MA 01720
tel: 001 (508) 428-9038
www.tokensandtrifles.com
For Stitching Cards

Zweigart/Joan Toggit Ltd
262 Old Brunswick Road, Suite E,
Piscataway, NJ 08854-3756, USA
tel: 732 562 8888
email: info@zweigart.com
www.zweigart.com
For cross stitch fabrics and pre-finished table linens

INDEX

Bold pagination indicates instructions